Years of Estrangement

Years of Estrangement

American Relations with the Soviet Union,
1933–1941

Thomas R. Maddux

A Florida State University Book

University Presses of Florida
FAMU / FAU / FIU / FSU / UCF / UF / UNF / USF / UWF

Tallahassee

University Presses of Florida is the central agency for scholarly publishing of the State of Florida's university system. Its offices are located at 15 NW 15th Street, Gainesville, FL 32603. Works published by University Presses of Florida are evaluated and selected for publication by a faculty editorial committee of any one of Florida's nine public universities: Florida A&M University (Tallahassee), Florida Atlantic University (Boca Raton), Florida International University (Miami), Florida State University (Tallahassee), University of Central Florida (Orlando), University of Florida (Gainesville), University of North Florida (Jacksonville), University of South Florida (Tampa), University of West Florida (Pensacola).

Library of Congress Cataloging in Publication Data

Maddux, Thomas R
  Years of estrangement.

  Originally presented as the author's thesis,
University of Michigan.
  Bibliography: p.
  Includes index.
  1. United States—Foreign relations—Russia.
  2. Russia—Foreign relations—United States.
  3. United States—Foreign relations—1933–1945.
  4. Russia—Foreign relations—1917–1945. I. Title.
E183.8.R9M247   1980   327.73'047   79–26489
ISBN 0–8130–0653–8

Typography by American Graphics Corporation
Fort Lauderdale, Florida

Contents

For Milli

Preface

America's relations with the Soviet Union from recognition in 1933 to the extension of Lend-Lease assistance to Moscow in 1941 lacked the dramatic developments of the subsequent wartime alliance and ensuing cold war. Consequently, historians have concentrated on the post-1941 period and neglected earlier relations except for the origins of recognition and the Lend-Lease decision. I have focused on the earlier period because it was a germinal stage in the molding of American attitudes and the shaping of Franklin D. Roosevelt's diplomacy toward the Soviet Union. Events of the 1930s were also very influential in shaping Joseph Stalin's attitudes toward Roosevelt and United States policy. Although there is very little available documentation on Soviet policy toward the United States, I have tried to assess Stalin's objectives and tactics, using the documents published by the Soviet Ministry of Foreign Affairs, *Dokumenty vneshnei politiki SSSR*, American documents concerning official discussions with Soviet officials, and secondary assessments of Stalin's diplomacy.

In his direction of America's relations with the Soviet Union, Roosevelt revealed his strengths and weaknesses as a diplomat while he sought friendly, cooperative relations with the Kremlin. The president's decision to extend recognition and Lend-Lease, as well as his unsuccessful efforts to expand relations with Moscow in the intervening years, illustrated his understanding of the challenges faced by the United States in the 1930s and his realistic assessment of ineffective policies. The president also repeatedly demonstrated his ability to manipulate domestic opinion, influencing both organized interest groups and news media—although for most of the period he lacked sufficient support to bring about effective cooperation with the Soviet Union. Yet at the same time Roosevelt's understanding of Stalin and Soviet policy remained superficial, and his tactics as a negotiator were unfruitful. The president's refusal to work closely with State Department specialists seriously weakened his efforts at negotiation, in which he demonstrated a reluctance to be firm, an excessive reliance on domestic considerations, and a tendency to advance proposals without sufficient investigation and reflection on their feasibility.

I have also given extensive attention to the external and internal influences on Roosevelt's Soviet policy, ranging from a desire to increase trade with the Soviet Union in the early years to an increasing preoccupation with strategic concerns after 1936, notably cooperation with the Kremlin against Japan in the Far East and Hitler in Europe. Private interest groups and governmental agencies, especially the State Department, influenced Roosevelt's approaches toward Moscow. The State Department and officials in the Moscow embassy, suspicious about Stalin's desire for expansion, usually resisted the president whenever he made a new approach to the Kremlin. Finally, the response of American observers to Stalin's foreign and domestic policies increased constraints on Roosevelt's options with regard to the Soviet Union. Reacting more to Soviet policies than to any diplomatic interaction between Washington and Moscow, American commentators increasingly criticized Stalin's domestic practices and distrusted his diplomacy.

I appreciate the assistance I have received in the writing of this book from many friends, librarians, archivists, and secretaries. Bradford Perkins supervised the beginnings of this book as a dissertation at the University of Michigan and patiently reviewed subsequent drafts. The example he set in his writings and his continued encouragement have helped me in the decade devoted to this study. John Lewis Gaddis has made helpful suggestions since our first meeting in the Security Search Room of the National Archives and carefully reviewed several drafts of the manuscript. Gaddis' approach to Soviet-American relations in his writings, most notably his attention to internal constraints on policymakers and his judicious assessments of responsibility, has clarified my perspective.

They have not done any of the research or revised any of the drafts or typed any of the chapters or struggled with the Russian language, dictionary in hand, but my parents, my wife, Milli, and my sons, Tim and John, have consistently supported my efforts and, most of all, have loved me despite my preoccupation.

Thomas R. Maddux

1

The Challenge to Nonrecognition

In 1920 Secretary of State Bainbridge Colby explained Washington's rationale for a policy of nonrecognition of the Soviet Union. Traditional American practice required recognition of any government, regardless of its character, that controlled a state and carried out its international obligations. President Woodrow Wilson, however, had rejected this tradition in 1913 when he refused to recognize the Huerta government in Mexico. Colby followed Wilson's precedent, arguing that recognition was more than a neutral act because it involved the extension of moral support to a government. The Soviet government did not merit this moral approval, Colby asserted, because the Bolshevik leaders had used force to obtain power and were maintaining their position through "savage oppression" of the Russian people. The secretary also emphasized the Kremlin's failure to fulfill its international obligations, especially Moscow's refusal to respect the financial responsibilities of prior Russian governments and its revolutionary actions and propaganda against existing governments.[1]

Although Washington would eventually discard Colby's characterization of the Bolshevik regime, Republican policymakers retained the policy of nonrecognition until leaving office in 1933. Hostility toward the Soviet government, reinforced by the Kremlin's revolutionary intrigues

1

and propaganda, caused the State Department to brush aside arguments that America's interests would be better served by recognition. Starting in 1929, however, Washington found it increasingly difficult to ignore the permanence of the Soviet regime as well as the potential economic and diplomatic benefits of recognition. A determined group of liberals and radicals attacked nonrecognition and, despite vigorous rebuttals from representatives of the Catholic Church, the American Federation of Labor, and patriotic organizations, contributed to the news media's endorsement of recognition in 1933.

Nonrecognition represented one element of Woodrow Wilson's response to the Russian Revolution in 1917. As the United States entered the First World War, Wilson tried to keep Russia in the war with aid, missions to Russia, and public declarations of support. When the Bolsheviks requested official American recognition after their takeover in Moscow in November, Washington ignored their request. Wilson and other American officials detested the Bolsheviks as much as Vladimir Lenin hated the Western capitalist powers. Bolshevik leaders challenged American beliefs about the intrinsic value of the individual, the importance of religion, and the virtues of representative government and free enterprise. Lenin, moreover, called for the workers of the world to unite and overthrow capitalism.

Faced with an openly hostile ideology, Wilson not only withheld recognition; he also reluctantly approved a limited military intervention at the northern Russian ports of Murmansk and Archangel and at Vladivostok, four months after Moscow withdrew from the war against Germany in March, 1918. Although he preferred to undermine the Bolsheviks by peaceful means, Wilson wanted to maintain cooperation with Great Britain and France and restrain Japanese actions in Siberia as well as facilitate the removal of Czechoslovakian troops from Russia. The president soon regretted his decision to approve the military intervention in Russia, but at the Paris Peace Conference he was unable to give adequate attention to it or to the Russian civil war; so American forces remained in Russia until 1920.[2]

Soviet-American relations thus began inauspiciously in a swirl of confusion, ideological antipathy, and bitter recrimination over the Allied intervention. Yet mutual interests, particularly economic interests in the early twenties, lessened somewhat the hostility between Moscow and Washington. Lenin, for example, encouraged economic ties with the United States as an avenue to American technological assistance and diplomatic recognition. Republican policymakers of the twenties rejected recognition but allowed substantial economic interaction, notably in famine relief in 1921–23, American concessions in the Soviet Union, technical aid contracts, and trade (despite restrictions on credit). However, Washington rebuffed several overtures from Moscow in the twenties, largely because of the Kremlin's use of the Comintern to advocate revolution around the world. Within the Department of State, the Division of East European Affairs, headed by Robert F. Kelley, closely followed the Comintern's activities and Moscow's clumsy direction of the American Communists. Kelley, a quiet bachelor with a scholarly interest in Russian history and culture, resisted recognition; he had the support of officials in the Commerce Department who shared Herbert Hoover's ideological distaste for the Bolsheviks.[3]

By the end of the twenties, Commerce Department and State Department leaders had to look more closely at U.S. interests with respect to the Soviet Union. Starting in 1929, the world depression undermined America's domestic market and important foreign markets except for the Soviet Union. In 1929 Joseph Stalin, omnipresent master of the Kremlin, launched the first Five-Year Plan, a program of massive industrialization requiring large orders for machinery and technical assistance from capitalist firms. U.S. machine tool and industrial equipment manufacturers eagerly competed with British and German corporations. By 1930 U.S. exports to the Soviet Union exceeded in value those of every other country, although the amount represented only about 3 percent of total U.S. exports.[4] The Kremlin, however, expanded Soviet exports to obtain foreign exchange to pay for imports. In 1930 and 1931 the Soviet Union was charged in Congress with "dumping" (selling below costs, which is illegal under U.S. law) and the use of forced labor. A legislative effort to embargo all Soviet exports to America was made. In the business community dissension among self-interested companies emerged. Paper manufacturers, for example, unsuccessfully opposed a Treasury Department ban on Soviet lumber. The steel industry overturned a similar ban on manganese; coal and wheat dealers defeated bans on Soviet anthracite and wheat sought by mine owners and the American Farm Bureau Federation.[5]

The Soviet Union naturally resented the Treasury Department's restrictions, and, using the trade issue, began to pressure the United States for diplomatic recognition. Nikolai N. Krestinsky, deputy commissar for foreign affairs, indicated the Kremlin's strategy in the fall of 1931 when he informed the Politburo that by stopping the purchase of American goods the Kremlin would "more quickly impel American business and political circles to reconsider their traditional position of not recognizing the USSR."[6] Soviet purchases fell off in the second half of 1931 and dropped 89 percent in 1932 from $103.7 million to $12.6 million. The world economic crisis also forced a general decline in Soviet imports; most were supplied by Germany and Great Britain which, unlike America, provided credits to the Soviet Union.

The Russian market, which had seemed within the grasp of American traders, slipped away; but the impact was not exactly what the Russians had anticipated. Representatives of the machine tool and industrial equipment industries, import-export companies, and investment corporations did blame the collapse of the Russian market on nonrecognition, arguing that it inhibited the extension of credit to Moscow and prohibited the use of Russian gold. But in 1932 and the spring of 1933, most interested corporations and business journals and associations asked merely for the removal of trade restrictions rather than for diplomatic recognition. Even the American-Russian Chamber of Commerce—the leading association of firms involved in the Russian market, such as General Electric, IBM, and Baldwin Locomotive Works—did not reverse its traditional stand against recognition until July 13, 1933.[7]

The absence of a concerted movement within the business community for recognition reflected several concerns in addition to the divided sentiment over Soviet exports to America. As long as the Hoover administration stood firm on nonrecognition, corporations pragmatically focused on trade and not on recognition. The vocal opposition to recognition also made business firms reluctant to make any moves that would attract public criticism. The importance of credit for Soviet purchases, moreover, was recognized by the leaders of the American-Russian Chamber of Commerce and by Alexander Gumberg, a leading intermediary between Soviet officials and American businessmen interested in the Russian market. Gumberg, a native-born Russian who advised Americans in Russia during 1917–18, privately pushed the appointment of Richard B. Scandrett, Jr., a director of the Chamber, as America's ambassador to the Soviet Union. In 1933 he reopened contacts with individuals like Sen. William Borah and Raymond Robins and with noneconomic groups that had advocated recognition during the twenties. Unlike Gumberg, who remained intensely sympathetic toward the Soviet Union despite the loss of a brother in Stalin's purge, many businessmen disliked Soviet domestic policies and foreign intrigue and insisted that Moscow pay its debts and end any interference in American domestic affairs.[8]

Despite the reluctance of American businessmen to push for recognition, the Kremlin's manipulation of trade to bring it about did not fail completely, inasmuch as the Soviet market for U.S. goods emerged as a pervasive issue in the 1933 debate on recognition. "Millions, and perhaps even billions, will be spent by the awakened Russian people," predicted the executive secretary of the National Committee for Recognition of Soviet Russia, "and only recognition is needed to start this tremendous financial ball rolling in the direction of American industry."[9] The news media also gave extensive and favorable attention to the trade issue. "America greatly needs the vast Russian market," announced the *Cleveland Plain Dealer,* and "Russia needs manufactured goods America has for sale. It is a natural process for the two to get together on terms agreeable to both."[10]

The depression highlighted the potential of the Soviet market and had an equally significant, although more subtle, influence on the 1933 debate. The impact of the depression moved American liberals to the left; they began to admire Soviet economic and social policies. Even liberals who rejected Marxist ideology and Stalin's dictatorship expressed some enthusiasm for the Soviet example in central planning.[11] Organizations such as the Friends of the Soviet Union and individual advocates of recognition like Jerome Davis and Raymond Robins hoped that recognition, signaling America's moral approval of the Soviet Union, might encourage the United States to move toward the new social experiment of the Soviets. Davis, a theologian at the Yale Divinity School, hoped to become America's first ambassador to the Soviet Union; he campaigned diligently for recognition, through articles and radio broadcasts and in conversations with Washington officials. Robins—an eccentric dilettante who had been at various times a progressive politician, cowboy, miner, minister to the Eskimos, Red Cross official in Russia, social worker, and experimental farmer—made a well-publicized tour of the Soviet Union, talking with Stalin for ninety minutes. Back in the United States he lobbied Washington officials, including President Franklin Roosevelt and a suspicious J. Edgar Hoover, and made public addresses, literally gushing with emotional enthusiasm for the Soviet experiment.[12]

These endorsements of the Soviet experiment disturbed the leaders of the opposition. They still considered the Soviet system an immoral, ungodly, repressive tyranny, and they rejected recognition as an undesirable extension of American moral approval. "For our Christian nation to officially sanction the policies of such defamers of God and all His teachings...," admonished the conservative *National Republic,* "would be to stultify all our traditions, and nullify all our free institutions."[13] Father Edmund A. Walsh, vice-president of Georgetown University, William Green of the American Federation of Labor, Ralph Easley of the National Civic Federation, Rep. Hamilton Fish of New York, and Walter L. Reynolds, editor of the *National Republic,* were among those who confidently dismissed the argument that recognition rather than credit would revive trade with Moscow.[14]

But Father Walsh and Representative Fish, an obdurate critic of Roosevelt and the Soviet Union, expediently shifted their position. To many American observers, nonrecognition represented an aberration in America's traditional policy, particularly since the United States recognized Mussolini's regime in Italy, Adolf Hitler's in Germany, and an expansionist regime in Japan. Rejecting recognition as an act of moral approval or disapproval, barrister John Foster Dulles argued that governments that effectively controlled a country should be recognized regardless of their internal policies. The Scripps-Howard chain of twenty-five newspapers, the Gannett chain of fourteen journals, and conservative Republican papers endorsed this position. As the *Dallas Morning News* put the issue, the Soviet government "fulfills the usual conditions demanded by our recognition policy. It is stable, accepted by the people of Russia, and is able to protect life and property."[15] When Roosevelt signaled his interest in recognition, Fish and Father Walsh said they would welcome the Kremlin into the family of nations, regardless of its form of government, if Moscow dropped its propaganda activities and paid its debts.[16] Fish did not expect Stalin to comply. He and Ralph Easley raided a deserted warehouse in Baltimore late in 1932 with the hope of finding secret files that would prove that Senator Borah and other advocates of recognition were Soviet agents. Instead, they discovered only a few crates of rotten cabbage.[17]

Father Walsh and other opponents of recognition also denied that any diplomatic benefits, especially in the Far East against Japan, would flow from recognition. Any diplomatic cooperation with Moscow was dangerous, according to Father Walsh, for the "rattlesnake" Soviet Union "would sink its fangs impartially into hands that caress or fists that menace."[18] After Japan moved into Manchuria in 1931, however, the Far Eastern situation seriously weakened the rationale for nonrecognition. Since Japanese expansion directly threatened the Soviet Union's hegemony in Outer Mongolia and the maritime territories as well as the Kremlin's interest in the Chinese-Eastern railroad, the tenuous link through Manchuria between the West and the vulnerable Soviet port of

Vladivostok, Moscow turned first to the issue of recognition. Mixing conciliation with firmness, the Politburo offered Tokyo a nonaggression pact and negotiations over the railroad. Turning to the United States in the spring of 1932 as a potential source of support for opposition to Japan's expansion, Stalin made many indirect appeals, through diplomats and the Soviet press, for American recognition.[19]

The United States opposed Japan's move into Manchuria but rejected the use of force or economic sanctions to restrain Japanese aggression. Secretary of State Henry Stimson did order review of the recognition issue by the Division of Far Eastern Affairs, which was under the direction of Stanley K. Hornbeck. Although Hornbeck suspected that Moscow hoped to profit from Chinese and Japanese conflict and eventual exhaustion, he believed that the Soviet Union would have to be involved in any solution of the conflict. The Chinese government and American officials in Japan and China gave similar warnings to Washington. Within Hornbeck's division, officials debated the question of how to approach the Soviet Union; at least one official urged an effort "to enlist Russia on the side on which her main interests lie rather than simply to ignore her or hold her at arms' length." When Stimson asked for a memorandum weighing the pros and cons of recognition in July, 1932, Hornbeck recommended against recognition, emphasizing the adverse effect that it might have on American relations with Japan.[20]

Stimson's evaluation of the issue centered on the Far Eastern conflicts and the nature of Soviet policy. He wondered if the Kremlin's designs for international Communism were too fantastic to merit serious consideration and whether American recognition would have any effect on them. By September, the secretary rejected recognition, perhaps because he sensed President Hoover's firm opposition. When Stimson revealed his decision, he explained it in a Far Eastern context. Russia's "very bad reputation respecting international obligations," the secretary wrote to Sen. William Borah, would prompt Japan and the rest of the world to interpret recognition as an expedient act. Japan "would regard us as merely an opportunist nation...," the Republican policymaker concluded, and Washington's "loss of moral standing would be so important that we could not afford to take the risk of it."[21]

Stimson brushed aside the diplomatic advantages of formal relations with Moscow, but by the fall of 1933 the news media were disagreeing with the secretary. Most journals pointed out the advantages of being able to discuss the Far East with Moscow through normal diplomatic channels, especially since the press noted a considerable reorientation in Soviet foreign policy. The revolutionary propaganda and actions of the Bolshevik regime, which encouraged unsuccessful revolutions in Germany, Hungary, and Poland between 1917 and 1921, had prompted Americans to endorse a policy of nonrecognition. After 1921, however, under the impact of Russian domestic problems and the failure of Bolshevism to spread abroad, Soviet policy focused increasingly on the interests of the Soviet state rather than on revolution. Yet Soviet leaders, including Stalin, retained their Marxist-Leninist ideology and hopes for the spread of Communism. The Kremlin's diplomacy thus evolved toward a traditional, nationalistic policy but retained the propaganda and apparatus of revolutionary Bolshevism. The Comintern had been established by the Soviets in 1919 to direct Communist movements throughout the world and, under Stalin's control, stepped up the militancy of its rhetoric in response to the world depression. At the same time Stalin initiated contact with the United States and in 1933 reoriented his diplomacy toward cooperation with the Western powers in the League of Nations.[22]

The U.S. news media responded favorably to the reorientation in Soviet diplomacy. Newspaper editors and journalists noted a significant shift in Soviet policy away from the earlier emphasis on the spread of Communism. Ten out of thirty-five newspapers (see Table 2), representing the major cities throughout the country, concluded that the Soviet Union had adopted a security-oriented foreign policy (see Table 4). Eleven other journals agreed with this assessment but also suggested that Moscow would continue a low level of propaganda activity favorable to Communism. Only three newspapers, the *Boston Evening Transcript*, the *Chicago Tribune*, and the *Seattle Times*, stated emphatically that Stalin retained the expansion of Communism as his most important long-range objective. This emphasis on security concerns also prevailed over the press's different perspectives on the Soviet Union (see Table 3). The twenty conservative newspapers, who were more critical of the Soviet system, Stalin's diplomacy, and the American Communists than were the fifteen moderate journals, tended to agree with the emphasis on security (see Table 6), despite reservations about the permanency of Moscow's reorientation.

"There is no ground for assuming that Russia has repudiated Communism with respect to domestic affairs," the *Philadelphia Inquirer* pointed out, but "...her idea of bringing about a world revolution has plainly been abandoned."[23] A surprising number of journals agreed with or came close to an endorsement of this conclusion. As the *Hartford Courant*, a moderate Republican supporter, expressed its view, "It is no longer, if it ever was, the Soviet policy to encourage revolution against established governments anywhere."[24] Most editors, however, doubted the permanency of Stalin's shift away from Communist expansionism, referring to it as a temporary change or agreeing with the *St. Louis Post-Dispatch*'s qualification: "...if it is true that the Russian Government has abandoned its dream of world revolution."[25] These journals, noting a considerable waning in Soviet revolutionary activity and only ritualistic support for the Comintern, hoped that Stalin would continue to move Soviet diplomacy down a traditional path.

A few American editors were more skeptical about Stalin's reorientation. Unlike the majority of the press, these observers considered the Kremlin's reorientation merely a short-range tactical maneuver, retaining a fundamental interest in the expansion of Communism. The *National Republic*, conservative and anti-Soviet, and the *Commonweal*, moderate and church-supported, basically agreed with the conclusion of the Jesuits' *America* that the Kremlin's objective remained world revolution. "Not content with enslaving the people of Russia," warned *America*, "it is their acknowledged purpose to spread that slavery throughout the world."[26] Several conservative newspapers also expressed strong doubts about Stalin's policies and emphasized the continued existence of Soviet revolutionary propaganda.[27]

On March 3, 1933, Under Secretary of State William R. Castle, Jr., reaffirmed the United States' refusal to extend recognition to the Soviet Union. Nonrecognition remained an appropriate policy, Castle argued, until the Soviet government would "carry out in good faith the international obligations which experience has demonstrated are essential to the development of friendly intercourse."[28] Castle's emphasis on the Kremlin's unpaid debts and its revolutionary propaganda campaign in the United States represented the position to which the Republican policymakers and their supporters had retreated. However, a vigorous minority of advocates of recognition, using the impact of the depression, the Far Eastern situation, and the reorientation of Soviet diplomacy, had challenged the stand-patters and eroded their strength. By the spring of 1933, editorial opinion had shifted: 66 percent of 1,141 newspapers favored recognition while 27 percent opposed it. Still, more than half of the editors who favored recognition qualified their support by insisting on Soviet payment of debts and noninterference in American affairs.[29]

Neither the business community nor the press insisted that President Roosevelt rush into recognition, and the opposition lacked sufficient strength and political influence to keep the president from exercising his prerogative. Consequently, Roosevelt retained considerable flexibility on the question of a change in policy toward Russia.

2

Roosevelt and Recognition

In October, 1932, *Soviet Russia Today* asked the presidential candidates to state their views about recognition of the Soviet Union. President Hoover refused to comment. Democratic candidate Franklin D. Roosevelt announced, with typical evasiveness, that if elected he intended to study the "different angles of this question and to reach the best decision within my power."[1] Roosevelt, however, had most probably made up his mind to recognize the Soviet Union when he entered the White House in March, 1933; he indicated such a desire to William C. Bullitt, who had served as a secret emissary to the Bolsheviks in 1919 for President Wilson, and to Henry Morgenthau, Jr., a personal friend and head of the Farm Credit Administration, who initiated discussions with Soviet representatives.

Yet Roosevelt moved very slowly, keeping the issue of recognition in the background until the fall of 1933. Although the depression certainly preoccupied the president, he generally preferred to move indirectly in his diplomacy. As Robert A. Divine has pointed out, "...movement in a straight and unbroken line seems to have been alien to his nature—he could not go forward until he had tested the ground, studied all the reactions, and weighed all the risks."[2] Characteristically, Roosevelt turned to advisors such as Bullitt and Morgenthau to conduct preliminary

discussions with Soviet representatives rather than to Secretary of State
Cordell Hull or other State Department officials. Except for his reciprocal
trade agreements designed to reduce trade barriers, Hull, a veteran
politician from Tennessee, reacted cautiously to any new initiative. In
order to get new policies off the ground, the president preferred to
postpone dealing with Hull's inevitable reservations until some momentum had gathered behind the new ideas. State Department specialists
were also eventually included in the negotiations, but Roosevelt suspected that they would resist any change in policy. So, he did not bring
them into the process of negotiations until he had tested the reactions of
the Soviets and the American public to the prospect of recognition.[3]

Roosevelt rarely indicated why he wanted to recognize the Soviet
Union. In March he provided the clearest indication of his views when he
said to Morgenthau that nonrecognition was futile and unrealistic. The
Kremlin controlled Russia, and most of the major powers had already
recognized this fact.[4] Nonrecognition had failed in practice, since the
Soviet leaders refused to recognize the financial obligations of former
Russian governments or to stop revolutionary propaganda. As the
president remarked to a Washington journalist, one "could not keep the
160,000,000 people of Russia silent and out of contact with us forever."[5]

The basic issues behind nonrecognition had lost some of their significance for Roosevelt. Of course he believed that states should fulfill their
international obligations, but circumstances had weakened the case
against the Kremlin. In 1932–33 many European countries defaulted on
their World War I debts to America. Although this was an emotional
matter for Americans and the White House had rejected any cancellation
or reduction of debts at the London Economic Conference in July, the
defaults by other European governments reduced criticism of the Soviet
Union. Roosevelt, moreover, was ready to write off more than half of the
American claims, specifically the obligations of the Tsarist regime and the
American investments made during that period, in exchange for a cancellation of the Kremlin's counterclaim for compensation for the American
intervention in 1918 in the Russian civil war. Soviet propaganda and
interference in American domestic affairs were more irritating, but the
president did not consider them impossible obstacles. After sixteen years,
Communism seemed confined within Russia, and Roosevelt was confi-
dent of his ability to lead the country out of the depression, despite the
American Communist party's efforts to exploit the crisis. Consequently,
the president wanted to return to a policy that would be a realistic one
rather than a symbol of moralistic disapproval.[6]

Roosevelt wanted to expand American trade with the Soviet Union and used this goal as the chief argument for recognition, perhaps because he recognized its popular appeal. In response to Morgenthau's complaint that Moscow was reluctant to negotiate trade agreements without recognition, Roosevelt replied: "...if I could only, myself, talk to some one man representing the Russians, I could straighten out this whole question. If you get the opportunity, Henry, you could say that you believe, but have no authority to say so, that the President would like to send some person to Moscow...in order to break the ice between the two countries and in that way gradually get the people of the United States used to doing business with the Russians." The president added that his representative might be a trade commissioner.[7]

As trade negotiations succeeded, momentum for recognition built up. Morgenthau finally obtained an agreement in July by which Moscow would buy approximately 80,000 bales of cotton from American firms, which would in turn receive $4 million in credits from the Reconstruction Finance Corporation. Encouraged by the favorable press reaction to this agreement, Roosevelt instructed Morgenthau to push negotiations for Soviet purchases of up to $100 million in machinery and raw materials.[8] In September of 1933 Morgenthau asked the president about the extension of an official loan to the Soviet Union for the purchase of American goods. A large loan would have implied at least de facto recognition of the Soviet government. Roosevelt ducked the question and instead asked his advisor's reaction to "bringing this whole Russian question into our front parlor instead of back in the kitchen." After Morgenthau's reserved reply, the president said, "Well, I have got a plan in mind." The plan involved an exchange of letters with the Soviet government concerning formal negotiations over recognition. Yet Roosevelt rejected William Bullitt's suggestion that he establish a semigovernmental corporation to control Soviet-American trade. When Morgenthau complained about Bullitt's emphasis on economic considerations, the president replied: "You are absolutely right. I want to keep these Russian negotiations on a high plane, and it will be time enough to talk about business after we have come to every other decision."[9]

The president expected recognition to provide diplomatic benefits, specifically with respect to the Far Eastern situation, but also on general matters like disarmament and world peace. Roosevelt realized that any successful solution of economic and disarmament problems required the participation of the Soviet Union. When in May of 1933 the president asked European governments to attend the London Economic Conference and to revive the Disarmament Conference, President Mikhail Kalinin of the Soviet Union was among the recipients of his message. This first direct communication between Washington and Moscow was to help prepare the American public for recognition of the Soviet Union.

Although Roosevelt's advisors have claimed that his motivation for recognition was cooperation with Moscow against Adolf Hitler, their hindsight assertions misinterpret the president's priorities.[10] When Hitler became chancellor of Germany in January, 1933, American officials were immediately upset. The president, for example, told the French ambassador in April that "Hitler is a madman." Hitler's persecution of Jews was criticized by Roosevelt, Germany's trade policies antagonized the State Department, and Hitler's rearmament policy frustrated the White House's hopes for the Geneva disarmament negotiations.[11] Roosevelt did discuss the German situation with Maxim Litvinov, the Soviet commissar for foreign affairs, after they settled the issue of recognition in November. During a review of the international situation, the president described Germany and Japan as the chief threats to peace, and the United States and the Soviet Union as the main defenders of peace. "The movement of Germany on the East he considers real...," Litvinov informed the Kremlin, but "he hopes that Hitler wouldn't endure and would collapse."[12] Yet Roosevelt devoted most of this discussion with Litvinov to the challenge of Japan, which seemed more immediate and pertinent to recognition than did Germany.

Roosevelt hoped that recognition by the United States would make the Soviets more resolute in opposition to Japan. By March, 1933, the ineffectiveness of Washington's nonrecognition policy toward Japanese expansion was clear: Japan had established the puppet state of Manchukuo in Manchuria, had taken over Jehol province and had moved south of the Great Wall to within thirteen miles of Peiping. In the Tangku Truce of May 31, Japan agreed to pull its troops back to the Great Wall but continued to exert military and diplomatic pressure on North China and the Nanking government. Tokyo also had increased the tension with the Soviet Union by stopping all through traffic on the Chinese Eastern Railway in April.

Roosevelt searched for new ways to restrain Japan. After March, he kept the American fleet in the Pacific, initiated a build-up of the navy, and quietly tried to win congressional approval of an arms embargo. Roosevelt privately expressed great interest in the "Russian-Japanese situation" and the Kremlin's military strength in the Far East.[13] William Bullitt also emphasized the Far Eastern situation. After a secret meeting with Maxim Litvinov at the London Economic Conference, Bullitt told Roosevelt that Litvinov wanted to connect recognition with the Far Eastern problem. "I think there is something in it," advised Bullitt, who also asked Morgenthau to support his idea of a loan to Russia in order to provide "the means by which the Soviet Union...could become a bulwark against the aggressive tendencies...developing in Japan."[14]

As Bullitt and Morgenthau talked with Soviet officials in the spring and summer of 1933, the president released enough clues to encourage support for recognition and to discourage the opposition, which, after July, maintained a less active resistance. When questioned by the press concerning a visit of Col. Hugh L. Cooper of the American-Russian Chamber of Commerce, Roosevelt went off the record and informed the press that he and Cooper had discussed only trade, not recognition. After a journalist asked if trade required recognition, he replied, "We have been selling some without recognition." In May the president skillfully handled questions about his inclusion of the Soviet Union among the recipients of his message on disarmament. Drawing the obvious conclusion that the White House was considering recognition, the press probed the president but obtained only repeated statements that the message had been sent to all countries in the economic and disarmament conferences. The game continued in July when the press asked him if the Reconstruction Finance Corporation credit for the Soviet purchase of cotton represented the first step to recognition. "I haven't heard a word about it until I saw the dispatch from London," replied Roosevelt.[15]

Roosevelt was also very circumspect with the Kremlin. On October 10, 1933, Bullitt and Morgenthau gave Boris E. Skvirsky, Moscow's unofficial representative in America since 1921, an unsigned invitation for Stalin to send a representative to discuss relations. If these overtures were accepted, Roosevelt would sign and release his invitation and Moscow's reply. "If they are not acceptable," Bullitt questioned Skvirsky, "will you give me your word of honor that there will never be any publicity in regard to this proposed exchange of letters and that the whole matter will be kept a secret?"[16]

After the Kremlin indicated its agreement, President Roosevelt released to the press on October 20 an exchange of letters with President Kalinin. "With indescribable gusto, he drew forth the Kalinin-Roosevelt exchange of cables, slowly eyed his tense audience, and read their text....He relished every moment," commented a press observer. Roosevelt stated his interest in recognition but proposed only friendly discussions about the "difficulties that have created this anomalous situation." Discussion, moreover, would "not commit either nation to any future course of action."[17] The president's restraint indicated not only his desire for negotiations before recognition but also his continuing concern about the public reaction. He closely followed public attitudes through his correspondence, conversations with journalists, and the half-dozen newspapers he read, paying special attention to columnists and editorials. The president also consulted a digest prepared from papers throughout the country.[18]

The very favorable reaction of the press to Roosevelt's announcement reaffirmed the wisdom of the president's cautious, indirect approach as well as the importance of preliminary negotiations. Only two journals out of thirty-six, the *Chicago Tribune* and the *Los Angeles Times,* expressed overt opposition.[19] This represented a significant shift from the spring of 1933, when 33 percent of the editors questioned by the American Foundation's committee had indicated opposition or neutrality. Most journals approved the planned negotiations, but they expected Moscow, in return for recognition, to pay its debts and to stop its interference in American domestic affairs.[20] Some Republican editors, however, rejected unconditional recognition and questioned the value of any agreements; they agreed with the *New York Herald Tribune*'s suggestion that "at the first sign of subversive operations by Russian Communist agents on American soil diplomatic relations should be severed instantly."[21]

The favorable assessment by the press encouraged Roosevelt to go after the leading opponents of recognition, notably Catholics and organized labor. Roosevelt realized that both groups, which approved his domestic policies, would not break with him over recognition; but he wanted to overcome their opposition. Using Smith W. Brookhart and other advisors as emissaries, the White House persuaded the National Federation of Labor not to oppose recognition. The American Federation of Labor was more difficult. After a number of conferences in Washington, President William Green reluctantly agreed to accept recognition if Roosevelt obtained agreements to end Soviet propaganda and Communist infiltration into organized labor.[22]

Although Catholics represented a more difficult problem, Roosevelt's charm, as well as the inevitability of recognition, brought them into line. Following several conferences with Brookhart, Father Edmund Walsh came to the White House. A sophisticated critic of the Soviet Union, Walsh warned Roosevelt about the difficulties involved in negotiations with the Kremlin. But the president, with typical confidence, replied: "Leave it to me, Father; I am a good horse dealer." After the president asked Walsh to prepare a report about the status of religion in Russia, Walsh promised to keep quiet and to swing "Catholics squarely behind the Administration's program for Russia." When Walsh called for silence about recognition, the Catholic press, including the staunchly anti-Soviet journal *America,* fell into line. Roosevelt's remarkable success with Catholics reflected their desire to avoid a break with the White House, their belief that he would improve religious conditions in the Soviet Union, and the president's flattery of Walsh, which briefly threw the Catholic leader off balance.[23]

With the press's endorsement in hand and the most vocal critics neutralized, Roosevelt still faced skepticism in the State Department. Although officials were reluctant to oppose the president directly, they rejected many of the arguments for recognition, particularly the repeated idea that trade and recognition would proceed happily, hand in hand. Robert F. Kelley, chief of the Division of Eastern European Affairs, which concentrated on the Soviet Union, insisted that an increase in American exports to the Soviet Union would come only with a vast expansion in American credits to Moscow, rather than with recognition.[24] The State Department also felt that the value of an observation post in Moscow did not outweigh the disadvantages of establishing relations with an unreliable, hostile government, particularly since it already had input from Kelley's division and from a special Russian section in the Riga legation which had collected information on the Soviet Union since 1922.

What bothered the State Department most about recognition was the widespread belief that Moscow would not live up to the "standards of civilized society" by paying its debts and ending its interference in American affairs.[25] Kelley's division and the Russian specialists at Riga predicted that Moscow would not make any significant concessions or keep any agreements. "The Communist leaders in Russia are unwilling to abandon their revolutionary aims with respect to the United States," Kelley warned Secretary Hull. "Even when these activities do not constitute a present menace . . . ," Earl L. Packer, assistant chief of the division, reminded Bullitt, they remained "a source of deep resentment and unavoidable friction."[26]

However, the State Department found it difficult to dismiss the potential benefits of recognition in the Far East. "We are handicapped in discussing matters relating to the Far East," Nelson T. Johnson, minister to China, complained to the chief of the Division of Far Eastern Affairs, "as long as we are cut off from a free exchange of opinions and ideas with the Soviet Government."[27] Within this division, officials disagreed about recognition; most of them supported it against the opposition of the division chief, Stanley K. Hornbeck. Secretary Hull was ambivalent, expressing interest in "friendly cooperation" with Moscow against Japan after a meeting with Soviet Commissar Maxim Litvinov at the London Economic Conference in September. Under Secretary William Phillips and Assistant Secretary Robert Walton Moore also worried about Japan's determination "to remove the Russian obstruction from the path of her ambitions at an advantageous moment."[28]

Perhaps Roosevelt noted the State Department's interest in Soviet-Japanese relations, for within a week after Hull's favorable comments to the president, William Bullitt approached Hornbeck with a reference to Moscow's interest in cooperation against Japan. Hornbeck vigorously argued that Washington should refuse to discuss the issue. The president's advisor tried again, mentioning "the possibility of an understanding with regard to steps which might be taken if Japan took the aggressive, an understanding in advance and to be invoked only in such eventuality, to which the U.S., G.B., France and Russia would be parties." Hornbeck, who favored a passive, unilateral approach in the Far East, flatly rejected this proposal and suggested that "we could not rely upon any one of them, least of all Russia, for performance on their part." Bullitt could only end the meeting with the weak remark that Hornbeck's views "all sounded very reasonable."[29]

When Roosevelt seemed determined to recognize the Soviet Union, the State Department tried to shape the negotiations. Robert Kelley and the Division of Eastern European Affairs prepared a series of memoranda during the spring and summer of 1933 which became the department's guidelines on issues such as debts, Communist propaganda, and the legal rights of Americans in the Soviet Union. With the approval of Hull and the top echelon of the department, Kelley strongly recommended in a memorandum to the president that the major issues be settled before the resumption of diplomatic relations. Moscow should be required to sever all ties with Communist activity in the United States, settle its debts, and protect the rights of Americans in Russia, Kelley argued, in order to have satisfactory diplomatic relations.[30]

In order to emphasize the importance of these guidelines, especially those concerning Soviet interference in American domestic affairs, some State Department officials in October leaked reports to the press about Soviet aid to Cuban revolutionaries. On October 20 Kelley's division warned that Moscow hoped "to undermine the position of the United States in its political and economic relations with the countries of Latin

America." On the same day Assistant Secretary Jefferson Caffery attempted to leak a story to the press about communications between Moscow and Cuban revolutionaries. To Raymond Clapper, head of the Washington bureau of United Press, Caffery's story looked like "a plot being hatched to spike the Russians." Samuel Harper, an academic specialist on the Soviet Union and a frequent visitor to the State Department, also reported that some "'antis' in the State Department were exploiting the Cuban situation."[31]

The State Department also moved to keep consideration of the Far Eastern situation out of negotiations with Moscow. After incoming reports about a Soviet-Japanese clash became less alarming, Stanley Hornbeck admonished Hull and other officials to avoid discussions about the Far East and to reassure Japan confidentially on this point: "Avoid saying anything which could encourage the inference that the American government expects within the course of the forthcoming conversations to discuss Far Eastern questions."[32]

At the end of the September Roosevelt asked for Secretary Hull's views in writing in order to clear the path for Bullitt's exchange with Skvirsky. The secretary endorsed Kelley's guidelines by insisting on a settlement of all outstanding issues, preferably in secret negotiations, before the White House invited a Soviet representative to Washington. Unless Washington used "every available means of exerting pressure on the Soviet government...," Hull warned Roosevelt, "there is little likelihood that such problems can be satisfactorily solved."[33]

The president only partially concurred with Hull's and the State Department's recommendations. As Bullitt informed Hull, the Kremlin would have to accept the draft agreements meticulously prepared by Kelley's division in order to obtain recognition and credits for trade.[34] But Roosevelt never agreed to keep the Far East out of the discussions, and he rejected his secretary's suggestion of secret negotiations preliminary to a settlement—primarily because the president felt that he could successfully negotiate a settlement.

Hull's proposal, however, had several advantages. First, negotiations would have taken place under less pressure, with more time for experts to keep track of the all-important details which Roosevelt frequently neglected. Second, they would have provided an opportunity, if difficult or insurmountable disagreements arose, for the president to separate recognition from agreements of a more specific nature. But Hull's proposal would not have guaranteed better agreements with Moscow, except on the debt issue, nor would it have ensured that the Kremlin would keep its agreements. Moreover, publicized negotiations (rather than secrecy) would put pressure on Maxim Litvinov to compromise in order to obtain recognition.

The day before Litvinov's arrival, Roosevelt met with Hull, Bullitt, Morgenthau, and other officials from the State Department for a final briefing session. Hull, who had postponed his departure for the Montevideo Conference in Uruguay, was to direct the negotiations with the assistance of Kelley, Under Secretary Phillips, Assistant Secretary Moore, and Bullitt. "We went over the subjects to be discussed with Litvinov," Hull recalled in his memoirs, "and agreed that the two most important were precautions against Soviet propaganda and illegal activities in the United States and freedom of worship for Americans in Russia."[35] Roosevelt had not asked Hull to delay leaving for the Pan-American meeting, perhaps doubting the likelihood of recognition resulting from negotiations directed by the State Department.

Litvinov, a portly, cosmopolitan negotiator who ably articulated the emerging Soviet policy of cooperation with the Western democracies, probably expected unconditional recognition, since other governments had granted it, followed by discussion of the major issues. He discovered on November 8 that the State Department had other plans. Hull and other officials insisted that Litvinov accept the department's memoranda about debts, noninterference, and rights of Americans in the Soviet Union. When Hull asked for guarantees on religious freedom, Litvinov misinterpreted this request as a demand applying to all Russians and not just to Americans in the Soviet Union. The commissar angrily and at length rejected any interference with internal Soviet policies. The issue of legal rights for Americans did not stimulate a similar exchange, but the question of debts brought a quick stalemate. After mentioning the complexity of the issue and Moscow's counterclaim against the American intervention at Vladivostok in 1918, Litvinov suggested either a mutual repudiation of all claims or postponement to future negotiations. He later informed the Kremlin that "Hull rejected unfairly our counterclaim on intervention." When presented with a demand for Soviet responsibility for the Comintern and a termination of Soviet ties with American Communists, Litvinov gave a "firm refusal."[36]

After two hours of unyielding exchanges, Hull took Litvinov to the White House for lunch, where the president not only reviewed the issues in a more friendly manner but also revealed some of the tactics that would characterize his discussions with Soviet officials throughout his presidency. After defending Hull's positions, Roosevelt informed the Soviet commissar that agreements were necessary to satisfy Catholics and critics in the Congress. Instead of defending Washington's demands as necessary for normal diplomatic relations, the president turned to domestic concerns. This tactic did not impress Litvinov, who informed the Kremlin that Roosevelt "really is scared of the recognized enemies of recognition." With Hull at his side, the president tried to ingratiate himself with the commissar by questioning the morality of American claims against the Tsarist regime, by admitting that "no one can make excuses for the intervention into Archangel," and by complaining confidentially about recent negotiations with Great Britain. On the subject of the Comintern, Roosevelt agreed that "it is impossible to demand removal of it from the Soviet Union," but recommended that it would be "best of all to move it to Geneva where the League of Nations is."[37]

After this introduction to Roosevelt's techniques, Litvinov went back to the State Department on November 9 for another session with Hull and his assistants, who, the commissar complained, were hostile and were trying to complicate the negotiations. After two hours of fruitless exchanges with an unyielding Litvinov, the secretary asked Roosevelt to try his hand at breaking the logjam at another White House meeting on November 10. "Somehow the President succeeded in changing the whole atmosphere," Under Secretary Phillips remarked in his diary, and "he did it by a combination of humor, sincerity, clearness and friendliness."[38] Roosevelt again emphasized the domestic importance of agreements guaranteeing religious rights for Americans in the Soviet Union, settling the debt issue, and providing restrictions on propaganda. Litvinov, who may have wanted all along to negotiate with the president rather than with subordinates, repeated his desire to discuss these issues *after* recognition, but he then agreed to review the problems with Roosevelt. The commissar and the president then immediately outlined the substance of the final agreements, described here by Litvinov: "Concerning propaganda, I let Roosevelt choose any formula from agreements concluded with other states or from a mixture of them, but I couldn't agree to go farther than these formulae. Roosevelt replied that he would not insist on the text adopted from his draft, and only on its essence. He is ready to agree that it is completely impossible to settle the question about claims, but wants to consider the possibility of agreement on some in principle."[39]

On the evening of November 10 Litvinov returned to the White House, where he and Roosevelt readily agreed on a guarantee of freedom of worship and conscience to American citizens in the Soviet Union. An accord on propaganda and noninterference in domestic affairs proved more difficult. Without mentioning the Comintern by name or demanding an end of Soviet Communist propaganda everywhere, the final agreement required Moscow to sever its ties with the American Communist party and other Communist-controlled organizations in the United States. Litvinov agreed "not to permit the formation or residence on its territory of any organization or group ... which has as an aim the overthrow or the preparation for the overthrow of, or the bringing about by force of a change in, the political or social order ... of the United States."[40] Although this statement described the Comintern in everything but name, Litvinov claimed in 1935 that he had warned the president that the Kremlin would not be responsible for the Comintern and that Roosevelt had replied that only a serious violation would force a Washington protest. Bullitt, who remembered the discussion differently, rejoined that the president had indicated that Moscow would be held strictly accountable for any actions of the Comintern.[41]

On the debt issue the White House obtained only an interim accord rather than a final settlement. Kelley had recommended earlier that Washington demand repayment only of its 1917 loan to the Kerensky government. When Litvinov refused to accept this claim of $150 million, Bullitt on November 15 threatened a withdrawal of governmental and private credit unless he came to terms. That afternoon, Roosevelt, with the assistance of Bullitt and Morgenthau, took a softer line and obtained a gentleman's agreement that set $75 million as a minimum settlement of the loan to the Kerensky regime. Moscow would repay the debt through extra interest on a loan granted by Washington or private sources. The negotiators also agreed to eliminate all other official and private claims.[42]

Negotiated in forty-five minutes by men who were not very concerned about the details of economic issues, the final agreement was full of unresolved problems. Roosevelt and his advisors were inexcusably hasty and careless about details on the debt issue. For example, they mentioned a loan to Moscow when they intended to extend only a credit. With the controversy over World War I loans causing repeated questions at press conferences, Roosevelt should have avoided such a mistake. Despite Litvinov's later insistence on a loan, he informed the Kremlin after the negotiations on November 15 that he had agreed to pay no more than $75 million on the loan to Kerensky "in the form of additional interest on the credit, obtained by us from America."[43] The White House also neglected to indicate that Washington expected interest on the debt and omitted any reference to the State Department's desire to exercise control over Soviet purchases. Roosevelt would have profited from the inclusion of experts from the State Department in the negotiations. If Moscow had rejected these specifics concerning interest and control, as well as a final fixed amount, the president then could have decided whether to proceed or to keep the debt question separate from recognition.

Roosevelt also ignored the State Department's warning that the Far Eastern situation be kept out of the negotiations with Litvinov. In his final discussion with the commissar on November 17, the president made several suggestions about Soviet-American cooperation against Japan which he kept secret from the State Department. After reviewing the German and Japanese threats to peace, Roosevelt suggested that the Kremlin and Washington exchange information about Japan and that (in Litvinov's words)

> America is ready to do everything in order to avert the Japanese danger from us. America will not wage war, for not one American favors that, but the president is ready to give us 100% moral and diplomatic support. As if reasoning aloud, Roosevelt asked why we did not subscribe to a non-aggression pact to which I gave immediate consent and also approved the idea of a Pacific pact, and Roosevelt on the spot charged Bullitt to busy himself with these questions and to make a report to him. Roosevelt, certainly, understands the unacceptability of even a triangular pact for Japan, but the rejection of Japan unties his hands for the conclusion of a pact with us. I asked him if he could make it for the preservation of peace and that he consider an agreement with us about joint actions in case of a threat to peace. Roosevelt, afraid of every doublesided obligation, replied that he prefers to make unilateral statements during the latter situation.[44]

Although Litvinov's account of the conversation cannot be compared with American records, the commissar depicted fairly accurately Roosevelt's hopes for limited diplomatic cooperation in the Far East (hopes he would raise again in 1937) and his habit of tossing out suggestions which had been neither cleared with the State Department nor studied by his advisors.

Shortly after midnight of November 17, Roosevelt and Litvinov signed the final agreements.[45] They had achieved their goal of recognition by accepting compromises on both sides. Litvinov had relinquished the Soviet desire for unconditional recognition and had agreed instead to a number of specific provisions. The president had surrounded recognition with guarantees; some of them, particularly on the debt issue, were imprecise. Smoothing over disagreements for the moment, Roosevelt had created a somewhat misleading impression of reconciliation which ensured a favorable immediate reaction from Americans but also laid the foundation for future difficulties.

American observers generally applauded Roosevelt's decision to recognize the Soviet Union. Many newspaper and magazines emphasized the potential trade benefits, although reservations about the extension of credits to Moscow increased.[46] Most commentators also hoped that recognition would have a favorable impact on the Far Eastern situation—on Soviet-Japanese tension immediately and on peace in Asia in the long run.[47] Unlike their reaction in October, editors now widely approved Roosevelt's abandonment of an ineffective, unrealistic policy. The president "saw the absurdity of a continued refusal to recognize a great Nation with a stable government and, with characteristic vigor, he cut the Gordian knot," applauded the *Dallas Morning News*. Other journals welcomed the removal of an "irritating absurdity," the "shedding of hypocrisy," and the "end of some fifteen years of elaborate up-stage pseudo-diplomacy."[48]

Many praised the president's cautions and careful approach. The *Wall Street Journal* called him "a master bargainer," and the *Commercial and Financial Chronicle* thanked Roosevelt for taking "care to guard scrupulously American interests."[49] Liberal and Republican journals added endorsements. The president "appears to have been a good trader and to have exacted from the Russians all the concessions and assurances that could reasonably be expected," concluded the *Chicago Daily News*. Very few observers questioned the firmness of the debt agreement.[50]

The initial reaction of those who had opposed recognition was subdued. Catholic spokesmen approved Roosevelt's action, particularly the agreement on religion, and Father Edmund Walsh briefly supported the White House. An announcement that "Roosevelt had put God back into Russia" brought cheers from the members of a large Catholic organization.[51] The American Federation of Labor and the American Legion promised that they would accept recognition but recommended continued vigilance against Soviet propaganda. "Litvinov came, conquered and departed with the spoils," complained the *National Republic*, which remained unconvinced that the Kremlin would abandon its revolutionary aims.[52]

State Department officials publicly endorsed recognition and privately believed that the president "drove a harder bargain than had been anticipated."[53] But Russian experts continued to doubt that Moscow would observe its agreements. George Kennan and other members of the Russian section at Riga retained their suspicions, as did Robert Kelley and members of the Division of Eastern European Affairs—particularly when they failed to obtain a definite debt agreement in negotiations with Litvinov after recognition. Litvinov's public statements, moreover, intensified their apprehension. Addressing the National Press Club, Litvinov casually denied any connection between Moscow and the American Communist party, and he also warned the press to leave the Comintern out of the agreements. "The Third International is not mentioned in the document," Litvinov stated, and "you must not read into it more than was mentioned."[54]

Undoubtedly President Roosevelt's satisfaction increased as Americans reacted favorably to recognition and extensively praised him. Indeed, the president deserved credit for his part in developing a consensus for recognition and negotiating agreements with Litvinov. Roosevelt understood that Americans would not approve an unconditional recognition and were particularly concerned about the issue of Soviet interference into American affairs. Using caution, indirection, delay, personal persuasion, and compromise, he had demonstrated his significant skills as a master politician. He had also adopted a realistic outlook when he dropped the ineffective policy of nonrecognition. Although he expected practical economic and diplomatic benefits from recognition, he was probably most concerned that "for sixteen long years a nation, larger than ours, has been unable to speak officially with the United States."[55]

Unfortunately Roosevelt's major weaknesses as a diplomat, as well as his strengths, had shaped the negotiations that began formal Soviet-American relations. His reluctance to work closely with the State Department had seriously weakened the settlement, most notably regarding the debt issue, where haste and carelessness about detail had generated problems that would surface in the future. He had also demonstrated a reluctance to be firm in personal negotiations; in particular, he should have insisted on a definite debt settlement and Soviet responsibility for the Comintern. Litvinov, moreover, had recognized most of Roosevelt's shortcomings, such as his failure to keep the State Department informed about the discussions; to the Soviet Foreign Affairs Ministry, he stated: "... it is our advantage to direct the negotiations in the presence of the President who will ... be more yielding than his counselors."[56]

Despite an apparently satisfactory beginning of Soviet-American diplomatic relations, the negotiations had produced serious misunderstandings on both sides which could quickly shatter a brief honeymoon atmosphere. Roosevelt had given Litvinov the impression that the agreements were designed primarily to appease public opinion, which increased the likelihood that the Kremlin would ignore them. The State Department, however, viewed the accords as a necessary test of Moscow's willingness to have normal relations with the United States. The president had also led Litvinov to expect Soviet-American cooperation against Japan when the White House had the support of neither the State Department nor Congress for any positive steps beyond recognition. On the other hand, Litvinov had given the president and his advisors the definite impression that the Soviet Union intended to make a partial payment of its debts and to seriously curtail its interference in American domestic affairs. The immediate future of Soviet-American relations depended on how these misunderstandings would be untangled.

3

Estrangement: Debts and Propaganda

Early in 1934, the American-Russian Chamber of Commerce announced plans for a "Recognition Trade Flight" to the Soviet Union. An airplane, full of manufactured goods, would fly to a number of Soviet cities and return with samples of Soviet goods. According to the Chamber's spokesman, this "missionary work" would encourage the sale of American products and assist Soviet industrialization. Washington and Moscow, however, turned down the Chamber's requests for official approval. The State Department refused permission to name the plane after President Roosevelt and would not support the flight. Moscow rejected the Chamber's request for permission to fly over and land on Soviet territory. Neither the State Department nor the Kremlin were ready to relax their reservations concerning the new Soviet-American relationship. In the spring and summer of 1934, reports came into Washington announcing the arrival of the "Recognition Trade Flight" plane in Bermuda; however, the plane never left the ground.[1]

Soviet-American diplomatic relations followed a similarly tantalizing but ill-fated course after recognition. The hopes for a substantial increase in trade and President Roosevelt's expectations of friendly diplomatic relations were both short-lived. Stalin and Litvinov also abandoned their expectations of substantial American assistance against Japan. The

27

estrangement that developed in 1934—35 resulted from the actions of Roosevelt and Stalin as well as from internal pressures on the White House. Roosevelt's mistakes during the negotiations on the debt issue and Stalin's overt violation of the agreement on noninterference precipitated friction. The president also found his flexibility limited by a rigid State Department, which insisted that Moscow make further concessions on the debt issue, and by the American public, which assumed that the debt question had been settled and that Soviet propaganda against the United States would cease.

The beginning of Soviet-American relations was also indirectly undermined by the absence of severe international crisis and the surge of isolationist sentiment in the United States. With the ebbing of tension in Soviet-Japanese relations, Stalin had less incentive to make necessary concessions to Washington and Roosevelt had less justification for making gestures of support for the Soviet Union that would antagonize Japan. In Europe Hitler moved unilaterally to rearm in 1934, but the most immediate threat to peace came from the Italian dictator, Benito Mussolini, who advanced against Ethiopia after December, 1934. Neither Moscow nor Washington considered the Ethiopian war a fundamental threat to their security or other interests.

Even if he had wanted to cooperate against Italian expansion, Roosevelt found himself increasingly restricted by isolationist sentiment and by a Congress trying to shape foreign policy that would avoid involvement in another war like World War I. For example, isolationists in Congress forced the White House in 1933 to abandon its efforts to win approval for an arms embargo against aggressors. Increasing hostility toward the European powers over their defaults on war debts combined with growing concern about the protection of American neutrality in 1934 to produce strong support for Sen. Hiram Johnson's bill to ban public financial transactions with foreign governments that were in default on their obligations to the American government. Despite the opposition of the State and Treasury departments, the Senate passed the Johnson Act, which infringed on the president's authority in foreign affairs. Johnson and other isolationists like William Borah backed a Senate committee investigation, headed by Gerald P. Nye, of the arms trade and its role in America's entry into World War I. Roosevelt, to the dismay of Secretary Hull, contributed to the erosion of his own authority when he handed the problem of neutrality, on which the State Department had prepared draft legislation, to the Nye committee in March, 1935. Hull tried unsuccessfully to kill the committee's recommendation of a ban on American citizens traveling in war zones, a prohibition against loans by private citizens to belligerent powers, and an impartial arms embargo against all belligerents. In August Congress passed a neutrality act which included a warning against traveling on belligerent ships, an impartial arms embargo, and a National Munitions Control Board to supervise the embargo. In asserting Congress's influence in foreign policy, the isolationists had also ensured that Roosevelt would not risk their wrath with any significant political cooperation with the Soviet Union.[2]

Roosevelt also continued to have problems with the State Department, which never fully agreed with him on the importance of Soviet-American relations. Nevertheless, as a result of the continuing depression and Hull's enthusiasm for trade expansion, the White House and the State Department did concur on the importance of encouraging trade with the Soviet Union. Shortly after recognition, Washington and Moscow removed discriminatory tonnage duties, and the Treasury Department annulled antidumping and convict labor rulings against the Soviet Union. In Washington, the first Export-Import Bank was established—a federal agency specifically designed to assist trade with the Soviet Union by extending credits for the purchase of American goods. Furthermore, Roosevelt and Assistant Secretary R. Walton Moore tried, without success, to persuade Congress to exclude the Soviet Union from the list of countries in default on their debts. They did obtain an exemption in the Johnson Act so that public corporations, like the Export-Import Bank, could extend credits to nations in default.[3]

Roosevelt and the State Department, however, could not agree on cooperation with the Soviet Union in the Far East. On November 17, 1933, the president had offered Litvinov "100 percent moral and diplomatic support" against Japan and had ordered Bullitt to study the idea of a nonaggression pact. After this discussion, Litvinov proposed to Under Secretary William Phillips the idea of a pact that would include China, Japan, the Soviet Union, and the United States. Phillips replied that the Kellogg-Briand Pact, which outlawed offensive wars, adequately covered the Far East. "I did not give him any encouragement," Phillips wrote in his diary, "because I am certain that Japan would not consent to a nonaggression pact with Russia."

According to another official, who shared the State Department's lack of knowledge about the president's remarks to Litvinov, Roosevelt had "made a particular point when the Russians were here of doing nothing that would offend Japanese susceptibilities or implying a support of Russia against Japan." The department had also immediately reassured the Japanese ambassador that recognition had "nothing whatever to do with the Far East."[4] Yet officials welcomed the impact of recognition on the Far Eastern situation. The Russians "have been talking much more decisively to the Japanese," Minister Nelson T. Johnson happily informed Stanley Hornbeck, and Ambassador Grew in Tokyo noted "a decidedly healthy, restraining and calming influence" in the Kremlin's firmer stance. When Soviet-Japanese tension increased in December, the State Department worried about the "possibility of Japan striking the Soviet in the spring." Showing a realistic flexibility, Russian specialist Robert Kelley advocated an immediate extension of long-term credits to Moscow in order to restrain Japan and "bring out a balance of power in the Far East which is essential to American interests."[5]

When tension ebbed in January and February, 1934, the State Department turned away from cooperation with Moscow. Officials never considered Moscow to be very reliable, especially since they suspected that the Kremlin would welcome an American-Japanese war. The general orientation of the United States toward Japan was also incompatible with any direct cooperation with Stalin. When in April Tokyo announced its opposition to foreign aid to China, the State Department cautiously rejected this stance on legal grounds but proceeded to curb American aid to China. Secretary Hull took a moral position of neither approving nor opposing Japanese actions, and Roosevelt concurred with an inactive policy designed to avoid provoking Japan.[6] Instead of advocating cooperation with Stalin, the State Department pointed to Moscow's problems with Japan as evidence that the Kremlin needed Washington much more than Washington needed the Kremlin; consequently, any concessions in the post-recognition negotiations should come from the Soviet Union rather than from America.

Roosevelt's selection of William Bullitt as ambassador to the Soviet Union also stimulated friction with the State Department. Although Secretary Hull approved the selection as a logical choice—considering the new ambassador's familiarity with the recent settlement and his enthusiasm for friendly Soviet-American relations—Hull and other officials may have accepted it only as a better alternative than Bullitt's continued presence in Washington. "What a travesty and how extraordinary, but it means his departure from the Department which will please Hull," commented one advisor regarding the appointment.[7] Hull indirectly indicated his displeasure with the ambassador in the almost bitter tone of his comments when problems developed over the debt issue. The State Department may also have feared that Bullitt would be too independent and too aligned with the White House to carry out the department's policies on relations with the Kremlin. Many officials considered the ambassador far too impulsive, and his public attack on President Woodrow Wilson after his mission to Russia in 1919 had not been forgotten.

Hull and other officials, however, did not anticipate Bullitt's most serious weaknesses with respect to the Russian post: his emotional enthusiasm for the Soviet Union and his need for intimacy and approval. The new ambassador had a mercurial temperament and knew little about the Soviet Union; his enthusiasm thus rested on a fragile base. Roosevelt did offer Bullitt a superficial intimacy and ready praise for his efforts. For Bullitt to expect a similar relationship with the Bolsheviks indicates not only how uninformed he was about Soviet history but also how he could later turn emotionally against Moscow.[8]

The Kremlin seemed to anticipate Bullitt's weaknesses when he made a quick trip to Moscow in December, 1933, and overwhelmed the new ambassador with everything from an American flag at his hotel to standing cheers at the Bolshoi Theater. Stalin capped this welcome by meeting Bullitt at a private dinner, assuring him that "at any moment, day or night, if you wish to see me you have only to ask and I will see you at once." Moscow intended more than flattery in this special treatment of Bullitt. All Soviet officials who met with him stressed the danger of a Japanese attack upon the Soviet Union and asked for assistance from Washington. Stalin, for example, expressed interest in the acquisition of American rails for the Trans-Siberian railway. Litvinov pushed even harder than Stalin for American cooperation, asking for a visit by American naval vessels to Vladivostok and suggesting that "anything that could be done to make the Japanese believe that the United States was ready to cooperate with Russia, even though there might be no basis for the belief, would be valuable."[9]

Stalin and his advisors definitely expected Bullitt to follow up on Roosevelt's offer of moral and diplomatic support in the Far East. On December 11 Litvinov questioned the ambassador about the prospects for a nonaggression pact and "my hints to the President on the desirability of a declaration in which we pledge ourselves to cooperate in case of the threat of war."

Bullitt, who proposed more ideas of Soviet-American cooperation against Japan than he later admitted to the State Department, avoided a direct reply to the commissar. Two days later the ambassador told Litvinov's deputy, Lev Karakhan, that Washington would find it difficult to make a nonaggression pact with Moscow since it had rejected a similar proposal from Tokyo. Nevertheless, Bullitt noted favorably Japanese suspicions about a Soviet-American alliance. "Such notions in Japan about our relations he considers extremely useful for us and for world affairs," reported the deputy commissar. Bullitt later informed Roosevelt and Hull that he had told Litvinov that Washington would extend only its moral influence for peace in the Far East. Yet, in his final talk with the commissar, the ambassador did not decisively reject a pact; after reviewing the difficulties involved with respect to Japan, he offered to "once again discuss this question with the President."[10]

The Soviet Union approached Roosevelt directly in February, 1934, when its new ambassador, Alexander A. Troyanovsky, called at the White House for the first time. American officials respected Troyanovsky as a moderate and articulate diplomat who had developed his skills as ambassador to Japan from 1927 to 1933. When the president asked him for his views on Japan's policies, Troyanovsky warned that "Japan will not listen separately to America or the Soviet Union, but to both together she will listen at the last moment; therefore, it is necessary for us to have contact." The ambassador recommended that Moscow and Washington consider cooperation "with respect to a Japanese attack on China and war on the Pacific ocean." Troyanovsky then informed the Kremlin that the president "is ready to agree with this," but Roosevelt instead turned to generalities about the peaceful aims of the Soviet Union and the United States.[11]

The Kremlin's approach backfired. Misinterpreting Moscow's requests as an indication of desperation, Bullitt concluded that Stalin would accept any American demands and quickly settle the debt issue. "The Soviet Government values so highly the moral support it may receive from the United States in the matter of preventing war with Japan," Bullitt informed Roosevelt, "that there is almost nothing we may not ask for and obtain at the present time."[12] By accepting this recommendation, however, Washington reduced the chances for a satisfactory resolution of postrecognition problems and the development of relations with the Soviet Union. Without gestures of U.S. support in the Far East, such as a joint aid program to China, Moscow would not pay its debt or permanently exempt America from its propaganda activities. However, the idea of such support was in conflict with the generally passive attitude of the United States toward Japan in 1934–35.

When Bullitt returned to Moscow in March, 1934, he immediately encountered the results of his miscalculation about Soviet policy. The ambassador "beamed happily from the train window as he saw a band

and a delegation laden with bouquets waiting on the station platform" in Moscow. The music and flowers, however, were for a delegation of women rather than for Bullitt, who barely concealed his disappointment from the minor official who greeted him.[13] Aloofness replaced the flattery lavished upon him earlier. Soviet officials continued to talk with the ambassador, but Stalin withdrew from personal contact, and difficulties developed over even minor issues, such as housing facilities for American officials, restrictions on travel by officials in the Soviet Union, and controversy over the value of Soviet currency. The diplomatic honeymoon had not even lasted one winter.

The first serious problem concerned the debt negotiations. Since Roosevelt was being questioned constantly by the press about negotiations on the general debt situation, a settlement with the Kremlin was imperative—particularly since the announcement in November of the gentlemen's agreement with Litvinov, which had not publicized the terms, had given the impression that a definite accord had already been reached. Roosevelt also had to settle this matter before the State Department would approve further cooperation with the Soviet Union. Although the president wanted only a token payment as a demonstration of Moscow's good will, the State Department considered the issue a serious test of Moscow's willingness to live up to the standards of civilized society. Several officials in the Moscow embassy confided to Ambassador Bullitt that Russian specialist Robert Kelley's "unaltered purpose in life for the last decade has been to achieve an explicit—not merely a tacit—debt acknowledgement from the Soviet Government."[14]

The Kremlin initially shared Washington's interest in a settlement, particularly when it realized that American financial assistance would depend on payment of its debt. Tension with Japan in the winter and spring of 1934 also kept Moscow interested in an accord that might lead to American support in the Far East. On Bullitt's second trip, at their first meeting on March 14, Litvinov immediately asked about cooperation in the Far East. Although the ambassador indicated that Roosevelt was not considering any concrete measures, he did suggest that Washington remained interested in a four-power nonaggression pact as well as a general Pacific nonaggression accord. "Bullitt communicated nothing of interest but everything stands clear that America has no intention to advance with other new suggestions," complained the disappointed Soviet commissar. Several days later Bullitt against expressed Roosevelt's interest in a nonaggression pact that would include Japan but, under questioning by Litvinov, admitted that "Roosevelt hardly intends to turn to the powers with suggestions about a pact. He would rather throw out an idea in order to catch up other governments and to get them to make appropriate use of it."[15]

The first exchange between Bullitt and Litvinov on the debt issue revealed the mistakes made in the Washington negotiations of 1933. The ambassador asked for a Soviet payment of $150 million with 4 percent interest and offered a credit with the first Export-Import Bank at 10 percent interest. In reply, Litvinov proposed a payment of $100 million without interest and an American loan with interest. Bullitt's argument that Roosevelt had used the words loan and credit interchangeably did not budge the commissar, whose proposal was closer than Bullitt's to the original agreement that mentioned a payment between $75 million and $150 million without any interest and a loan with interest. Litvinov also emphasized the Kremlin's concern about the establishment of a precedent which could be used by France and England, who had much more substantial claims against the Soviet Union than did the United States. The commissar's demand for a loan must have been a negotiating ploy since, despite his disclaimer to Bullitt, he had informed Moscow that they would receive a credit.[16]

Litvinov's proposal produced dismay in Washington. Assistant Secretary Moore wired Bullitt that the president "was very much astonished that Litvinov should talk about a direct loan to the Soviet which ... was never discussed." Secretary Hull shared Roosevelt's surprise and disappointment. Under Secretary Phillips noted in his diary that "Litvinov is now going back on his oral pledges.... Bullitt's honeymoon is over," Phillips concluded, and "we are taking a very stiff attitude."[17] The State Department moved immediately to prevent the Export-Import Bank from extending any credits to Moscow. Litvinov subsequently agreed to pay interest on the debt, dropped his demand for a loan, and proposed instead a twenty-year credit with interest. Although Bullitt favored Litvinov's new offer, Hull strongly rejected it as "wholly unacceptable." After twenty years Moscow would have paid off its original debt, Hull complained, but would then owe twice as much for the new credit.[18]

Most American officials opposed any compromise of the original American position. Ambassador Bullitt, who incorrectly assumed that Litvinov and Stalin disagreed over the debt, tried to circumvent Litvinov through other officials. Bullitt also recommended to Roosevelt that he inform the Russians that "if they are unwilling to move forward and take the carrot they will receive the club on the behind." Bullitt's club included a warning to Litvinov that Washington might extend the credits of the

Export-Import Bank to Japan. The State Department supported Bullitt's position but rejected any bluffs about American aid to Japan.[19]

President Roosevelt favored a more conciliatory approach. "The President seems inclined to go much farther than I would in modifying the original debt proposals ... ," Moore wrote to Bullitt, "but I did suggest to him the difficulty he would find in doing what he has tentatively in mind." After reviewing the earlier discussions with Soviet Ambassador Alexander A. Troyanovsky on April 30, 1934, Roosevelt modified the original American position in response to a new proposal from Litvinov. Roosevelt reduced the level of interest and promised to supply a credit up to double the debt if Moscow liquidated each transaction within five years.[20]

Despite Roosevelt's intervention, the Kremlin and Washington remained at odds over the question of control, an issue that had been left out of the gentlemen's agreement. Moscow wanted complete freedom in its use of the American credits; the State Department insisted on control by the Export-Import Bank. "Litvinov's attitude," Secretary Hull exclaimed, "is wholly inconsistent ... and from every point of view absurd." Hull worried about Soviet purchases of arms and bitter competition among American businessmen for Soviet orders.[21]

Sometime in April or May, 1934, the Kremlin decided to reject any further compromises on the debt. An improvement in Soviet-Japanese relations after Moscow offered to sell its interest in the Chinese Eastern Railway contributed to this decision. Ambassador Troyanovsky reported from Washington that Roosevelt favored a more moderate approach than did Bullitt or the State Department, but he suggested that only an increase in American-Japanese tension would prompt Washington to "repudiate their own unreasonable obstinacy."[22] Litvinov frequently suggested to Bullitt that they drop the debt issue. Although upset by Litvinov's lack of interest, Bullitt recommended "no other policy than unruffled patience." We should "preserve our wrath for major issues," the ambassador advised Hull, for "we cannot forget that at any time the lines of major policy of the United States and the Soviet Union may run parallel."[23] Hull and the State Department, however, believed that Moscow never intended to fulfill its agreements.

Despite Soviet apathy, President Roosevelt remained very interested in a settlement. He would have liked to satisfy interested exporters who were urging the administration to make a quick settlement that would open credit to Moscow before it turned to British and German corporations. The State Department received "constant inquiries from American businessmen as to the prospect of a debt agreement," though they expressed little criticism of Washington's strategy.[24]

The November congressional elections also entered into Roosevelt's calculations. He believed that a favorable settlement would help Democrats in the elections. Washington had kept the negotiations from receiving public attention partially through the president's deceptive replies at press conferences. When asked on May 9 if Moscow had made an offer, Roosevelt replied, "No." On August 15 the press asked if the president had reviewed the debt situation. "I have not had time to talk about it at all," he commented.[25]

After Roosevelt persuaded the State Department to modify its demand for complete control over Soviet purchases, Washington engaged in another round of unsuccessful negotiations. On August 29 the president told Assistant Secretary Moore: "Try to bring the Russian matter to a conclusion. I do not think the coming election presents a valid reason for delay and I am inclined to think that an honorable settlement between us and Russia would help rather than hurt. At all times it should be made very clear, of course, that the credits we extend will result in immediate orders for American goods and thus put American workmen to work."[26]

Roosevelt finally seemed to realize that only American support in the Far East would persuade Moscow to accept a settlement. On October 3, he expressed interest in a multilateral nonaggression pact for the Pacific that would include Moscow, and Bullitt tried to entice Litvinov with the possibility of general cooperation. Litvinov recorded the exchange: "Roosevelt planned a rapprochement with us in the interests of peace.... He has made many steps already in this direction, and he could make many more in the future. But if we will hold to these positions, then Roosevelt could do nothing since in America there will be very few people interested in relations with us." Later in October Roosevelt raised the idea of a nonaggression pact with Under Secretary Phillips. After Phillips and Pierrepont Moffat expressed reservations, Roosevelt decided to "let this matter rest."[27]

Negotiations over the debt finally collapsed in January, 1935, when Ambassador Troyanovsky returned from Moscow with a rejection of Washington's latest proposal. After criticizing the Soviet position for five minutes, Secretary Hull ended the negotiations and soon afterward abolished the first Export-Import Bank. The State Department, which could not openly blame Roosevelt for the result, found Ambassador Bullitt a convenient target. "Litvinov won his victory when he obtained recognition," Hull coldly reminded Bullitt in September, "and regards everything else as of minor importance." Roosevelt kept out of the issue by referring press questions back to Secretary Hull: "Try him again," he would say in response to probing questions.[28]

Moscow and Washington shared responsibility for the unsuccessful negotiations. The State Department's inflexibility prevented a realistic compromise like the one Roosevelt proposed in April. Secretary Hull and other officials, who insisted that Moscow prove its good faith, exaggerated the strength of Washington's position (especially as European states also repudiated their debts) and worried too much about the dangers of uncontrolled trade with Moscow. On the other hand, Stalin gave only perfunctory attention to Roosevelt's various proposals after April, 1934. For the American negotiators, a debt settlement had become a necessary prelude to expansion of Soviet-American relations; the failure to obtain it started the slide toward estrangement.[29]

The White House profited from public ignorance and confusion about the terms of the negotiations. Assuming the Soviets to be at fault for the breakdown in negotiations, most Americans approved the administration's stance. Hull's public statement and Litvinov's reply reinforced the impression that the question of a loan to Moscow was crucial, along with disagreement over the amount of the debt payment and rate of interest. Very few commentators focused on the main obstacles, the issue of long-term credits and control over Soviet purchases.[30] Interested exporters, who sadly noted the "vanishing prospect of Soviet trade," and liberal journals, which blamed the State Department, expressed the greatest disappointment.[31]

A few Republican editors called for a return to nonrecognition. "The indisputable fact is that recognition has failed of its purpose," argued the *Philadelphia Inquirer*. The *Seattle Times* agreed that "two nations fundamentally antagonistic on every principle of government and common honesty can't stand with hands clasped across either sea." But most journals either ignored this recommendation, disputed its relevance, or vigorously criticized it. Even a staunch critic of the Soviets like the *Boston Evening Transcript* attacked nonrecognition as an extremist measure which "cooler heads" would reject.[32] Instead of criticizing Washington, many editors recommended a resumption of negotiations; the *Richmond Times-Dispatch*, for example, urged Roosevelt to keep negotiating, for "our army of unemployed can never be put back to work unless foreign markets for the country's industrial products can be found."[33]

The reaction of the press probably reinforced Washington's interest in making a settlement to obtain "a market for raw cotton and textiles and other American products." Some officials also wanted to increase Moscow's "economic strength" in order to "divert the attention of Japan and ... discourage reckless adventuring on Japan's part."[34] Moscow also remained interested in a resumption of negotiations, although Soviet officials were unwilling to modify their position. In his assessment of the breakdown in the talks, Ambassador Troyanovsky placed the blame on Washington's disappointment over Moscow's independent foreign policy and on the internal American political situation, most notably a rising reactionary mood and the president's movement to the right. Litvinov and his deputy, Krestinsky, were not as pessimistic as the ambassador. The White House had not broken relations, Krestinsky reminded Troyanovsky, and the State Department not only wanted to negotiate a trade agreement but also, like England and France, would probably extend credit pretty quickly without a debt settlement. "In the next couple of years which appear the most acute in our relations with Japan," the deputy commissar recommended that Moscow try to stay close to Washington and especially to Roosevelt.[35]

In June, Roosevelt encouraged Moore and Bullitt to approach Moscow about a new interim settlement, but negotiations over the debt would not resume again in earnest until 1938. Instead, Washington negotiated a trade agreement with Moscow in July, 1935. The White House promised to extend most-favored-nation treatment to the Kremlin if it purchased $30 million of American goods in the next year. Secretary Hull endorsed the agreement as a favorable expansion of trade that was within the spirit of his general reciprocal trade program and was acceptable to the department's Russian specialists, since it would not require close cooperation with the Kremlin.[36] The accord also reduced the inquiries and complaints that the department had been receiving from business firms.

The trade agreement partly reduced the disappointment over the unsuccessful debt negotiations, but Roosevelt soon faced a more serious challenge over the issue of Soviet interference in American domestic affairs. In November, 1933, Litvinov had explicitly promised that Soviet organizations would not advocate the overthrow of the American system or interfere in American internal affairs. Washington did not insist on full observance of the agreement and did not protest as long as Stalin avoided an overt, public violation of the pledge. The White House, however, had to be watchful on this issue, particularly since anti-Communist spokesmen, immediately after recognition, had renewed their criticism of Soviet interference in American affairs.

Before the Special Committee on Un-American Activities, established by the House in 1934, Ralph Easley of the National Civic Federation and Walter S. Steele of the *National Republic* pointed out evidence of Soviet propaganda in violation of Litvinov's pledge. The committee attacked Moscow's involvement in American affairs in its final report.[37] Anti-Communist leaders worried about a spread of radical ideas encouraged by the Kremlin; among them was the Liberty League, a coalition of conservative Democrats and wealthy businessmen formed in August, 1934.[38] The American Vigilant Intelligence Federation and writer Elizabeth Dilling alleged the existence of a subversive conspiracy, abetted by Moscow, which controlled Roosevelt's New Deal. Dilling's *The Red Network*, an indiscriminate catalogue of individuals and organizations, appeared in April, 1934. Even more sensational was Dr. William A. Wirt's accusation that Roosevelt's brain-trusters were plotting to overthrow the social order.[39]

The response of the press to the Wirt affair indicated that Roosevelt had some flexibility in his reply to charges of Soviet interference. When a congressional hearing revealed Wirt's lack of evidence, most editors expressed amusement over the whole affair. "Flatter than a crepe suzette fell the Red Scare of 1934," concluded *Time*.[40] Yet the charge of Communist influence in the New Deal had potential as a political issue against Roosevelt.

Washington initially tried to keep the interference issue quiet and out of the debt negotiations. When Matthew Woll of the American Federation of Labor and Easley presented evidence of Soviet interference to Assistant Secretary Moore, he urged them "not to agitate the subject in any way, pending our effort to conclude an agreement as to debts," although the State Department already had "pretty definite" proof of Soviet violations. The evidence consisted of articles in Soviet publications urging American Communists to launch strikes, the discussion of policies for the American Communist party at Comintern meetings, and Soviet direction of the American Communist party's efforts to acquire positions of leadership in the American Federation of Labor. President Roosevelt also kept away from this volatile issue. When asked by a reporter about reports of Soviet propaganda, Roosevelt replied: "I have not heard anything about it at all. Have you any reports, specific ones?" The reporter answered, "Quite a few," and Roosevelt ended the exchange by saying,"Ask the State Department; I haven't any."

Assistant Secretary Moore and Secretary Hull privately warned Ambassador Troyanovsky and the Kremlin about the violations of Litvinov's pledge, specifically the points about noninterference in the internal affairs of the United States and preventing the activity of organizations which aimed at the overthrow of the political and social order in the United States. Counselor Wiley was not very impressed with Washington's complaint. "There is nothing particularly unexpected in it, no allegations of subversive undercover activities are made...," Wiley informed Ambassador Bullitt, and "formal representations in the matter might be equivalent to shooting sparrows with heavy artillery."[41]

The Kremlin's obvious preparations for the Seventh Comintern Congress in the summer of 1935, despite Litvinov's denials to Bullitt, brought stronger warnings from Washington. In July, Hull instructed the ambassador to tell the Kremlin that any involvement of America or Americans in the meeting would constitute a violation of Litvinov's agreement. Bullitt favored measures that would be commensurate with the severity of the Comintern's statements. "Some people in Washington will doubtless want to break relations even if the violation is merely technical," he wrote to Roosevelt, "but I can hear you roar with laughter over the idea of breaking relations on the basis of a mere technical violation of Litvinov's pledge." If Moscow avoided giving offense to America, Bullitt assumed the president would wish "to ignore the Congress altogether." However, if a "gross and insulting" violation occurred, he recommended that a break in relations would be justified.[42]

Stalin forced an official American response to the Comintern Congress by permitting a limited violation of Litvinov's agreement. Earl Browder and William Z. Foster, leaders of the American Communist party, attended the conference and were elected to the Presidium; Browder reviewed the status and activities of the American Communist party before the Congress. Other Americans served in offices or on committee assignments and made speeches. Georgy Dimitrov, the new secretary-general of the Comintern, suggested the application of the new united-front tactics to the United States. Most officials, however, focused on the new united front against Fascism rather than the immediate overthrow of American capitalism.[43]

"The main point" about the Comintern Congress, Bullitt suggested to Roosevelt the day after it ended, "is to handle the matter from the domestic, not the foreign, political viewpoint."[44] This reference to the domestic reaction was very pertinent to the calculations of the Roosevelt administration. Since the Comintern Congress lasted for almost a month, American observers had ample time to assess it. The press reacted very mildly. Most journals either completely ignored the Congress or did not request action by Washington, although there was some criticism of

Moscow for at least a "technical violation" of Litvinov's pledge, and many editors were suspicious about the Kremlin's united-front policy. Despite Earl Browder's claim of great advances for the American Communist party with youth, organized labor, and the Farm Labor party, most editors agreed with the *Denver Post*'s conclusion that "the menace of Communism should be among the least of our worries."[45] Only a few anti-Communist leaders and Republican newspapers suggested that Washington had a "plain duty ... to withdraw recognition."[46]

Ironically, Bullitt—ignoring his own advice—overreacted to the Comintern Congress. Since he had helped to obtain Litvinov's pledge, the ambassador regarded its violation as a personal insult. He opposed a break in relations, for he favored the retention of the Moscow embassy "to measure and report on the increasingly noxious activities and breach of faith of the Soviet Union." Instead, he asked Washington to make an oral protest about the Comintern, to revoke the exequaturs of Soviet consuls, to restrict American visas for Russians, and to inform the American public about Moscow's lack of faith. The ambassador's telegrams to Washington on the night of August 21, 1935, marked the end of his sympathy toward the Soviet Union.[47]

Roosevelt and Hull rejected all of Bullitt's recommendations (although an oral protest would have minimized the public reaction as well as reduced the likelihood of an official Soviet reply). However, they did decide to protest in writing. Roosevelt may have realized that an official complaint would be popular despite the press's failure to demand one. He also may have wanted protection against Republican criticism, particularly since a rumor appeared in the press that the American Communist party, under orders from the Comintern, would support Roosevelt in the 1936 election.[48]

On August 23, Secretary Hull instructed Bullitt to send a message to the Kremlin, warning that its "flagrant violation" of Litvinov's pledge would preclude the "development of friendly relations." Further violations, Hull cautioned, would bring the "most serious consequences." Washington hoped to end the affair with this written protest, but the Kremlin made a formal reply, denying any violation of its agreement on noninterference and disclaiming any responsibility for the Comintern.[49]

"The stern rebuke administered to the Moscow government ... will be universally approved in the United States," the *Atlanta Constitution* confidently concluded. Americans endorsed Washington's protest, but the Soviet reply precipitated a demand by Republican leaders for a break in relations. Republican editors argued that the domestic political thrust of

Roosevelt's protest should not obscure the total bankruptcy of his Russian policy, another unsuccessful New Deal experiment. "It now appears that the Roosevelt Administration committed a dangerous and expensive blunder in recognizing the Soviet Government," suggested the *Philadelphia Inquirer.*[50]

Most commentators, however, opposed a return to nonrecognition. Liberal journals, for example, admitted a technical Soviet violation but criticized Hull's protest as a serious overreaction which might increase international instability. "Hull merely succeeded in making this country look silly," complained the *New Republic*.[51] Other editors, who emphasized Moscow's opposition to Fascism and support for the status quo, worried about the unfavorable impact of Soviet-American tension on the European and Far Eastern situations. The "interests of both countries are now identical in the desire to avert any extension of the area of political instability," the *Washington Post* pointed out, with specific reference to the Italian-Ethiopian crisis. "Now, more than ever, in this time of acute international tension, these relations should be maintained," insisted the Republican *Chicago Daily News*.[52]

The Soviet denial of any violation prompted a Washington reply, although Roosevelt again rejected Bullitt's recommendation for minor retaliatory measures. Hull advised Bullitt that the president "feels we should proceed step by step in this matter and desires that our action at the present time be confined to the making ... of a formal statement clearly and forcibly setting forth our position ... with great dignity." In a statement to the press on September 1, which Washington did not present to the Kremlin, Hull rejected the Soviet reply as untrue and warned that further violations would seriously impair Soviet-American relations.[53] Despite some criticism and demands for more action, most American observers approved Hull's statement.[54]

Although they were glad that the affair was over, most editors put the Soviet Union on probation because of the failure to resolve the debt issue and the noninterference issue. The press wanted to break relations immediately if another Soviet violation occurred. "Russian-American relations have been conducted for nearly two years past on a basis of Soviet bad faith and American credulity," complained the *New York Herald Tribune*.[55] Few editors indicated much interest in diplomatic cooperation with Moscow in the future. American opinion about the potential benefits of Soviet-American relations had significantly deteriorated.

An even greater disillusionment pervaded the attitudes of Moscow and

Washington officials. As Secretary Hull recollected in his memoirs, Soviet-American relations were "back almost to where we started." Moscow's petty harassment of American diplomats in Moscow on issues such as their housing and the goods they imported or exported, as well as the numerous difficulties the American embassy encountered in its efforts to protect American nationals, further reinforced the State Department's belief that friendly relations with the Soviet Union were impossible. Ambassador Bullitt urged foreign correspondents and diplomats in Moscow to attack the Kremlin in their articles and reports. By the second anniversary of recognition, Moscow was also indicating little interest in the relationship; according to Ambassador Troyanovsky, Washington "was so determined to remain aloof from foreign affairs that it was relatively unimportant to maintain good relations with the United States."[56]

Washington and Moscow both contributed to the failure of Soviet-American relations to move very far beyond recognition. Stalin lost interest in a debt settlement when Roosevelt refused to provide substantial aid against Japan, and the Soviet leader then antagonized Americans with the Comintern's interference in domestic affairs. Roosevelt's mistakes came in the area of tactics, most notably his handling of the State Department on the debt issue and the form and tone of the first protest against the Comintern. However, the president should have gained valuable insight into negotiations with the Soviet Union. He should have learned to avoid agreements with Moscow that could not be fulfilled, regardless of their favorable impact on the American news media. And he should have questioned his belief in the possibility of friendly relations with the Kremlin, considering Stalin's refusal to keep the agreement on noninterference.

Yet the emerging estrangement did not entirely undermine the advantages of recognition. American exports to the Soviet Union increased gradually, especially after the trade agreement in 1935. The United States also enhanced its expertise on the Soviet Union through the training of officers in the American embassy in Moscow. As Stalin advocated cooperation with the Western powers and launched a devastating purge, the embassy became an increasingly valuable source of information and interpretation for the United States.

4

American Diplomats and
Stalin's Diplomacy

After the frustrations of 1934 and 1935 and as a response to the rising isolationist sentiment in the United States, American relations with the Soviet Union settled into a period of drift. The White House was uninterested in new initiatives, as Roosevelt focused on domestic issues and the upcoming election of 1936. The State Department was content to concern itself with matters of trade and sought no closer cooperation with Moscow. Yet American observers in the United States and American diplomats abroad, especially those serving in the U.S. embassy in Moscow, watched Soviet foreign and domestic policies after 1934 and developed attitudes which increased the estrangement in Soviet-American relations. When Roosevelt tried again to promote cooperation with the Kremlin in 1937–38, he encountered intensified opposition from diplomats, who questioned Stalin's reliability and motives, and from the news media, which denounced Stalin's bloody purge.

Throughout the thirties, American diplomats who watched Stalin maneuver between Nazi Germany and the Western powers retained a strong suspicion about his tactics and objectives. Despite a general difference in assessment of Soviet policy between Soviet experts who increasingly emphasized the dominance of nationalistic self-interest and other officials who stressed the importance of Marxist-Leninist ideology, most officials believed that the Kremlin's commitment to eventual Communist expansion discredited current policies and made the Soviet Union unacceptable as a potential ally. Since Russian specialists were suspicious of Stalin's objectives, they accurately recognized the ambiguity in Soviet policy, most notably the Kremlin's efforts to cooperate with the Western powers against Nazi Germany combined with its secret approaches to Hitler. Yet American diplomats underestimated the importance of Stalin's overtures to the West and the potential benefits in the encouragement of these overtures—if only to keep Stalin away from Hitler.

Historians of Soviet-American relations have generally neglected the evaluations made by Russian specialists. William A. Williams, for example, in his pioneering study of American-Russian relations, fails to consider the Moscow embassy's reports, although Williams emphasizes the importance of George Kennan's post-1945 recommendations in the development of Washington's containment policy. Like Williams, Robert Paul Browder and other specialists concentrate on the origins and results of the United States' extension of diplomatic recognition to Moscow in 1933. The only exceptions are Beatrice Farnsworth's analysis of Ambassador William C. Bullitt and several unpublished dissertations. Farnsworth judiciously mixes praise of Bullitt's prescience concerning Moscow's future expansion in Eastern Europe with criticism of his emotionalism and the policies he recommended to Washington. Yet Farnsworth necessarily focuses on Bullitt's handling of bilateral issues such as Soviet propaganda and the debt issue, rather than his and the rest of the Moscow embassy's evaluations of Stalin's diplomacy.[1]

This neglect reflects in part an underestimation of the importance of the American diplomats' appraisals of Soviet diplomacy. The experience of living in Moscow in the 1930s and making evaluations of Stalin's domestic and foreign policies had a lasting impact on officials who not only influenced American policy toward Moscow during World War II but also played an important role in the cold war years after 1945. The general views that ambassadors and career officers formed in the 1930s tended to mold their continuing interpretations on crucial issues such as Stalin's objectives after 1945. Despite the voluminous literature on Soviet-American relations after 1941, historians of this latter period have also not recognized the critical influence of the 1930s experience on American officials.[2]

Important social and institutional pressures shaped the attitudes of American officials who went to the Soviet Union or followed Stalin's policies from within the State Department. Personal temperament and

ambition as well influenced the evaluations of America's three ambassadors to Moscow. William Bullitt, who committed his emotions and his
prestige to expectations of friendly, intimate relations with the Kremlin,
became a hostile opponent by 1935 when Soviet officials withdrew both
personal intimacy and cooperative relations. Joseph E. Davies, who
replaced Bullitt in 1937, also wanted friendly relations with Stalin. A
successful corporation lawyer and financial supporter of the Democratic
campaign in 1936, Davies was asked by Roosevelt to carry out a brief
"mission" to Moscow in 1937. The president wanted to find out which
side Moscow would support in the event of war between the Western
democracies and the Fascist powers. Davies' earnest desire for diplomatic
cooperation with the Kremlin caused him to exaggerate Stalin's general
reliability and the firmness of Soviet opposition to Hitler.[3]

Laurence A. Steinhardt, who arrived in Moscow in August, 1939, came
from a similar background but had a different ambition. After starting as a
political appointee in 1933 with inherited wealth and legal training,
Steinhardt became a career officer. At his posts in Sweden and Peru,
Steinhardt cultivated the image of the professional who reported cautiously about current developments. Before coming to Moscow, he
accepted the interpretations advanced by Russian specialists in Washington who recommended a hard line against the Kremlin, matching annoyance for annoyance.[4]

As chief of the Division of Eastern European Affairs from 1926 to 1937,
Robert Kelley played a crucial role in the institutional molding of young
Russian specialists. Kelley impressed upon officers like George Kennan
and Charles Bohlen the importance of taking a cautious, objective approach with as much factual verification as possible in evaluating Soviet
policies. Yet Kennan later remarked that Kelley took "a sharply critical
view of Soviet policies and methods" primarily because he believed that
the "communist leaders in Russia are unwilling to abandon their revolutionary aims with respect to the United States." Loy W. Henderson, who
as first secretary of the embassy directed the political reporting from
Moscow until 1938, had, next to Kelley, the most influence over new
recruits. Henderson impressed subordinates as a man of "deep serious-
ness and impressive sincerity," with an "unbending conscientiousness."[5]
He strove for objectivity in his evaluations but remained suspicious about
the Kremlin's long-range intentions.

Special training shaped the attitudes and interpretive approaches of the
younger Russian specialists. Most of them spent some time in the Russian
section of the American legation at Riga in Latvia. Under Kelley's supervi-

sion, Kennan and Bohlen received intensive training in Russian history, culture, and language rather than exclusively in Soviet politics and economics. Kennan and Bohlen, who specialized in political reporting during their tours of duty in Moscow, frequently turned to past Soviet and Russian history when preparing their memoranda. "Politically, I had to go back into Russian history and to probe the origins of the traditional suspicion and diffidence on the part of the Russian rulers," comments Kennan in his memoirs. Kelley's demand for caution in generalization and attention to facts also influenced Bohlen's analysis.[6]

Even when nonspecialists such as Alexander Kirk and Stuart Grummon entered the embassy staff, which usually had eight officers, they readily accepted the interpretations of the Russian specialists. Although the staff frequently debated the meaning and implications of Stalin's policies, they rarely failed to develop a consensus—undoubtedly bolstered by the experience of living in Moscow in the thirties. American officials were plagued by annoyances: the Kremlin restricted travel, isolated foreign representatives, and refused to reply to diplomatic notes. The Soviet bureaucracy made housing facilities, currency exchange, and a steady supply of hot water unpredictable. Close exposure to Stalin's totalitarian system, climaxed by a massive purge, could only increase the doubts of embassy officials about any diplomatic cooperation with Stalin.[7]

American diplomats disagreed somewhat about the influence of Marxist-Leninist ideology in Stalin's diplomacy. Ambassadors Bullitt and Davies were furthest apart in their views. After Bullitt became disillusioned with the Kremlin, he criticized the Soviet Union as a "nation ruled by fanatics who are ready to sacrifice themselves and everyone else for their religion of communism" and felt that world revolution remained the Kremlin's primary goal. "Neither Stalin or any other leader of the Communist party has deviated in the slightest from the determination to spread communism to the ends of the earth," he reminded the State Department.[8] On the other hand, Davies and Philip R. Faymonville, the American military attaché in Moscow from 1934 until 1939, emphasized Stalin's concern for security as opposed to ideology. "There is no danger from communism here, so far as the United States is concerned," Davis confidently remarked in his final dispatch from Moscow.[9]

Russian specialists increasingly emphasized the importance of national interest in Stalin's calculations, although they remained suspicious about the Kremlin's future intentions. After 1933 the Division of Eastern European Affairs, the Russian section at Riga, and the Moscow embassy pointed out a "subordination of the aims of 'world revolution' to the interests of the Soviet State in foreign policy."[10] Loy Henderson, Charles Bohlen, and George Kennan considered national defense to be the most important, immediate Soviet objective. "The essential element of Stalin's policy," Bohlen notes in his memoirs, "was to protect, above all, the Bolshevik regime in Russia."[11] However, they also worried about Stalin's manipulation of foreign Communist parties to disrupt American interests in Latin America or to encourage China's resistance to Japanese expansion.[12] When Stalin aided the Loyalist government in the Spanish Civil War, the Moscow embassy suggested that the Kremlin wanted to retain its influence with the world revolutionary movement as well as establish a Communist satellite in Spain.[13]

This assessment headed in the right direction but did not move far enough. Contrary to Bullitt's view, Stalin generally subordinated ideology to the interests of the Soviet Union. Although the Soviet leader pursued power as a revolutionary well-versed in Marxist-Leninist theory, he seemed to use ideology as a tactic rather than allow it to shape his diplomatic objectives. The idea of world revolution gave Stalin a rationalization for the hegemony of the Soviet Communist party as well as an instrument, in the international communist movement, for influencing the policies of other countries. The pursuit of power—both the creation of it and the removal of any potential opposition to his exercise of it—had a greater influence on Stalin than an unrealistic, millennial desire for world revolution.

This suspicion about Stalin's ultimate objectives seriously weakened the assessments made by American diplomats. To be sure, the Kremlin's policies, despite its collective security rhetoric, had an ambiguous quality which made analysis difficult. The Kremlin remained interested in territorial expansion, particularly with respect to Russian territory lost in 1918–19, and exaggerated the degree of its opposition to Berlin and Tokyo. Like the Western powers, the Soviet Union wanted much more to avoid war than to overthrow Hitler or to drive Japan out of China. Without putting everything into one policy, the Kremlin engaged in a largely verbal war with Berlin, mixed appeasement with force against Japan, and tried to cooperate with France, Great Britain, and the United States. Stalin also made overtures to Hitler, which made his ambiguity obvious. Instead of having a master plan for either war in Europe, from which communism would emerge triumphant, or rapprochement with Hitler, the Soviet Union responded to diplomatic problems with almost as many puzzling, shifting tactics as did the Western powers. Although distrustful of the intentions of the capitalist powers, Stalin might have cooperated more, especially with France, if they had reciprocated his gestures.[14]

When the Soviet Union approached France and joined the League of Nations on September 10, 1934, most American diplomats viewed this shift with suspicion. The Riga legation and Moscow embassy, both of which correctly evaluated Stalin's policies as tactical maneuvers to obtain an agreement with France, slighted other considerations. "The Russians hated entering the League of Nations," Bullitt informed the State Department, "and did so only as a preliminary step to a defensive agreement with the French."[15] He failed to recognize that the Kremlin also gained prestige and a forum from which it could encourage opposition to Germany and could work to prevent a British or French rapprochement with Hitler. American officials disliked the presence of Moscow in the League, for they expected—unfairly, as it turned out—many Soviet provocations. For example, Hugh Wilson, who served as minister to Switzerland, accused Litvinov of getting a "mischievous pleasure in putting the others in the most embarrassing possible situation."[16]

American diplomats were concerned about a Soviet-French alliance. As Norman H. Davis confided to Roosevelt, "France is playing too much into the hands of Litvinov, who ... is going to lead them into all sorts of trouble."[17] The Moscow embassy officials considered the Kremlin reluctant to make any long-term commitments and doubted the advantages of the mutual assistance pacts Moscow signed with France and Czechoslovakia in May, 1935. "The Soviet Union, by maneuvering the positive and negative forces which dominate conflicting German, French, Italian and British policies," John Wiley suggested to Kelley, "may eventually see the enemy confounded and her own allies fall like ripe fruit from their capitalistic tree tops."[18] Bullitt went further, emphasizing that the pact did not change Stalin's determination "to produce world revolution." According to Bullitt, the entente represented Moscow's current tactic to keep Europe divided until the Soviet Union was strong enough to spread Communism by means of an "inevitable and *ultimately* desirable" war. The State Department echoed Bullitt's observations.[19]

The Moscow embassy also suspected a Nazi-Soviet rapprochement. After Hitler's takeover, the Kremlin tried unsuccessfully to avoid a break with Berlin; Stalin only reluctantly turned away from traditional cooperation with Germany and occasionally sent secret feelers to Berlin seeking better relations. Moscow and Berlin ended their secret military relationship but continued economic arrangements throughout the thirties. Although lacking concrete information about this dimension of Stalin's diplomacy, the Moscow embassy was looking for invisible forces "behind the scenes." Shortly before the Franco-Soviet pact, Ambassador Bullitt partially raised the curtain by suggesting that "Russia would doubtless follow the example of France and attempt to develop close relations with Germany."[20]

Moscow did make several unsuccessful overtures to Berlin. When Germany proposed expanded trade relations in June, 1935, Stalin recommended an improvement in political relations. After France delayed ratification of the pact with Moscow, dropped the planned military convention, and tried for an accommodation with Hitler, the Kremlin made another unsuccessful approach to Berlin. Such maneuvers foreshadowed the Nazi-Soviet negotiations in 1939. Instead of encouraging a European war to facilitate Soviet territorial expansion, Stalin tried to improve relations with Berlin out of concern about German intentions toward the Soviet Union. Like Great Britain and France, the Kremlin attempted to pacify Hitler in order to avoid war.[21]

The Franco-Soviet rapproachement should have been supported by American diplomats, despite the maneuvering by Paris and Moscow, for it had potential value as a counter to Hitler and a check to any improvement in Nazi-Soviet relations. A more favorable, continuing response by the Western powers to Stalin's overtures might have encouraged him to move further toward France and Great Britain and away from Hitler. Instead, Ambassador Bullitt urged French officials to scrap the pact and turn to Berlin. Russian specialist George Kennan, who underestimated the Nazi threat to the Soviet Union, felt that Stalin wanted to stay out of any European war until he could enter "in the capacity of a vulture." By focusing upon problems in military logistics, William E. Dodd (ambassador to Germany), like many officials, downgraded the value of the new alliance. Assistant Secretary George Messersmith disagreed: "If France and Czechoslovakia give up their agreements with Russia, Germany and Moscow will be on the fairway towards making their peace within six months." Europeans and Americans "have only this fear of communism which blinds them to the fact of Russia and to a consideration of the realities which have to be faced," Messersmith complained to the State Department.[22] American diplomats, however, continued to sidestep Messersmith's realistic appraisal.

Starting in 1936, American officials placed increasing importance on Stalin's desire to avoid involvement in war, as he backed away from active pursuit of cooperation with the Western powers and continued to offer secret negotiations to Berlin. Both Ambassador Bullitt and Charles

Bohlen noted considerable caution in Moscow's response to German and Italian expansion.[23] The Kremlin "is endeavoring to work out formulas whereby, upon short notice, it might ... come to at least a temporary understanding with Germany," Loy Henderson warned Washington.[24] As the Western powers demonstrated weakness toward Hitler, Stalin turned more to a unilateral defensive posture, but not as exclusively as Bullitt (who left Moscow in June, 1936, and became ambassador to France in August) suggested to Roosevelt. "The Russians ... are completely out of the picture so far as Europe is concerned ...," Bullitt reported from Paris, and "have now apparently retired behind their swamps."[25]

American officials did not always agree in their appraisals of Stalin's policies, especially Ambassadors Bullitt and Davies, who disputed extensively about the relative influence of ideology and national interest in Soviet diplomacy. Bullitt and Hugh Wilson (ambassador to Germany after Dodd) favored a Western rapprochement with Berlin instead of cooperation with Moscow. "Russia's great wish," Bullitt told the British ambassador in Paris, "is to provoke a general conflagration in which she herself will play but little part, beyond perhaps a little bombing from a distance, but after which she will arise like a phoenix ... and bring about a world revolution."[26] Emphasizing the importance of security concerns, Ambassador Davies argued that Moscow would come to the aid of Prague in the Czechoslovakian crisis of 1938, even if it had to violate Polish and Rumanian territory.[27]

Russian specialists agreed with some of Bullitt's suspicions in 1938. The Moscow embassy, under the direction of Alexander Kirk with Charles Bohlen in charge of political reporting, emphasized Moscow's prudent refusal, based on the terms of the Soviet-Czechoslovakian pact, to assist Prague unless France fulfilled her obligations. Since the Soviet Union lacked a contiguous border with Czechoslovakia, any Soviet aid looked insignificant, especially after military attaché Philip Faymonville told Kirk and Bohlen that Moscow could send only two of its forty-five squadrons of bombers to help Prague. The embassy staff also believed that Stalin would prefer to remain on the sidelines, ready to profit if war ensued. "The Soviet Union is in a position to derive maximum profit with the minimum risk," Kirk informed Washington, and would welcome a war "which might result in the substitution of social and economic orders more in harmony with its own."[28] After the isolation of Moscow from the Munich Conference, embassy officials expected Stalin to take a unilateral approach and stay out of any conflict unless Soviet security were threatened. If events forced Stalin into a war, Kirk suggested that he would "look to the advantages which may be derived from internal upheavals in other countries."[29]

Ambassadors Bullitt and Davies, agreeing perhaps for the first time, approved when the British and French turned to the Soviet Union in the spring of 1939. Without shedding any of his hostility toward the Kremlin, Bullitt urged French officials to move quickly, emphasizing the possibility of a German-Russian rapprochement and arguing that "Stalin has had enough of being treated like an outcast when at the same time Russian assistance is essential if the democracies are to be saved." Davies emphatically agreed. If the Russians did not "get a practical reciprocal alliance with the West," he warned Roosevelt, "it is clear as a pike staff they will do the next best thing and get a nonaggression pact with Hitler."[30]

The Moscow embassy closely followed Stalin's maneuvers in the spring and summer of 1939 without reaching any firm conclusions. Under the impact of Kelley's training and Kirk's influence, Bohlen cautiously qualified most of his predictions. When Stalin removed Litvinov as foreign commissar on May 3, Bohlen and Kirk carefully referred to the move as either a step toward Hitler or an effort to pressure Britain into an anti-Nazi coalition. "The real direction and portent" of this maneuver, they cabled Washington, "... will only be apparent in light of further development."[31] A major intelligence coup, moreover, did not remove the embassy's uncertainty about Stalin's intentions. Starting in May, Bohlen obtained confidential information from Hans Heinrich Herwarth von Bittenfeld, a second secretary of the German embassy. During May and June, Bohlen and the new chargé, Stuart Grummon, informed Washington about secret Nazi approaches to the Kremlin, but evidence of continuing Soviet suspicion toward Hitler prompted them to remain cautious in their predictions about the direction in which Stalin would head.[32]

By the time Laurence A. Steinhardt arrived in Moscow as the new ambassador, Stalin was moving close to an agreement with both Germany and the Western powers. On July 22, Moscow announced the resumption of trade negotiations with Berlin, and on July 27 London announced that a military mission would leave for Moscow in a few days. After August 5, however, Bohlen obtained increasing evidence of Soviet interest in an agreement with Berlin, culminating in an August 16 report which outlined the general nature of the agreement. Bohlen, however, still hedged his conclusion: "Although it is possibly too soon to speak of a definite German-Soviet rapprochement at the present time, ... a steady progress can be noted." Steinhardt even expected Moscow to stall with both sides "in the hope of thereby avoiding the outbreak of war" before winter arrived.[33]

But Stalin opted for an agreement with Hitler. American diplomats had underestimated Stalin's flexibility and his mistrust of the British government. British appeasement of Hitler to avoid war looked, from the Kremlin's perspective, like a maneuver to turn Hitler against the Soviet Union. Also, London and Paris could not match Hitler's offer. Unwilling to accept Hitler's control of Eastern Europe, the British also refused to give Stalin a free hand in the Baltic states. Moreover, since London could not provide effective aid to Poland, the main burden of defending Poland would have fallen upon the Red army. On the other hand, Hitler offered the Kremlin a slice of Poland, a sphere of influence over Finland, Estonia, and Latvia, and an exchange of German machinery and armaments for Russian raw materials and agricultural supplies. Most important, Stalin could stay out of the expected European war.[34] By ignoring the course Steinhardt thought he would follow, a course which avoided the risks of an alliance with the West or the infamy of a pact with Hitler, Stalin obtained only temporary defensive benefits. The pact precipitated the German invasion of Poland and, in the long run, brought destruction and discredit to the Soviet Union.

On the morning after Stalin and German Foreign Minister Joachim von Ribbentrop negotiated the Nazi-Soviet Nonaggression Pact, Herwarth called Bohlen and asked him to come to the German Chancery. While Ribbentrop slept in an upstairs bedroom, Herwarth gave Bohlen the details of the secret protocol on territorial arrangements. Stalin's stunning move did not surprise Bohlen and other Russian specialists. They had always been skeptical about Nazi-Soviet conflict, looking behind the hostile rhetoric for signs of a detente. Instead of reevaluating their general views on Soviet policy, American diplomats considered the pact, with some justification, as an endorsement of their analysis of Soviet diplomacy in the thirties. Both Ambassador Steinhardt and Loy Henderson reaffirmed the central emphasis of Russian specialists on opportunistic power politics as the polestar of current Soviet policy. Moreover, the pact seemed to confirm their belief that Stalin wanted to avoid direct involvement in war but profit from it; the Kremlin's promise of neutrality enabled Hitler to move on Poland while Moscow regained former Russian territory and moved toward a sphere of influence in Eastern Europe. The pact also reinforced the deemphasis of ideological influences in Soviet policy by officials like Henderson who wondered if "Stalin is really fulfilling

Trotsky's prophecies in deserting the world revolutionary movement."[35] A few diplomats like William Bullitt found confirmations of a somewhat conflicting view: that Stalin wanted to provoke a European conflict in order to spread Communism. Initially, the Kremlin would nibble from the sidelines, but ultimately it would seek to spread Communism over a prostrate Europe.[36]

Bullitt typically exaggerated Stalin's interest in the extension of Communism just as Ambassador Davies had overestimated his commitment to cooperation with the Western powers. Soviet specialists followed a middle course, emphasizing Stalin's defensive orientation, his caution toward the Western powers and Hitler, and his declining interest in ideological expansion. But they, like other American diplomats, missed the potential importance of Stalin's overtures to the West. Their ingrained hostility toward the Soviet Union prompted them to view too critically the Kremlin's entry into the League and detente. Henderson's speculation in 1939 that Stalin had abandoned world revolution indicates how long it took Russian specialists to shed their suspicions about Stalin's long-range interest in world revolution. This left them with a somewhat inadequate analysis of Stalin's ambiguous diplomacy in the thirties as well as a misunderstanding of contemporary power realities which required cooperation with Stalin, the sooner the better, in order to contain Hitler.

The assessments made by American diplomats had a lasting, significant impact upon the officials themselves. Ambassador Bullitt, for example, retained a strong hostility toward the Soviet Union, despite his support for cooperation in 1939, and warned Roosevelt during World War II about a Soviet attempt to communize Europe. In contrast to Bullitt, Ambassador Davies continued to recommend cooperation with the Soviet Union during and after World War II. Davies urged Roosevelt and his successor, Harry S Truman, to view Stalin as a nationalistic dictator concerned about security and cooperation with the West.

Even more important was the influence of this experience upon Loy Henderson, George Kennan, and Charles Bohlen, who were starting influential careers in Soviet-American relations. This was the formative period in the development of their basic attitudes about Stalin's diplomacy. They agreed with Bohlen's conclusion that the "essential element of Stalin's policy was to protect, above all, the Bolshevik regime in Russia." Yet they believed that the Bolshevik political philosophy of Marx and Lenin continued to guide Stalin and other Soviet leaders who considered the spread of Communism a desirable secondary objective if they could retain Stalinist control over Communist regimes. Con-

sequently, the Russian specialists felt that Soviet policy was fundamen- ·
tally unreliable since Stalin would change his policies and repudiate any
agreements depending upon Soviet interests. The implications of this
assessment were not very promising for the long-term future of Soviet-
American relations. Unless American negotiations were truly inspired,
Kennan "could see little future for Russian-American relations other than
a long series of misunderstandings, disappointments, and recriminations
on both sides."[37] Similarly, Henderson and Bohlen never could believe in
the possibility of friendly relations with Stalin and, consequently, opposed
in various degrees Roosevelt's strategy during World War II. During the
preliminaries of the cold war, these officials played an important role in the
State Department and advocated a strategy of firmness against Stalin.

The interpretations of those in the Moscow embassy and other American officials increased the estrangement in Soviet-American relations. By
recommending that the United States keep its distance from Stalin,
officials found a receptive audience in the State Department, from Robert
Kelley in the Division of Eastern European Affairs to Secretary Hull. The
members of the State Department relied on the evaluations of Russian
specialists for confirmation of their belief that Washington could not count
on any cooperation from the opportunistic, unreliable Soviet Union. In its
management of relations with the Kremlin, Kelley and other officials kept
the Soviet Union at arm's length and cooperated with Soviet officials only
on the yearly trade agreements. Consequently, Washington and Moscow
drifted further apart.

The Moscow embassy's assessments also widened the difference
between the State Department and President Roosevelt concerning
relations with the Soviet Union. The president had neither the time
(because of the depression) nor the interest or patience to read the
Moscow embassy's evaluations. Bullitt and Davies, however, did present
their views to Roosevelt in correspondence and during visits to Washington; the president listened more to Davies than to Bullitt on the question
of cooperation with the Kremlin in 1937. Roosevelt remained somewhat
suspicious of the professional diplomats and never indicated much
confidence in the views of Hull and the State Department on the subject
of relations with Moscow. Always hopeful about achieving cooperation
with Stalin, he encountered intensified opposition from the State Department whenever he considered such a possibility.

5

The Soviet Experiment
and the Moscow Embassy

The estrangement in Soviet-American relations was further intensified by the evaluations made by American diplomats in the Moscow embassy concerning Soviet domestic developments in the thirties, most notably Stalin's massive purge. Added to the view of Stalin as an unreliable diplomat was the image of a bloody tyrant determined to wipe out both actual and potential opposition to his hegemony. This elicited a powerful moral censure that made it even more difficult for Roosevelt to overcome the State Department's reluctance to cooperate with Moscow.

Although American diplomats were not free from bias regarding the Soviet regime nor from preconceptions that weakened some of their evaluations, they understood the larger domestic developments of the thirties. The embassy staff, for example, provided a reliable analysis of Soviet industrialization, although their attachment to American capitalism produced some misinterpretation about the character of the Soviet economy. With more discernment than most foreign observers, embassy officials understood Stalin's ruthless tactics to remove any opposition and developed an insightful analysis of the mixed results of Stalin's domestic policies. They understood the weakness produced by the general purge, which at the same time increased Stalin's dominance. Even Ambassador Davies, who disagreed extensively with the career officers, recognized that the Soviet experiment had become a totalitarian system.

Davies and Faymonville sharply dissented from the basic consensus among the career officers in the Moscow embassy. Unlike the Russian specialists, Davies interpreted Soviet developments from an American perspective founded upon a faith in capitalism, American institutions, and businesslike compromise. He frequently exaggerated the capitalistic aspects of the Soviet economy, and his faith in public trials and confessions made it difficult for him to assess the real meaning of the Moscow trials. His evaluations suffered from his inability to see Stalin's Russia from the perspective of Russian history. Davies also frequently relied on Faymonville, a veteran of the American intervention in Siberia in 1918, for information and interpretation. Somewhat sympathetic toward the Soviet Union, Faymonville generally tried to defend Soviet policies such as the purge.[1]

Professional and personal factors intensified the differences between Davies and the Russian specialists. The embassy staff responded to the news of the ambassador's appointment with "dismay, bewilderment and discouragement." Kennan and others disliked his amateurish status and approach to problems and interpreted his selection as an indication of Washington's lack of interest in the Moscow embassy. After Davies' first day in the embassy on January 19, 1937, the staff, led perhaps by Kennan, considered a mass resignation. Rebuked by Loy Henderson, the younger secretaries decided to give the ambassador a chance to prove himself.

Since Davies considered himself to be on a special mission involving extensive travel in Russia and neighboring European countries, he neglected the daily duties of an ambassador—an attitude which reinforced the initial disapproval of the embassy staff. In addition, his personal treatment of the officers hardened their resentment against him. In his memoirs, Bohlen recalled that the ambassador and "his wife treated the staff as hired help and rarely listened to its views." At the time of the Moscow trials, though Kennan and Bohlen served as interpreters for him, Davies failed even to seek their private assessments. Instead, he sent them to pick up sandwiches during the intermissions in the trials, while he exchanged opinions with Western journalists.[2]

Before American diplomats had returned to Moscow after recognition, Stalin had laid the foundation of his totalitarian regime. By 1929 he had defeated his political opponents and controlled the major sources of power: the Soviet Communist party, the Red army, and the secret police (NKVD). In 1929 the Kremlin launched a massive industrialization program, the first Five-Year Plan, with emphasis on developing heavy industry while transferring land from individual peasants to collectives directed by the state. Collectivization of agriculture provided capital for industrialization, and both policies tightened the Kremlin's control over peasants and workers. By 1933 Stalin had broken the resistance to collectivization, and agriculture very slowly revived. A rapid expansion in heavy industry began shortly thereafter, although the production of consumer goods fell far behind.[3]

The Moscow embassy correctly reported the Soviet Union's renewed industrial expansion. Starting with the embassy's first major evaluation in October, 1934, Ambassador Bullitt, Elbridge Durbrow, and Bertel Kuniholm (the latter two being specialists on economic issues) reported continuous increases in industrial production, although they noted such problems as bureaucratic mismanagement, a lack of skilled labor, and uneven product quality.[4] When Soviet industrialization slowed down in 1937, and even declined in some areas, the Moscow embassy quickly detected this trend. Loy Henderson and the staff considered the Second Five-Year Plan a general success until June of 1937, when they noted a drop in industrial production. Henderson attributed the decline to a general purge of management and labor as well as overly intensive pressure for increased production. Ambassador Davies accepted Henderson's analysis but tried to minimize its importance. Arguing that agriculture "produces the wealth which enables the government" to industrialize, Davies believed that he could reject the "...criticism that the Soviet governmental structure is breaking down because its industry isn't functioning."[5]

Davies and the embassy staff characteristically disagreed about the extent and implications of Stalin's economic problems. Although the ambassador recognized certain problems, such as the "inefficiency of bureaucracy and political control of industry," he remained enthusiastic about Moscow's economic accomplishments. "This great bear is lumbering along and with impressive results," Davies happily concluded in April, 1938.[6] Career officers, however, observed the symptoms of a serious economic crisis stemming from industrial stagnation, inadequate skills, widespread corruption, and the debilitating effects of the purge. Loy Henderson in Washington believed the "inherent defects of the Russian people, the effects of the purge on industry, and the increasing hesitancy of Soviet officials to accept responsibility" checked progress even in heavy industry, the strongest sector in the Soviet economy.[7]

The officers and the ambassador also differed over the importance of capitalistic methods in Soviet industrialization. On August 31, 1935, a worker in the Donets coal mines set a new production record. The Stakhanov movement, named after this miner, was a massive campaign to increase production by providing special privileges and higher wages to workers who fulfilled new production quotas. The embassy staff stressed the similarity between the Stakhanov movement and traditional capitalistic methods of increasing labor production. "The whole purpose of the Stakhanov movement," George Kennan concluded, "is to prepare the ground for a forced increase in the productivity of Russian labor." When the Kremlin quietly ended the movement—but not the principles behind it—Loy Henderson suggested that Stalin had increased production "in very much the same way as this has been done in capitalist enterprises for decades."[8]

Davies took a far more optimistic view of the incipient capitalism in the Soviet economy. Upon discovering several private flower and perfume shops on the main business street near the embassy, Davies happily recorded in his diary another example of budding entrepreneurship. Within a month after his arrival, Davies confidently informed Roosevelt that the "communist principle here has in actual fact been abandoned." The Soviet experiment "is a socialist enterprise based upon capitalistic principles of profit and self-interest." Davies also expected the Kremlin to move further in this direction, with the state controlling large industry and small business "working under capitalistic, property and profit principles."[9]

Career officers shared some of Davies' conclusions but not his prediction of an irresistible movement towards capitalism. They readily affirmed the differences between Communism and Soviet industrialization. A few officers also concurred with Davies' depiction of the Soviet economy as "state capitalism"; Alexander Kirk, Norris B. Chipman, and Edward Page, for example, mentioned Moscow's "extreme form of state capitalism." When Davies asked the embassy staff to prepare a study of Soviet violations of Communist principles, Loy Henderson pointed out Moscow's use of such capitalistic practices as the speed-up, pay differentials, and decentralization of industrial enterprises. But Henderson warned Davies about reading too much into Stalin's tactics: "I don't believe that Stalin or the leaders around him have any intention to permit the Soviet Union to develop into a capitalistic economy."[10]

The Moscow embassy developed a fairly reliable and sophisticated understanding of Soviet industrialization. Officials recognized both the quantitative industrial development and the many problems in the Soviet economy, although Ambassador Davies continuously minimized these.

The most significant error in their evaluations was rooted in their latent sympathies with capitalistic enterprise. Since Davies, Bullitt, and a few career officers noted so many capitalistic practices in the Soviet economy, they tended to view it as state capitalism. Given the Kremlin's total control of the economy, state socialism would far better have described the Soviet system.

The Soviet experiment involved more than massive industrialization, for Stalin also precipitated important shifts in politics and social policies in the thirties. To some foreign observers these developments heralded an end to dictatorship and terror in the Soviet Union. American diplomats, however, saw the shifts—notably the restructuring of the Communist party and the new Constitution of 1936—as signs of a conservative retreat from earlier policies. The Moscow embassy also attentively watched Stalin wipe out opposition to his brand of totalitarianism, a system that increasingly veered away from formal communist theories.

Without exception, all American officials comprehended Stalin's rigid control of the Soviet Union (a crucial point which some foreign observers missed); but they had more difficulty, just as historians do today, under-standing Stalin's motivations. Ambassadors Bullitt and Davies, as well as Loy Henderson, felt that Stalin was a sincere revolutionary whose original aim had been the triumph of communism.[11] This view, however, greatly exaggerated Stalin's idealism, for he seems to have used ideology more as a means to an end than as an end in itself. Although Stalin understood the tenets of Marxist Leninism and used them to rationalize his actions, his policies discredited, and diverged from, communist theories. Stalin sought power, and some embassy officials, such as George Kennan, recognized that a quest for power was at the heart of Stalinism. Their "abundant cruelties, their claims to infallibility, their opportunism and unscrupulousness of methods, their disregard for the truth..., and espe-cially their love of power that so often and so obviously lurked behind the pretense of high-minded ideological conviction" were the distinguishing traits of Stalin and his supporters in the Kremlin, according to Kennan.[12]

During the early thirties Kennan found confirmation of his assessment in Stalin's purge of the Communist party. From 1933 until 1938 Stalin removed over 850,000 members of the party and filled vacant positions with officials whose interests and loyalties were aligned with his own. Henderson analyzed the purge as a source of weakness, for poor disci-pline and morale in the party are "likely to weaken the unity of the whole country."[13] To Kennan, however, the most important result of the purge seemed to be an enormous expansion of Stalin's hegemony. By giving the party control of the economy, Stalin not only tightened his mastery over the population but also created a new party bureaucracy completely loyal to himself. Ambassador Bullitt described Stalin's freshly purged party as an "enormous switchboard with wires touching every nerve center in the country."[14]

The embassy staff retained this understanding of Stalin's dominance despite the Constitution of 1936, which looked like a step toward democracy in the eyes of many foreign observers. Although the new constitution established the Supreme Soviet and the Presidium, laid down procedures for elections, and enumerated the rights of Soviet citizens, it neither contained any means for an individual to defend his rights nor allowed any political party, other than the Communist, to present candidates for elections. Instead of a step toward democracy, the constitution marked the spread of Stalinism.

Loy Henderson and Kennan considered the constitution to be propaganda designed for foreign and domestic consumption. Its coincidence with the Comintern's popular front movement and the Kremlin's overtures to the Western powers seemed significant to them. If Moscow could be made to look more like a democracy than a dictatorship, then perhaps the Western powers would side with Stalin against Hitler. On the domestic side, Henderson felt that Stalin wanted to elevate the peasants nearer to equal rights with workers and instill a new sense of responsibility in minor officials. Ambassador Davies typically chose to report the more favorable aspects of the constitution, notably the shake-up of local party organizations and the stimulation of American-style campaigns in the first election of 1937. Yet even Davies recognized the serious limitations in the constitution; a secret ballot did not mean very much when only one party ran candidates. The provisions for individual rights "had to be exercised and enjoyed only if consistent with Communistic principles," Davies confided to a friend, and "that is the 'nigger in the woodpile'."[15]

When the Moscow embassy assessed Stalin's social policies, they emphasized a conservative retreat from earlier Marxist-Leninist policies. By 1937 embassy officials remarked on new social trends, notably growing class stratification and renewed emphasis upon marriage and patriotism. Henderson and his staff, moreover, expected Stalin to accelerate the "rapid restratification of Soviet society."[16] Moscow's emphasis on marriage, motherhood, and other "bourgeois concepts" reinforced Ambassador Bullitt's conclusion that "in the sphere of morals as in so many other spheres, the Russian Revolution is in a Cromwellian phase."[17] Yet Moscow's determined campaign against traditional religions, which resumed in 1937 after a brief lull, forced most officials to recognize the tactical quality of Stalin's policies.[18]

The embassy's keen appreciation of Stalin's preoccupation with power and control, even in his social policies, was crucial to their analysis of Stalin's massive purge. After 1935 the focus of foreign debate on the Soviet experiment shifted from industrialization to the purge itself, with the greatest emphasis on the public trials of former Bolshevik leaders. The trials were just the tip of an iceberg, for the purge decimated the leadership of all important Soviet institutions and bureaucracies—including the purging agent itself, the NKVD—and the mass population of workers and peasants. During the purge approximately one million Russians were executed, twelve million died in labor camps, and countless individuals were stripped of their strength, nerves, and courage. Stalin emerged as the unquestioned master of the Soviet Union, supported by a new elite of fearful, loyal, and self-interested leaders and bureaucrats.[19]

On December 1, 1934, Leonid Nikolayev, a young and psychologically unbalanced Communist, assassinated Sergei Kirov, head of the Communist party organization in Leningrad. Nikolayev had already made two unsuccessful attempts but each time had been released by the NKVD. Stalin had possibly directed the plot in order to get rid of the popular Kirov and to break down resistance to a general liquidation of party officials. The Kirov incident signaled the onset of the purge.

Basing his assumptions upon a report by the Lithuanian minister, Bullitt at first believed that Nikolayev had shot Kirov in a moment of passion, after an unsuccessful attempt to exploit Kirov's alleged love affair with his wife. But Bullitt soon concurred with Henderson and Bohlen, who perceived a deep political conflict behind the affair. The embassy heard rumors about Stalin's complicity in Kirov's death but neither reached a consensus on this issue nor reported it to Washington. "It would be stretching the truth to say that anyone in the foreign colony seriously suspected...that Stalin himself was behind Kirov's murder," recollected Bohlen in his memoirs.[20] Instead, the staff emphasized the conflict between Stalin and advocates of earlier Communist policies. "The 'shot from the Left'," counselor John Wiley advised Washington, "illustrates the losing struggle of Communism versus Sovietism and of dissatisfaction of younger Communist elements with the conservative trend of Stalin's policies." When Stalin used the Kirov incident to order the execution of over seventy individuals in Leningrad and Moscow, and the deportation and imprisonment of thousands in Leningrad (including two of his former opponents, Grigori Zinoviev and Lev Kamenev), the embassy considered this a reaffirmation of the essentially political nature of Stalin's action.[21]

Until the summer of 1936, the Moscow embassy reported some evidence of a general purge but did not detect Stalin's preparations for a massive purge, especially the NKVD's arrangements for public trials of old Bolsheviks. On August 19, the trial of Zinoviev and Kamenev opened with the accusation that they and other Bolsheviks had formed a terrorist group with the exiled Leon Trotsky in order to liquidate Kirov, Stalin, and most of their colleagues in the Kremlin. In fact, the charges were totally false, the confessions were lies induced by mental and physical torture, and a massive purge was beginning.[22]

Loy Henderson, who daily watched the sessions of this trial, formulated the embassy's interpretation, for Kennan was visiting America at the time. According to Henderson, Stalin desired to remove former leaders, silence criticism of his "moving from Communism in the direction of state capitalism," find a scapegoat for economic failures, and further discredit his arch enemy Leon Trotsky. The confessions did not convince Henderson, who described the trial as a circus with the "director putting a group of well-trained seals through a series of difficult acts." Since an admission of guilt was at most an indication of opposition to Stalin's policies rather than involvement in a bloody conspiracy, officials suspected that the defendants confessed to save their own lives as well as those of their families and friends. Finally, Henderson alerted Washington to a general purge in which "hundreds of persons have been arrested on charges of disloyalty to Stalin and the Party."[23]

The second trial, in January, 1937, led to a division of opinion in the Moscow embassy. The Kremlin now charged veteran Bolsheviks like Karl Radek, Grigori Pyatakov and Grigori Sokolnikov with a fantastic conspiracy: a Trotskyite plot, abetted by Berlin and Tokyo, to eliminate Soviet leaders and dismember the Soviet Union. But Ambassador Davies, having recently arrived in Moscow, was very reluctant to write off Stalin as a tyrant. Davies' background in American law gave him an overly sanguine view of public trials and confessions. This attitude, plus his enthusiasm for Soviet industrialization and his desire for Soviet-American diplomatic cooperation, governed his ambivalence toward the purge.[24]

After attending the trial in the company of George Kennan, Ambassador Davies reported that "on the face of the proceedings so far...the Government has overwhelmingly established its case." Davies, however, was troubled by the confessions; "motives for sincerity of confession" were a "...matter of conjecture." By February his misgivings had grown more pronounced, and he suggested that although the Kremlin had found "a widespread plot," the trial was "more or less of a propaganda enterprise."[25]

Kennan and Henderson expressed far more reservations about the official charges and confessions, although Davies' partial acceptance of the Kremlin's case prompted these officers to tone down their criticism of Stalin's tactics. Kennan, for example, avoided a complete rejection of the charge of conspiracy and equivocated over the confessions. "It is doubtful whether the western mind could ever fathom the question of guilt and innocence, of truth and fiction," he concluded in a long memorandum. "The Russian mind... knows no moderation; and it sometimes carries both truth and falsehood to such infinite extremes that they eventually meet in space... and it is no longer possible to distinguish between them." Henderson, however, privately maintained his original analysis. As he confided to Robert Kelley, "the dictatorship is doing its best to discredit" former leaders and "old grudges are being paid off."[26]

The final public trial, in March, 1938—of Nikolai Bukharin and Alexei Rykov, two eminent old Bolsheviks, and Genrikh Yagoda, former head of the NKVD—again troubled Davies. After a series of confusing qualifications, Davies admitted that "not all charges as alleged were proved." Yet after observing the daily sessions, he decided that he had heard enough evidence to prove that "these defendents had plotted to overthrow" the Kremlin.[27]

Charles Bohlen, who returned to Moscow in 1938 to replace Kennan, also had difficulty interpreting the trial, although he knew it was "phony." After attending the daily sessions as Davies' interpreter, Bohlen and the staff discussed the reasons for the trial and the issue of guilt. Bohlen pointed to a number of Stalin's objectives, notably the efforts to blame economic failures upon the accused, to arouse antiforeign sentiment, and to "blacken the opposition to Stalin and render it incapable of organizing any movement against him." However, he found it difficult to ascertain the truth or falsity of the specific charges. Too many of the episodes, as well as the confessions themselves, seemed fantastic and unbelievable. He was particularly troubled by Bukharin's ambiguous general confession of guilt despite his denial of specific criminal acts. Carefully trained to support his interpretations with facts, Bohlen found it impossible to "separate fact from fiction at the trial," or to determine "whether a statement or an event was a total invention or had some semblance of fact behind it." For over a month he tried to prepare a convincing case against the validity of the trial but finally had to admit defeat despite his belief that the trial had "no relevance to reality."[28]

Thus, career officers made a fairly reliable evaluation of the public trials except when Ambassador Davies' ambivalence and the problem of ascertaining facts hindered their criticism of the official charges and confessions. Unfortunately the trials distracted attention from the simultaneous purge, which affected every stratum of the Soviet population, from party leaders at all levels through officials directing every institution, and even nonparty workers and peasants. It was very difficult for any observer, inside or outside the Soviet Union, to obtain a clear understanding of the qualitative and quantitative nature of the purge. Within these limitations, the Moscow embassy provided an insightful analysis of the nature and impact of Stalin's assault on the Russian people.

The purge of the Red army, which received more attention from the Moscow embassy than any other aspect of the purge, highlighted the different emphases of Ambassador Davies and the career officers. Starting with a secret trial and execution of military leaders in June, 1937, Stalin went after the army with a vengeance in order to eliminate its potential threat to his hegemony. By 1938 Stalin had removed 90 percent of the army's generals—including the replacements of the original leaders—and 80 percent of its colonels, and had reintroduced political commissars. Stalin thus retained the loyalty of the army and made it more subservient, but in the process it lost most of its combat-tested leaders and much of its prestige.[29]

Davies and Philip Faymonville, the military attaché, underestimated the impact of the army purge. Initially, Davies accepted the existence of a "definite conspiracy in the making to a coup d'etat by the army—not necessarily anti-Stalin, but antipolitical and antiparty." As the Soviet press made more and more accusations against the generals, Davies and Faymonville found less and less evidence for a conspiracy. Nevertheless, these officials concluded that the purge increased the army's loyalty, morale, and strength, despite a loss of prestige.[30] Henderson and Kennan, however, disagreed with this interpretation. They rejected the charge of an army conspiracy and considered the purge a serious weakening of the army. "The morale and self-confidence of the armed forces had received a severe shock from which they cannot recover for some time," Henderson predicted.[31]

In the spring of 1937 the Moscow embassy detected another wave of arrests and watched Soviet leaders and personal acquaintances disappear. The impact of the purge on the leadership was partially obtained by watching posters and pictures during the May Day and November 7 celebrations and by following the reports of arrests and trials in the newspapers of the various republics. Henderson, who directed the embassy's evaluation, initially interpreted the purge as a result of Stalin's fear of sincere Communists who charged him with the betrayal of Communism at home and abroad. The effects of this phase of the purge seemed severe in the disruption and spread of panic in the bureaucracies, but not among workers and peasants, who seemed indifferent to the fate of their superiors. The embassy staff, moreover, began to sense the mixed results of the purge; the Soviet Union had lost strength, but Stalin had increased his personal control. Henderson concluded that "there is no organization other than the Red Army, which appears powerless at present, through which dissatisfaction or discontent can be expressed."[32]

Ambassador Davies accepted his staff's analysis of the nature of the purge but minimized its impact on the Kremlin's strength. Davies admitted that by 1938 the terror was a "horrifying fact" that reached "down into and haunts all sections of the community," but he expected the inherent strength of the Soviet Union, notably its resources, agricultural production, and industrial achievements, to counteract the effects of the purge. Nonetheless, the ambassador's enthusiasm for the Soviet experiment in general had been diminished; in his view, the purge had revealed the dark side of Stalin, "the exercise of horrifying oriental ruthlessness and cruelty."[33]

As the embassy staff watched the spread of the purge, they related it to other aspects of the Soviet experiment. By the end of 1937 they had noted that the purge was accentuating economic problems and was slowing Soviet industrialization. The liquidation of Stalin's old allies and opponents reinforced his conservative retreat from communist theories in economic and social policies. It was another proof that the "early Marxian dreams of 'pure communism' have lost...," George Kennan remarked. "Like the cardboard rocks and wire mesh trees of stage scenery—the closer one approaches them, the more ridiculous and implausible they become."[34]

The purge also strongly reaffirmed the career officers' conclusion that the Soviet experiment was a ruthless totalitarian system and not a progressive social experiment. The Soviet Union functioned through the "existence of a complicated and delicately-wrought system of social control, the brain center of which in Moscow shoots off numerous nerve branches into every human activity and into every town and village," commented Loy Henderson. Henderson expected the system to collapse if Stalin lost control or the system broke down, but the purge indicated that Stalin would intensify control even at the expense of weakening the Soviet Union.[35]

The Moscow embassy made a first-rate analysis of the Soviet experiment. Unlike many foreign observers, American officials successfully combined skepticism about the Kremlin's rhetoric and bias against Stalin's system. Too much skepticism and bias would have led the embassy staff to underestimate the quantitative industrial expansion and necessary costs of this process. Instead, American diplomats presented an able evaluation, although they did introduce a serious misconception when they identified the Soviet economy as state capitalism instead of state socialism. In addition, Ambassador Davies underestimated the continuing problems in Soviet industrialization.

American diplomats were even more perceptive concerning Stalin's social policies—the public trials and the general purge. Although Davies made an inferior analysis, the embassy staff recognized that Stalin was tightening his control by removing any potential opposition. The Kremlin's accusations and the defendants' confessions were properly dismissed, except when Davies' influence inhibited frank reporting. Henderson and the staff realized that Stalin had disrupted the economy with an unnecessary purge that had weakened the Soviet Union while at the same time increasing Stalin's hegemony. Instead of a bold, progressive social experiment based upon socialistic industrialization, the Soviet experiment had become a totalitarian system of coercion, terror, and liquidation.

Of all their experiences in the Soviet Union, the purge had the most lasting impact upon Henderson, Kennan, and Bohlen. Kennan asserted that "to be forced to follow their course, day by day, and to write analytical dispatches about the entire process, was unavoidably a sort of liberal education in the horrors of Stalinism." Although Bohlen and Henderson were not as emotional as Kennan, the purge also hardened their views: "Obviously there must have been something wrong with a man who would send millions of people to senseless deaths," Bohlen remarked. "So insistently were the evidences of Russia's degradation borne in me...so prolonged and incessant were the hammer-blow impressions, each more outrageous and heartrending than the other," Kennan declared, "that the effect was never to leave me."[36]

This perception of Stalinism as an immoral system intensified the estrangement in Soviet-American relations, for it reinforced the State Department's rejection of cooperation with Moscow and broadened the differences between Roosevelt and the State Department. Henderson and the embassy staff, for example, noted a withdrawal of Soviet interest in diplomatic cooperation as the purge intensified; they came to believe that friendly relations with Stalin were impossible. Stalin's assault on the Russian people also raised questions in their minds about the solidarity of the Soviet Union. Roosevelt, however, showed scant interest in Soviet domestic developments and instructed only Davies to make a specific assessment of Soviet industrial strength. The ambassador's exaggeration of the strength of the Soviet Union, as well as his minimal criticism of the public trials and the purge, bolstered the president's interest in cooperation with Stalin. But Roosevelt needed the more balanced, reliable assessment of the Russian specialists so that his understanding of the Soviet Union would move beyond a superficial level.

6

Watching Stalin's Russia
from America

As Stalin's purge gathered momentum in the spring of 1937, Alfred M. Bingham, editor of the liberal *Common Sense,* announced that "it is beginning to dawn on those who are able to face facts that Fascism and Russian Communism are more alike than unlike. ... The man in the street has had a pretty sound hunch, when he lump[s] Fascism and Communism together." Bingham, who felt it was time for the left to speak out on the issue and end the "pussyfooting," pointed out similarities between the two in dictatorial control, economic practices, and political fanaticism.[1] He touched on a central theme in the American reaction to Stalin's domestic and foreign policies. Although the Soviet reorientation toward cooperation with the Western powers had received substantial approval from American commentators, the trials and the purge undercut much of this endorsement.

The erosion of favorable opinion about Soviet policies, which began gradually in 1934–35, reflected a change in the limited sources of information about the Soviet Union. American journalists in Moscow were the most important source, along with the accounts of travelers, visiting students, scholars, and temporary residents. By 1934 the small community of journalists in Moscow was less sympathetic to the Soviet Union, whose censorship of dispatches and manipulation of visas reinforced their reservations.

Although William Henry Chamberlin of the *Christian Science Monitor* and Eugene Lyons of the United Press gladly left the Soviet Union in 1934, they published critical evaluations of Soviet affairs throughout the thirties. Chamberlin, who prepared a study of the Bolshevik Revolution and spent five years as a correspondent in Tokyo, increasingly criticized the repressive features in Stalin's dictatorship and focused on the parallels in Nazi-Soviet-Italian techniques of tyranny.[2] Lyons contributed books and articles on Soviet affairs and took editorial positions in the *American Mercury* and *Reader's Digest* that helped to shape a critical outlook on Stalin's system.[3]

Stalin's purge and the Moscow trials further alienated journalists, although some of them found it difficult to reject evidence presented in court. Chamberlin's successor, Demaree Bess, almost accepted the official explanations but became more skeptical in 1937 and 1938. The court confessions also troubled Harold N. Denny, who spent five years in Moscow for the *New York Times*. During a Paris vacation in 1937, away from the Moscow censor, Denny resolved some of his doubts in an influential series of articles which gave Americans the most revealing view they had had of the general purge and Stalin's system. After his return from Moscow in 1940, Denny recounted his reactions: "I sat through some of these trials and tried to understand them, but didn't very well. After five and one half years there I began to feel it was the biggest hoax on earth and the biggest hoax in human history."[4]

A few journalists who continued to provide favorable assessments of Soviet policies bolstered the interpretations of liberal journals. As a correspondent for the *New York Times* during the twenties and thirties, Walter Duranty usually approved Soviet policies like the Moscow trials and ignored the general purge except for infrequent reports about an "administrative readjustment ... carried out in a very Russian manner."[5] Louis Fischer, the *Nation* correspondent, had an even more significant impact in reinforcing liberal sympathy toward the Soviet experiment. Fischer vigorously praised the Five-Year Plans, the Soviet constitution, and Stalin's diplomacy and avoided criticism of the trials and the purge.[6]

Academic specialists and students of Soviet affairs, who received some attention from the media and foreign policy elite in round-table discussions, turned against Soviet policies in response to Stalin's purge. Bruce Hopper, a Soviet specialist at Harvard University, frequently argued in favor of the Soviet experiment until a visit to Moscow in 1938 turned him against Stalinism. "Virtue had departed from the leaders in Russia," Hopper complained, and "dog eat dog with personal fear is the governing motive."[7] The purge also put Samuel Harper, a leading specialist at the University of Chicago, on the defensive. After his fifth visit to Moscow in 1936, Harper endorsed Stalin's diplomacy, but the trials soon troubled him. "The new trials have me guessing again," Harper confessed, before addressing the Council on Foreign Relations. "I had more or less successfully explained away the 1937 purge when, bang ... along came the new trial."[8]

Soviet policies also weakened the enthusiasm of students and semipermanent American residents in the Soviet Union during the early 1930s. The Institute of International Education established the Anglo-American Institute of the First Moscow University in the summer of 1934. Two hundred American students attended classes presented by Soviet professors, but Moscow canceled the session planned for 1935. By 1937 students began to return home. Many still praised the Soviet experiment without qualification, particularly in pro-Soviet journals. However, the purge cooled the enthusiasm of John Hazard, who studied law in Moscow from 1935 to 1938 under the sponsorship of the Institute of Current World Affairs. Like many students, Hazard was sympathetic toward the Soviet Union and accepted official explanations of the public trials; in his last memorandum from Moscow, he admitted that what he learned in Moscow "so often coincided" with the Kremlin's line that "... I am being pushed towards acceptance of the official interpretation." But reservations had developed. "We are torn by the desire to condemn the regime as brutal and question the advisability of pushing any program at such a cost," remarked Hazard.[9]

The Kremlin also drove out many Americans who had come to the Soviet Union after 1929 in search of employment and a new life-style. Engineers and workers left quickly if they had not lost their American citizenship or acquired a Russian one. Some Americans acquired editorial positions in the pro-Soviet press on their return to the United States. Typical of the few who stayed in Moscow was journalist Anna Louise Strong, who experienced a number of disappointments, notably the pettiness of Moscow's censors and a conflict with party liners on the staff of the *Moscow Daily News*. When the Kremlin required her to wait six weeks for a visa to reenter the Soviet Union, Strong left for China instead.[10]

Moscow's treatment of individual American travelers followed a similar pattern. In the early thirties the Kremlin tried to present a favorable view of the Soviet experiment to summer tourists, numbering from 5,000 to 10,000 every year, who arrived on guided tours or on short excursions from cruise ships that stopped at Soviet ports. The purge and a general antiforeign campaign abruptly curtailed travel in 1937–38, and all but a few Americans stayed away until 1955.[11]

Although the experiences of travelers, students, and American residents in the Soviet Union initially influenced only individual attitudes, there was potential for a larger impact. John Rothschild of the Open Road, an organization that directed guided tours to Russia, reported that over half of American travelers to the Soviet Union in 1935 had an educational occupation and about half lived in New York City. These travelers could spread their impressions through their teaching activities and through journals, both conservative and liberal, centered in New York.[12]

The decline of favorable assessments of Soviet policies influenced the general American reaction. Yet many commentators in the United States responded more directly to actual Soviet developments than to interpretations by observers of these events. The response to the Kirov affair, for example, which attracted more attention than had any Soviet event since recognition, was very critical. Although *Soviet Russia Today* and columnist Louis Fischer approved the executions as a necessary response to a counterrevolutionary conspiracy, most liberal spokesman condemned them. "Circumstances provide no excuse for the ruthless and bloody reprisal of the Soviet government," complained the *Nation*.[13] Other commentators were more vigorous in their criticism. "There is a businesslike brutality and intolerance about it which will suggest, in this country," remarked the *Minneapolis Tribune*, "nothing but naked terrorism" and the continuation of a repressive dictatorship in Moscow.[14]

Many American observers compared the Kirov purge with Hitler's purge of the SA, the first Nazi political-military force, in June, 1934, and raised the larger issue of the relationship between Stalin's and Hitler's systems (see Table 8). Even liberal journals admitted a significant similarity in methods: *Common Sense* stated that there was "considerable justification" in the comparison of Stalin's and Hitler's tactics; the *New Republic* confessed that the Kirov purge "forcibly recalls the thirtieth of June in Germany"; and the *Nation* more obliquely lamented that before the Kirov affair the "world had come to look to Germany for exhibitions of frightfulness and to Russia for an example of orderly progress."[15] Most commentators, however, went further than this and found a similarity in objectives as well as methods. "One finds it difficult to distinguish," pointed out the *Omaha Morning World-Herald*, "between its [Communism's] absolutism, its cruelty, its terrorism and that practiced by Hitler,

a Dollfuss or a Mussolini." Despite the absence of an extensive comparison of Nazism and Stalinism, there was widespread agreement with the
Chicago Tribune's stress on the "essential unity of the two forms of
government."[16] William Henry Chamberlin, who made the most comprehensive analysis of this issue, expressed the general viewpoint when
he noted a strong possibility for convergence between the two systems
"into something that might reasonably be called Red Fascism," despite
the different characters and temperaments of the two nations.[17]

In 1936, American observers had not completely identified Nazism and
Stalinism as "Red Fascism." Instead, many journals, especially liberal
organs and editors concerned with international developments, withheld
final judgments, primarily because the difference between Nazi and
Soviet foreign policy up until this time seemed so great. As Hitler left the
League of Nations, Stalin joined it; as Berlin demanded revisions of the
status quo, Moscow moved to defend it; and as Hitler attacked the
Western democracies, Stalin offered them cooperation and a united front
against Fascism.

Americans welcomed Stalin's diplomatic reorientation. Liberal journals, for example, increasingly supported Stalin's efforts to cooperate
with the West, climaxed by his united-front policy, which called for
cooperation against Fascism in domestic and foreign affairs. Even the
Christian Century, which vigorously criticized Stalin's domestic policies,
applauded the new direction in Soviet diplomacy.[18] Most journals approved Moscow's move into the League as beneficial for the maintenance
of the status quo and balance of power in Europe, although some editors
worried about the League becoming nothing more than a weapon of the
anti-German coalition. The Franco-Soviet alliance received a more
neutral reaction. A few newspapers openly endorsed the alliance as a
deterrent to German expansion and consequently a strong force for
peace; more, however, pointed to continuing mutual suspicion between
Paris and Moscow as a limiting factor.[19]

The greatest disagreement and uncertainty emerged over whether or
not Stalin's maneuvers reflected a basic change in Soviet objectives. In
1934–35, twenty-two of thirty-five newspapers (see Table 4) considered
security the most important concern of the Kremlin, and only ten believed
that the expansion of Communism was Moscow's central goal. The
increase in the latter viewpoint came primarily from conservative journals
that had not commented on the subject in the fall of 1933. The division
between conservative and moderate journals (see Table 6) continued to
shape their assessments of Stalin's actions. None of the fifteen moderate

editors emphasized the expansion of Communism, and none of the conservative newspapers endorsed the security interpretation without a qualification about the continuation of Soviet propaganda advocating Communism. The degree of interest the editors expressed in foreign affairs had a secondary but important impact. All nine of the journals with the strongest orientation toward foreign affairs (see Table 7) supported the security interpretation. Considering their extensive coverage of Stalin's collective security demarches, it would have been difficult for the editors to dismiss the Kremlin's public preoccupation with security, especially since most of the newspapers favored Western cooperation with Moscow. The eleven journals with a moderate interest in foreign affairs were divided, with seven emphasizing security and four, Communism. The fifteen newspapers with little interest in international relations, of which eight either made no comment or endorsed the Communist category, found it easiest to dismiss Stalin's policies and reiterate the traditional view that the Kremlin wanted world revolution.

Stressing the threat of Berlin and Tokyo, most editors noted a significant erosion of Soviet interest in the spread of Communism and confidently announced that Moscow had abandoned propaganda and foreign intrigue in order to concentrate on its internal affairs and on cooperation with the Western powers. "The Soviets have withdrawn their propaganda and sought to win friendship abroad," stated the *Cincinnati Enquirer.* The *Philadelphia Inquirer* agreed: "Russia now wishes to live at peace with her neighbors and is willing to refrain from interfering with their internal affairs."[20] Some journals, remembering earlier Soviet denunciations of the League of Nations and revolutionary ambitions, responded to Stalin's demarches with greater reservations. "Should this new attitude be verified and confirmed," the skeptical *New York Times* announced, "it would be a wonderful turn about in policy, and marvelous in the eyes of the world."[21] Conservative observers rejected Stalin's reorientation as a mere change in tactics. When Moscow entered the League, *America*'s editor, John La Farge, argued that the Kremlin only wanted protection from imperialists while it continued to push civil war. The *National Republic* insisted that Stalin would not drop his preparations to conquer the world for Communism.[22]

In 1936 Stalin briefly reinforced the favorable assessment of his diplomacy with a new constitution, which he publicized as a major step toward democracy. It "goes a long distance toward liberal, democratic organization," the *New Republic* concluded, and Louis Fischer and the *Nation* proclaimed the arrival of democracy.[23] Most commentators were more cautious, expecting Stalin and the Communist party to maintain control but hoping the constitution would start a move toward a representative system. Even the conservative *Chicago Tribune* considered the constitution a very favorable development because it repudiated Communist dogma and contained the "essentials of real democratic government."[24]

By November, 1936, when the constitution was formally approved, editorial opinion had become more critical, although the *Richmond Times-Dispatch* endorsed the economic and welfare guaranties and the *New York Herald Tribune* found hopeful signs in the increased participation of the people in the government, the establishment of the "rudiments of civil rights," and a less arbitrary court system.[25] Most journals hedged their views, warning that only the future implementation of the constitution would demonstrate its true significance. By December the *New Republic* admitted that the Communist dictatorship "still goes on," and conservative spokesman William Henry Chamberlin denounced the constitution: "No shoddier goldbrick has been turned out in the long historical process of masking the ugly facts of despotic rule."[26]

The cautious attitude of most editors toward the constitution reflected their observation of the first Moscow trial in August, 1936, which had signaled the start of Stalin's massive purge. The press found the Moscow trials, which received more editorial evaluation than any other Soviet affair until the Nazi-Soviet pact, difficult to interpret. The first trial attracted extensive acceptance of the official charges, primarily because of the dramatic confessions. The *San Francisco Chronicle,* the Louisville *Courier-Journal,* and Eugene Lyons correctly dismissed the trial as a staged demonstration with coerced confessions.[27] Most journals, however, accepted the confessions even if they had initially doubted the official accusations. "There is every reason to believe that the plot existed, as the confessions have indicated," remarked the *Dallas Morning News.*[28] Editors criticized some aspects of the first trial, especially the inevitability of secret conspiracies in a dictatorship and the long-term struggle for power between Stalin and Trotsky.

During the second trial many observers still found the confessions confusing. An increasing number of journals, faced with "a tale so weird, told under circumstances so extraordinary, as to justify suspicion that in it fact and fiction are mixed in unknown proportions," concurred with the *Boston Evening Transcript*'s advocacy of a neutral position.[29] Some began to express doubts about the validity of the confessions: "There is something fantastic and weird here," commented the *Des Moines Register.* "It doesn't ring true."[30]

As the trials continued, criticism grew stronger. Moscow's "dreams of liberating humanity became a ghastly joke; its new and 'democratic' constitution is something to stir ironic smiles," remarked the *Washington Post*. An increasing number of newspapers agreed with the *Baltimore Sun*'s characterization of the Soviet Union as "murderous and relentless dictatorship."[31] Even liberal journals intensified their criticism. "If the defendants are not guilty as charged, no liberals can excuse the resort by a government to such measures . . . ," the *Nation* suggested; but, even if the charges were true, "a Socialist government that . . . is so riddled with conspiracies cannot lay claim to the trust that liberals have thus far accorded it." Within a month, however, the *Nation* reverted to a position of sympathetic criticism.[32]

When one defendant denied any guilt and then confessed the next day during the third trial in March, 1938, American spokesmen concluded that the confessions were coerced. They also began to view the trial as part of a continuing purge in which even the original leaders of the purge were being liquidated. "Practically everybody who had an important part in building up the Soviet Union apparently will soon be either dead, in prison or in exile," concluded the *Richmond Times-Dispatch*. Most journals agreed with the *Cincinnati Enquirer*'s conclusion that the trials "are a systematic terror calculated to keep leaders, as well as mere citizens, cowed before an all-powerful dictatorship."[33] The trials further discredited Stalin's domestic system, which the *Philadelphia Inquirer* denounced as the "blackest despotism in the world's history." The *New York Times* vigorously attacked the Kremlin: "We are witnessing today the moral and intellectual collapse of communism. We are back in the torture chambers of the Aztecs and the Druids."[34] Many commentators asserted that violence and "reoccurring bloody purges" now dominated the Soviet scene, where the Revolution was over, replaced by a "hierarchy determined to preserve its power" at all costs.[35] Even some of the liberal journals like the *Christian Century* extensively criticized the purge and eschewed the *Nation*'s rather feeble defense of it as a valuable "cleaning" (of incompetent or dishonest officials) that had gotten out of control.[36]

The trials and the purge not only turned American spokesmen against Stalin's regime but also strengthened the comparison between Stalin and Hitler. Contrasting their use of the purge, some journals concluded that Stalin had far exceeded Hitler in the liquidation of his people. The "practical operations of both," noted the *San Francisco Chronicle*, "have seemed strangely alike in some particulars."[37] Fourteen of thirty-five newspapers (see Table 8) affirmed the essential similarity of the two systems, and twelve noted significant parallels in the repressive methods used by Stalin and Hitler. Conservative papers like the *Philadelphia Inquirer* argued that "there is little to choose between the tyranny of Communism and the despotism of Fascism."[38] Eugene Lyons judged that the differences between the two systems were minor—differences as "there are between arsenic and strychnine"—and that they were shaped by forces that were essentially the same—"the political Tweedledum-Tweedledee which is Fascism and Communism."[39] Although the *New Republic* and the *Nation* avoided this issue, other liberal spokesmen turned against all forms of totalitarianism, including the Soviet Union. Under the impact of the purge, the *Cleveland Plain Dealer* admitted that Stalinism and Nazism, despite different stated motives, were "functioning" as "repressive and tyrannical" regimes.[40]

The general deterioration after 1936 of American opinion about Stalin's domestic system carried over into attitudes toward Soviet diplomacy. It was difficult even for liberal spokesmen to advocate support for Stalin's foreign policies. "In the United States any concrete proposal of cooperation with the Soviet Union, difficult as it would have been at any time," complained the *New Republic,* "is now sure to be buried under popular disapproval." When in 1938 Moscow proposed a general conference to plan ways to stop aggression, the *Christian Century* rejected the proposal because of the purge: "It is just not possible to get up any degree of enthusiasm for going hopefully and trustfully into a conference with Russia."[41]

However, Stalin's diplomacy—contrasted with Hitler's expansion and Japan's activities in China—stopped American spokesmen from completely rejecting Moscow. The Kremlin's policies conveyed a somewhat contradictory image; observers noted defensive characteristics as well as the old, if more subtle, exportation of Communism.

The outbreak of civil war in Spain in 1936 did not immediately focus the attention of commentators on Soviet interests in international Communism. A majority of the press did not even refer to Communism or Moscow in the first weeks of the crisis, instead emphasizing the reactionary, monarchist, Fascist character of the rebellion against the government. A significant minority, however, expected the Republican government to move to the left; the *Washington Post* expressed this view: "Every day the intimations grow stronger that the government cause is moving swiftly toward that of an outright Communist dictatorship."[42] A few conservative journals focused almost exclusively on the threat of Communism and agreed with the *Seattle Times* that "every anti-Communist element of the Spanish population is lined up against the murderous Reds who have been running the government."⁴³ By the end of August, however, the press considered Communism as big a threat as Fascism in Spain. The *Pittsburgh Post-Gazette* remarked that "unfortunately, democracy seems to be wholly out of the picture; Fascism and Communism cast a baleful shadow."⁴⁴

When the Soviet Union provided aid to the Spanish government, journals split into two camps concerning Stalin's objectives. To check the spread of Fascism and improve the Soviet defensive position vis-à-vis Hitler seemed to be a crucial Soviet aim to some, especially liberal journals.⁴⁵ From another perspective, Stalin's intervention looked more like an effort to make Spain a "great Communist headquarters, fronting on the Mediterranean and the Atlantic." Soviet involvement in Spain, according to conservative spokesmen, confirmed their view that when the time was right, Stalin would spread Communism.⁴⁶ Some (but not all) American observers viewed Soviet policy as double-edged, aiming at security and revolution.

Yet American observers considered Communism a secondary threat compared to Fascism, and Soviet policy defensive compared to German and Japanese expansion. This viewpoint emerged most clearly in response to the Anti-Comintern Pact of November, 1936, between Berlin and Tokyo, which ostensibly aimed at the containment of the Communist International. Only the *Atlanta Constitution* wholeheartedly welcomed the pact as an "outstanding move for world peace" because it would contain Communism. The vast majority of the press did not believe that the pact really aimed at defense, but viewed it as an aggressive alliance to take away Soviet territory. The stated purpose of the pact appeared to be, as the *Des Moines Register* put it, "pure camouflage" for a desire to acquire Russian territory and disrupt the Soviet alliance with France. The pact "may be regarded as a combine of land-hungry nations feverishly preparing for territorial acquisitions and conquests," concluded the Louisville *Courier-Journal.*⁴⁷

The Soviet Union's reoccurring problems with Japan along the Manchurian–Outer Mongolian border reinforced this image of Stalin's diplomacy. In infrequent comments before 1938, most editors emphasized the cautious, defensive stance of Moscow in contrast to an aggressive Japan. When full-scale fighting occurred in the summer of 1938, the press devoted more attention to it than to any other Soviet diplomatic affair in 1937–38. After extensive speculation about who started the border war, with most journals undecided, the press focused on the question of Soviet motivation. The strategic importance of Changkufeng Hill to Possiet Bay—a potential port—and the defense of Siberia and Vladivostok were widely discussed.[48] When the conflict continued after Moscow rejected initial feelers from Tokyo concerning an armistice, the press noted with favor a Soviet desire to aid China by pinning down Japanese troops along the northern border and weakening the current Japanese offensive on the Yangtze River toward Hankow. "In a very practical way Russia is aiding its Chinese ally," concluded the Louisville *Courier-Journal*.[49]

This favorable assessment of Soviet policy in Asia did not significantly influence the press's evaluation of the Soviet Union's role in the European crisis of 1938. Despite the Red army's firmness in the Far East, serious doubts about the strength of the Soviet Union and censures of the purge persisted. As the *Richmond Times-Dispatch* pointed out, the "Soviet Union's brutal terrorism has so alienated world opinion that France and Britain will certainly be less zealous for its help than in earlier days."[50] When the Czechoslovakian crisis peaked in September, most editors felt that Stalin would take a cautious approach. In very limited references to the Soviet Union, journals alluded to the refusal of Poland and Rumania to provide access for Soviet aid to Prague and Moscow's reluctance to aid Czechoslovakia unless France kept its commitments.

Before and after the first settlement at Godesberg, members of the press expressed a variety of views about Stalin's stance, none of them very enthusiastic. Most considered Stalin's position enigmatic and unreliable and approved the isolation of the Kremlin. Even liberal journals, noting the decline of Soviet interest in cooperation with the Western powers, fatalistically accepted the isolation of Moscow. The prospect of Hitler turning on the Soviet Union after the settlement also caused little apprehension. "Those who recall how the Bolsheviks sold out at Brest Litovsk," the *Washington Post* and the *New York World-Telegram* reminded their readers, "will see less cause for breaking a quixotic lance in behalf of Stalin now."[51]

The Munich Conference strengthened this attitude toward Moscow's isolation. Although editors referred favorably to a report of British-French-Soviet cooperation against a German military move on Prague before the conference, most failed to mention the Kremlin in their final assessments of the conference. This in itself indicated apathy about Stalin's policy and, indirectly, acceptance of the refusal to cooperate with him against Hitler; a few journals approved outright of keeping Stalin out of the conference in order to prevent war. "The democracies and the fascist states might well have fought through to mutual exhaustion," observed the *Portland Oregonian,* which would have been "very pleasing to the communists."[52] Only a few editors criticized the exclusion of Moscow. "The fact that the Russians were not even invited to the Munich conference," complained the conservative *Denver Post,* "was an insult they are not likely to forget."[53]

"Any plan for the appeasement of Europe that does not include reconsideration of Godless Russia's trouble-making ideology and stupendous army is perilously short-sighted," warned the conservative *Philadelphia Inquirer.*[54] This statement illustrates the somewhat unpredictable views of the press; most newspapers mixed criticism and approval of Soviet policies. Political affiliation exercised some influence over the general division between conservative and liberal viewpoints. Some conservative Republican journals consistently criticized Stalin's domestic policies and worried about Communist expansion, and some liberal Democratic journals usually presented the best possible explanation of Soviet behavior—to a certain degree mirroring the sharper division between liberal journals like the *Nation* and conservative spokesmen such as Chamberlin and the *National Republic.* Another division appeared in journals that had a strong interest in international affairs and were reluctant to dismiss Stalin's diplomacy.

Overall, however, an unfavorable consensus of opinion emerged about the Soviet Union, and Stalin was primarily responsible. Initially, Americans had welcomed Stalin's reorientation toward cooperation with the Western powers, especially since it had suggested to them a decline of Soviet interest in world revolution. But Stalin undercut this with his public trials and general purge, which prompted the news media to emphasize the increasing similarity of Stalinism and Nazism as bloody totalitarian systems. This perspective affected all subsequent assessments of Soviet diplomacy and raised serious doubts about the strength, reliability, and morality of the Soviet leadership and system. Nonetheless, most commentators (except the most conservative) stopped short of a total rejection of the Soviet Union as "Red Fascism," because Stalin's attitude toward Berlin and Tokyo seemed cautious and defensive.

Stalin's domestic policies seriously broadened the already deep estrangement in Soviet-American relations. By turning Americans against the Soviet experiment, he raised another obstacle to any effective cooperation between Moscow and Washington. President Roosevelt would have to contend not only with the resistance of the State Department but also with the opposition of the news media.

7

Roosevelt's Unsuccessful Reorientation

Late in April, 1936, before his departure for Paris, Ambassador Bullitt summed up the advantages and disadvantages of formal relations with the Soviet Union. He believed that "We should not cherish for a moment the illusion that it is possible to establish really friendly relations with the Soviet Government"; yet he recognized that official contact with the Kremlin provided economic and diplomatic benefits. The yearly trade agreements steadily increased Soviet purchases of American goods, and the Moscow embassy obtained valuable information about the Kremlin's foreign and domestic policies. Bullitt also noted the advantage of being able to influence the Far Eastern situation: "We should use our influence quietly to oppose war in the Far East between the Soviet Union and Japan," he advised Secretary Hull, both as a matter of principle and in the interests of encouraging a Far Eastern balance of power.[1]

Bullitt's dispatch touched on many of the pressures that shaped Soviet-American relations until World War II, but he underestimated President Roosevelt's interest in the Soviet Union as a counterweight against Japan and Germany. After the election of 1936, the president attempted to remove some of the obstacles to Soviet-American cooperation, despite stubborn opposition from the members of the State Department, who argued that Stalin's diplomacy was too unreliable and his

81

domestic purge morally repugnant. With Congress still advocating an isolationist approach toward the European powers and the news media increasingly critical of Stalin, Roosevelt lacked substantial support for an approach to Moscow. The president's domestic critics stressed the issue of an internal Communist threat, and any overtures to the Soviet Union were politically risky. Nevertheless, Roosevelt tried, with more boldness than historians have recognized, to reorient relations with Moscow and initiate cooperation in the Far East.

Isolationist sentiment in Congress and throughout the country represented an insurmountable barrier to the president's maneuvers. Congress continued to block new policy initiatives with neutrality legislation, which was broadened after 1935 to forbid loans to belligerents and travel on belligerent ships. "Cash and carry" was extended to raw materials like copper and oil, which were important to belligerent powers. Roosevelt did not significantly resist the neutrality legislation. Instead, he encouraged Congress to extend the legislation to the civil conflict in Spain in 1936–37.[2]

The peak in isolationist influence in Congress came in 1938, when Rep. Louis Ludlow, an Indiana Democrat, tried to win approval for a constitutional amendment that would require a direct vote of the people before Congress could declare war. Ludlow, who hoped to increase popular control of American foreign policy and keep the United States out of another European war, excluded an attack on the United States from his original proposal in 1935 and in 1938 extended the exception to the entire Western Hemisphere. When Ludlow finally persuaded the House to consider a motion to discharge the Judiciary Committee from further considering his legislation, Roosevelt unleashed administration lobbyists against the bill. On the day of the vote, January 10, 1938, the president sent a letter to be read to the House, in which he rejected the war referendum and its isolationist limited-defense concept as "impracticable in its application and incompatible with our representative form of government.... It would cripple any President in his conduct of our foreign relations, and it would encourage other nations to believe that they could violate American rights with impunity." The House voted 209 to 188 against the motion to discharge the Ludlow bill.[3] A few days later Roosevelt confided to his son James that "national defense represents too serious a danger, especially in these modern times where distance has been annihilated, to permit delay and our danger lies in things like the Ludlow Amendment which appeal to people, who, frankly, have no conception of what modern war, with or without declaration of war, involves."

In 1938 and 1939 the president could barely defend the status quo against the isolationists. His political opponents, Republicans and conservatives, also put him on the defensive with a two-pronged campaign against Communism. The conservative Liberty League and the Republican National Committee initiated one part of the campaign with the charge of alien, Communistic influences in Roosevelt's New Deal. The coalition of Father Charles E. Coughlin, Rev. Gerald L.K. Smith, and Frances E. Townsend went beyond this accusation. "The hand of Moscow," Father Coughlin charged in July, supports Roosevelt "where Communism stands"; on August 2 he directly accused the president of being a Communist. Reverend Smith and extremist author Elizabeth Dilling agreed, suggesting that Roosevelt had a "deliberate, comprehensive plan to change the American form of government to a Red dictatorship" and lead America into a world war to support Stalin.[4]

The White House did not ignore these charges. When rumors circulated about Communist support of Roosevelt in the 1936 election, Secretary Hull ordered the Moscow embassy to check with Soviet officials, who denied the reports. At the New York Democratic convention, Roosevelt made a direct rebuttal: "I have not sought, I do not seek, I repudiate the support of any advocate of Communism or of any other alien 'ism."[5] Rather, the president argued, his New Deal attacked the social roots of Communism, whereas Republicans encouraged the social unrest that aided Communists. Roosevelt's speeches and the support he received from the press, which ignored or ridiculed the charges, effectively buried this attack until conservatives revived it in time for the congressional election of 1938.

Another dimension of the campaign of 1936 received less publicity but had more impact. Commander Frank L. Belegrando of the American Legion, in a 1935 national radio broadcast, warned that the "agents of Moscow have invaded our public rostrums, our factories, our schools and colleges, our press and our churches." A national campaign against Communism received extensive support in 1936 and afterwards from patriotic societies, the American Federation of Labor, anti-Communist organizations, and Catholics. The campaign had only mixed results. When several of these groups asked the Republican platform committee to include a plank advocating a return to nonrecognition, the committee rejected their request.[6] However, this crusade laid the groundwork for a congressional investigation in 1938.

Martin Dies' special committee to investigate subversive activities, a predecessor of the House Committee on Un-American Activities, brought together the two different themes of the campaign launched in

1936. When Dies started hearings in August, 1938, anti-Communist groups, led by Walter Steele of the American Coalition and the *National Republic,* presented massive documentation of Communist penetration into various organizations. Dies, a Texas Democrat, and other conservative members of the committee aimed their attack at the New Deal and liberal Democrats. Although the press heavily criticized the committee, public opinion polls by George Gallup reported that of the 61 percent of Americans who had heard of the Dies committee, 74 percent favored its continuation.[7]

Roosevelt responded cautiously to this revival of organized anti-Communist sentiment. After publicly criticizing Dies for accusations against individual Democrats, Roosevelt privately asked Democratic leaders to warn Dies about the unfavorable impact of his hearings upon the party. The White House also ordered the Justice Department to investigate Dies' charges.[8] Roosevelt allowed Soviet-American relations to drift in 1936 by not appointing a replacement for Bullitt until after the election, and he also disregarded relations with Moscow as the congressional elections of 1938 approached. With little countering pressure from liberals or the press favoring cooperation with the Soviet Union, Roosevelt moved very warily, hoping to avoid bitter criticism from anti-Communist groups and the Dies committee.

Any attempt by the president to reorient relations with Moscow also faced serious resistance from within the government. For over a year the State Department and the Moscow embassy had implemented their Russian policy—a cautious approach which encouraged only trade—without any interference from the White House. From Moscow, Ambassador Bullitt, Loy Henderson, and the embassy staff argued that Washington "should neither expect too much nor despair of getting anything at all" from the Kremlin. In a review of the first three years of formal relations, Henderson also warned that any attempt to cooperate with Moscow, which wanted "definite treaties of mutual military assistance in case of unprovoked attack," would be risky, since world revolution remained the Kremlin's long-range goal despite its current tactics. In Washington, Robert Kelley, who still directed the Division of Eastern European Affairs, fully agreed with the embassy's position.[9]

The Russian experts felt that they had provided a successful economic focus to relations with Moscow. They had encouraged economic relations with the Kremlin partially because trade did not generate pressure for political cooperation; interested exporters and the American-Russian Chamber of Commerce, which continued to assist American firms, asked only for favorable trade conditions. With yearly trade agreements, the Kremlin's purchases of American products reached $70 million in 1938, which made America the leading exporter to the Soviet Union. Most of Moscow's purchases were for products in the machine tool and industrial equipment industries, to replace Russian equipment worn out by rapid industrialization. In addition, the Kremlin considered the United States the most important source of military technology and war materials, and in July, 1936, established a special corporation, the Carp Export and Import Corporation of New York City, to manage its technological acquisitions. The Carp firm increased the Soviet Union's purchases, especially in aircraft technology. More than twenty American corporations sold aircraft, accessories, and technical assistance to the Soviet Union. The Glenn L. Martin Company, for example, agreed in 1937 to provide Moscow with the world's largest plane (the Martin Ocean Transport), the design of a new bomber, and the training of Soviet engineers. The Soviet Union also purchased specialized tools, engines, and DC-3 aircraft under an agreement with the Douglas Aircraft Company. Some firms had disappointing interactions with Moscow. The United Fruit Company, which shipped bananas to Moscow in 1936 "for the purpose of enabling your medical authorities and dieticians to study the food values and therapeutic values of bananas," did not obtain any lucrative Russian orders.[10]

In November, 1936, the Kremlin attempted to purchase naval vessels from the United States, as part of a general naval strategy to construct a big, balanced navy, primarily for the purposes of deterrence and prestige. Faced with German and Japanese expansion, the Soviet Union wanted battleships to discourage invasion by sea. Moreover, Stalin had discovered in the Spanish Civil War that the Soviet Union's submarine force, which was the world's largest and constituted the main striking unit of the Soviet fleet, could not be used effectively to support Soviet diplomacy. Consequently, Stalin expanded the improvement of Soviet shipbuilding yards and the construction of capital ships, most notably heavy cruisers and three large battleships. However, the Soviet Union's limited shipbuilding facilities and inadequate capacity for equipping capital ships with large-caliber naval guns, armor plate, and fire control equipment prompted the Kremlin to turn to the United States.[11]

Roosevelt and the State Department approved the Kremlin's effort to purchase various components of a battleship. Joseph E. Green, chief of the State Department's Office of Arms and Munitions Control, endorsed the transaction, as did Robert F. Kelley. "Assuming the evolution of the

Soviet Government eventually into a purely national Government," Kelley argued, "the strengthening of the naval forces of the Soviet Union would not run counter to the national interests of the United States."[12] Secretary Hull reviewed and approved a proposed contract between the Carp firm and the Bethlehem Shipbuilding Corporation for the sale of a disassembled battleship.

Senior career officers in the Department of the Navy, however, opposed any naval assistance to the Soviet Union. Adm. William D. Leahy, chief of naval operations, Rear Adm. W.R. Furlong, chief of the Bureau of Ordnance, and Rear Adm. Ralston S. Holmes, chief of the Office of Naval Intelligence, emerged as the main sources of navy resistance. These officials thoroughly disliked the idea of the United States providing any aid to a Communist government, basing their objections on legal grounds and established policy.[13] Under the Espionage Act of June 15, 1917, the revelation of military secrets of interest to the national defense was prohibited, and the Navy Department had the responsibility to enforce this legislation in matters concerning the sale of naval vessels and equipment. Consequently, any Soviet contract with an American shipbuilding firm had to be reviewed and approved by the navy. Furthermore, as Admiral Leahy repeatedly pointed out to the State Department, official policy precluded any navy assistance to private shipbuilders, and these firms could not supply the necessary armor plate and guns without active help from the navy.

When the proposed contract between Carp and Bethlehem was resisted, Roosevelt tried to bring the navy into line on official policy. At a Cabinet meeting on April 3, 1937, Roosevelt instructed the secretary of the navy, Claude A. Swanson, to encourage any shipbuilding firm to accept a contract for a Soviet battleship. "It was evident that the President saw no objection to this ship being built in one of our yards, and neither did Hull," remarked Harold Ickes, secretary of the interior. Roosevelt also told Admiral Leahy that he approved the transaction because it would be a propitious move from an international viewpoint.[14]

Despite Roosevelt's endorsement, officials in the Navy Department maintained a somewhat oblique but nevertheless effective opposition to the president. Admiral Leahy, who had stated that he agreed with the White House's position, indirectly encouraged this resistance by expressing little enthusiasm for the project and by not reprimanding subordinate officers when they maneuvered against it. Two days after Roosevelt's discussion with Admiral Leahy, for example, navy officials probably leaked information to the press about the proposed contract to arouse unfavorable publicity.[15]

Officials in the Navy Department were also using the issue of military secrets and the Espionage Act of 1917 to disrupt a March, 1937, agreement between the navy and the Electric Boat Company of Groton, Connecticut, which wanted to build a submarine for the Kremlin. Leahy insisted that the company withhold any data that the navy considered confidential, exclude Soviet officials from the construction plant, and accept all navy rules and regulations. The admiral's demands were so stringent that the Groton firm put aside the submarine project.

As negotiations over the Bethlehem contract continued into the summer of 1937, a third method of obstruction by navy officials emerged. Subordinate officers, including Furlong and Holmes, privately warned shipbuilding firms to reject a contract with Carp because of their aversion to any assistance to a Communist government. Since the navy was the principal customer of these firms, they feared reprisals on future contracts.[16]

The White House sent Joseph Green to intercede with Admiral Leahy. Asked about the comments of subordinate officers, Leahy said that "it was more than possible that some officers of his Department who were strongly opposed to sales of arms to a communistic government might have made indiscreet remarks." Green responded by pointing out that this had created "a highly embarrassing situation." Leahy expressed agreement; according to Green, "he did not, however, appear to be particularly impressed by what seemed to me to be the serious implications of the situation which has arisen as a result of statements made by his subordinates." Moreover, in his diary Leahy revealed his considerable reservations, referring to the directors of Carp, Morris Wolf and Sam Carp, as international villain types and to the Soviet Union as a "menace" and expressing skepticism about Ambassador Troyanovsky's comments on the similarity of Soviet-American interests in the Far East.[17]

In 1938 the Soviet Union shifted its primary attention to an effort to obtain plans for a battleship but again encountered opposition from the Navy Department. Gibbs and Cox, Inc., leading naval architects, prepared plans for a 35-knot, 60,000-ton battleship with 18-inch guns; it would be 15,000 tons larger than any battleship in existence. Roosevelt reviewed the plans with Charles Edison, assistant secretary of the navy, in March, 1938, expressed approval for the construction of a battleship for the Soviet Union, and indicated that the United States also might want to use the new plans. Edison told the president that "there was strong opposition to the proposed transaction on the part of several high ranking officers of the Navy Department." On April 8 Roosevelt met with Edison, Admiral Leahy, and several navy bureau chiefs in a fruitless effort, according to Joseph Green, "to dragoon the naval officers in question into a state of at least apparent conformity with the policy of the government."[18]

At a White House conference on June 8, Edison and Secretary Hull reviewed the impasse, suggested that a Soviet battleship stationed at Vladivostok "might be of positive advantage to" the United States, and urged the president "to take definite action." Roosevelt approved a 45,000-ton battleship with 16-inch guns and recommended that the government "give all help" to interested shipbuilders and naval architects. The president also suggested that a special officer under Edison's supervision handle the navy's involvement with the plans, probably in order to circumvent the entrenched navy opposition to the project. Roosevelt good-naturedly advised the participants in the conference to "start clubbing the resisting naval officers over the head."[19]

Although Roosevelt's intervention finally prompted the navy to approve the battleship, the issue was soon overshadowed by the Kremlin's desire to purchase two destroyers. Navy officers again dragged their feet, objecting to numerous aspects of the plans prepared by Gibbs and Cox, and Roosevelt again had to force the issue. The president's wishes "were clear," complained Assistant Secretary Edison, who promised to "prevent delays and petty attempts to make difficulties" by appointing three senior officers to carry out Roosevelt's instructions.[20]

But time ran out on the whole project, as the navy's own building program preempted construction in the shipyards and the outbreak of World War II scuttled the plans. The navy officers emerged the winners even though they appeared to lose each specific round to Roosevelt, the State Department, and Assistant Secretary Edison. Considering the restrictions on Roosevelt's time and the limited importance of this issue as a gesture to improve relations with Moscow, he had devoted considerable attention to it. The only measure he had not tried in his effort to circumvent navy opposition was the removal of some of the opposing officers—probably out of concern about an adverse reaction from the press. Since the president was sensitive to the news media's critical perspective on the Soviet Union, as well as isolationist criticism of any governmental involvement in arms trade with European powers, he wanted to avoid any step that might attract public attention. For example, he rejected a suggestion in 1936 that he ask Congress for a special endorsement of the navy's cooperation with shipbuilders on the Soviet battleship.

Roosevelt also had only limited success when he attempted to improve the framework of relations with Moscow by shifting personnel in the Moscow embassy and the State Department. William Bullitt in 1936 and Robert Kelley in 1937 lost their positions and Kelley disappeared in diplomatic exile as first secretary in Istanbul. The Division of Eastern European Affairs which he had headed since 1926 was abolished, its research activities ended and its files deposited in the Library of Congress. Many diplomats felt that the changes foreshadowed a new, more friendly policy toward Russia. More recently, George Kennan has alleged that the removal of Kelley was the result of Ambassador Davies' hostility. Various rumors also placed responsibility for the division's demise on Eleanor Roosevelt's determination to protect fellow travelers, particularly members of the American Youth Congress, with whom she was friendly.[21]

The removal of Kelley probably did reflect an emerging conflict between Roosevelt and the Russian specialists over cooperation with Moscow in Europe and the Far East, although this remains difficult to document. Unfortunately, Kelley, who had made an admirable contribution in the training of Russian specialists, became a symbol in this conflict, which spilled over into the State Department and overseas missions. Kelley and Arthur Bliss Lane, minister to the Baltics, for example, had clashed over Lane's desire to reduce the Russian section at Riga in order to advance cooperation with Moscow against Berlin. Lane believed that the Russian section's attitude toward the Soviet Union was too negative. When Kelley blocked Lane's proposals to remove Felix Cole and limit the section's operations to research and translation, Lane went to a higher official, R. Walton Moore. Following a formal investigation, Lane received most of what he wanted.[22]

Within the State Department, Charles Bohlen had watched and then participated in a political struggle which focused on Kelley and his division. Bohlen supported Kelley with somewhat mixed emotions; he recognized the need for a "fresh view" of Moscow in the State Department, but also believed that Kelley's skepticism was necessary when dealing with the Kremlin. The conflict, which pulled one of the young Russian specialists, Norris B. Chipman, over to the anti-Kelley faction, became emotional and vindictive. Kennan and Bohlen, for example, partially defeated an effort to break up the research files of Kelley's division by hiding reference books in the attic of the State Department and by arranging for the transfer of the rest of the collection to the Library of Congress.[23]

Elimination of Kelley's division was part of a larger reorganization carried out by Sumner Welles in June, 1937, shortly after he became under secretary. With Roosevelt's support, he sought to modernize the State Department's operations. Just as the various divisions dealing with Latin America were melded into one Division of the American Republics, so the Division of Eastern European Affairs disappeared into a new Division of European Affairs; the elimination of its research functions, however regrettable, merely placed it on a par with other components of the new, larger division. This bureaucratic shuffle, which seemed to reduce the influence of the Moscow embassy's Russian specialists, did not have this effect within the department. The chief of the new bureau, Pierrepont Moffat, and Kennan, who was brought home from Moscow to become the Russian desk officer, were at least as critical of the Soviet Union as Kelley had been. Although Kennan had little influence on policy, Moffat and Secretary Hull consistently expressed to Roosevelt the skeptical viewpoint of the Russian specialists. Despite the reorganization, Ambassador Troyanovsky considered "almost all of the American career diplomats to be reactionary."[24] Consequently, to the extent that the removal of Kelley and his division represented an attempt to weaken the State Department's opposition to cooperation with the Kremlin, the changes were rather ineffectual.

Roosevelt had more success in his appointment of Joseph E. Davies as ambassador to Moscow in November, 1936. Davies, who had refused a similar offer from President Wilson in 1913, accepted the post in Moscow after he missed his first choice, Berlin. Roosevelt's selection of Davies, who gave financial support to the Democratic campaign of 1936, represented more than a political plum to reward a wealthy contributor. The president immediately asked Davies to carry out a brief "mission" to ascertain which side Moscow would support in a war between the Western democratic powers and the Fascist powers; he also wanted Davies to evaluate the Kremlin's industrial and military strength as well as its policy in the Far East. "It is a matter of real importance ... ," Sumner Welles told Davies, elaborating on Roosevelt's instructions in December, "that friendly relations and cooperation should be restored particularly in view of the Chinese-Japanese situation and the possibility of world war starting in Europe."[25]

The special-mission dimension of Davies' ambassadorship had an impact on Roosevelt. As Bullitt predicted, Soviet officials covered "Joe Davies with tons of the very best butter," greeting him with open arms, flattering him with luncheons attended by Marshal Voroshilov and by Anastas Mikoyan, a member of the Politburo, and urging him to push for Soviet-American cooperation. Undoubtedly this flattery contributed to

Davies' friendly response to the Soviet Union, although he was not uncritical of Stalin's dictatorship. Before he reported back to Roosevelt in March, Davies told Litvinov that he preferred the American system but "was very much impressed with what they were doing, with the strength of their leadership, the difficulties they were overcoming" and with their devotion to peace. Like Roosevelt, Davies emphasized the Kremlin's strength and determination to check Germany and Japan.

Pleased with Davies' report, Roosevelt asked him to return to Moscow, although Davies wanted to move on to Berlin. Davies resumed his travels in Russia and Europe and recommended Soviet-American cooperation in his final report. He noted "no conflicts of physical interest" and little ideological conflict with a Soviet Union moving faster and faster toward capitalism. According to Kennan, Davies brought a "different tone in reporting, a different analysis of Soviet motives and intentions" from those of the Moscow embassy. More significantly, Davies' belief that Moscow was sincerely interested in cooperation with Washington reinforced Roosevelt's movement in this direction.[26]

Roosevelt was considering an alliance with the Kremlin, Great Britain, and France because of the increasing prospect of war in July, 1937. Both situations threatened a variety of American interests and, ultimately, America's security. Nazi Germany, for example, offended ideals with its racist posture, challenged Secretary Hull's trade policies in Latin America and elsewhere, and menaced America's economic and political ties with Western Europe. Every general war in Europe had, sooner or later, involved the United States. The isolationist viewpoint was that America should avoid involvement in a European war at all costs, since Hitler did not threaten America—but Roosevelt understood earlier than most officials that Hitler was ultimately capable of attempting anything, including a direct attack on the United States. The conflict with Japan was more immediate but less important in the long run. Japanese expansion after 1931 had violated the Nine Power Treaty of 1922; it upset minimal U.S. economic interests in Manchuria but increased the more valuable U.S. trade with Japan; and Tokyo threatened the State Department's institutional commitment to the Open Door policy in China, a policy with limited relevance to the contemporary situation. By invading China in 1937, Japan became a potential threat to the Philippines, which America still controlled, and thus the object of public and official criticism by Americans. Roosevelt correctly considered Japan an important problem but not of the magnitude that Hitler was.

After his victory in the 1936 election, the president intermittently tried various measures to check Germany and Japan, without much success. In the spring of 1937, he considered an embargo against Germany and Italy because of their involvement in the Spanish Civil War. Legal technicalities, the opposition of London, and the obvious futility of this proposal—since Berlin and Rome purchased few arms from America— prompted Roosevelt to drop this plan. With the support of Norman Davis, Secretary Morgenthau, and later Sumner Welles, Roosevelt considered various other schemes, including secret talks with London and an international conference to check German expansion. London's guarded replies and Hull's opposition shelved these ideas.[27]

When Japan attacked China in July, Roosevelt and the State Department searched for ways to restrain Japan. For example, they did not impose the Neutrality Act, hoping this would help China more than Japan—although it had the opposite effect. Washington also supported the League of Nations' ineffective condemnation of Japan. At the same time the president tried to cooperate with London without giving the impression, as he warned his private contact with the British, that Washington was "a tail to the British kite," as isolationists charged. On October 5, Roosevelt made his famous quarantine speech in Chicago, hinting at the need for a joint quarantine against aggressors. The next day Welles urged Roosevelt to call an international conference. Despite the favorable reaction of the press to the speech, Roosevelt's and especially Hull's extreme sensitivity toward isolationist critics prevented any change in policy.[28]

Great Britain was the most important source of cooperation, but Washington and London seemingly could not cooperate, partly because Americans still opposed active involvement with the European powers. Roosevelt, who shared the people's desire to keep out of war, did not explain the facts of the international situation to them with consistency and forcefulness. Instead he wavered, both in public statements and in private pronouncements—thus reinforcing the opinion of Neville Chamberlain, who became prime minister in 1937, that one could not expect much from the president.

Cooperation with the Soviet Union was part of Roosevelt's general strategy, but the prospects were not very good because of the likelihood of intense public criticism and because of the State Department's resistance. The Kremlin indicated an interest in such cooperation, probably in response to the Far Eastern situation. Tension between Japan and the Soviet Union increased, especially after Germany and Japan signed the Anti-Comintern Pact in November, 1936. Shortly before launching the undeclared war against China, Japan tested the Soviet Union's strength in the Far East by attacking Soviet forces on the Amur Islands, one of the many contested areas between Russia and Japan's puppet, Manchukuo. After an armed clash on June 30, 1937, Moscow withdrew its troops; over Soviet protests Japan occupied one of the disputed islands.

Although Adam Ulam, a leading specialist on Soviet policy, argues that Moscow had almost given up on Washington by 1937, Moscow's diplomatic gestures suggested a continuing interest.[29] In 1936 Soviet officials publicly and privately called for friendly Soviet-American relations. America and the Soviet Union "can exist and compete peacefully," Stalin told Roy Howard of Scripps-Howard Newspapers, ". . . if we do not indulge in too much fault-finding about trifling things." The Soviet press matched the Kremlin's semiprivate gestures with frequent calls for Soviet-American cooperation in support of collective security.[30]

During the U.S. election campaign of 1936, Ambassador Troyanovsky reported that a victory for the progressive forces led by Roosevelt over the reactionaries supporting the Republican candidate, Alfred Landon, would keep the door ajar for Soviet-American cooperation if another world war broke out. Roosevelt's victory prompted Troyanovsky to conclude that "for the present the situation here for us is favorable. The fascist states here are not popular, and if the obvious sympathy is not to us, it is possible, however, to anticipate that the choice will be made to our side."[31] The Soviet ambassador did not expect a change in the isolationist stance of Washington, but throughout 1936 and 1937 he suggested that the Kremlin should "cultivate friendship with the United States" and try "to draw them to our side" before the outbreak of war.[32]

The Kremlin followed Troyanovsky's recommendation in June, 1937, during the Amur Islands conflict with Japan. Moscow proposed a settlement of the debt issue through private parties appointed by both sides and instructed the ambassador to confer with Roosevelt about a nonaggression pact in the Far East. Since Japan probably would not participate, Litvinov suggested, a pact among Great Britain, the United States, China, and the Soviet Union "would to some extent be a mark of solidarity among these countries, especially if it provides for consultations in the event one of the signatories is threatened." After a reception in Washington for several Soviet aviators, Troyanovsky discussed the proposal of a nonaggression or collective security pact with Roosevelt, who commented that "pacts won't give any guarantees and no trust. America can't enter into an alliance or anything like that. In any case, a pact without Japan will not have meaning. The main guarantee is a strong fleet, our American one, the English, and perhaps, the Soviet one."[33]

Despite this rebuff, Roosevelt discussed the idea of cooperation with various U.S. officials in the fall of 1937, without ever stating precisely what he had in mind. On August 11, he mentioned his review of alternative means to check Japan and Germany to Ambassador William Dodd. Later in August, Dodd strongly recommended that Roosevelt cooperate with Moscow against Japan, "even to send American-British navies across the Pacific." When they met again in October, the president said that one thing troubled him: "Could the United States, England, France, and Russia actually cooperate?" Dodd replied affirmatively.[34] Assistant Secretary of State George S. Messersmith also favored cooperation with the Soviet Union, even though he considered Communism and Fascism to be "equally dangerous." If the Western powers quickly stopped Hitler, Messersmith argued, they would have enough strength to stop the Soviet Union "if Moscow gets strong enough to carry out her ultimate objectives."[35]

Roosevelt had less success with Secretary Hull and most of the leaders of the State Department. On August 19 he asked Hull and the top echelon if they thought the United States could cooperate with Moscow and received a negative response.[36] A number of considerations probably shaped the views of these officials. They may have agreed with the Moscow embassy's assessment that Stalin would not do very much unless Japan directly attacked the Soviet Union.[37] They also shared the Moscow embassy's doubts about the strength of the Soviet Union, particularly the Red army. "Russia has sunk into nothing," former Secretary of State Henry Stimson noted in his diary, after listening to accounts by Moffat, Hornbeck, and Herbert Feis about the impact of the purge on the Red army.[38] From this perspective, any agreement with Moscow seemed to offer only the risks of involvement to the United States without any concessions from Moscow, since Stalin was already doing as much as he could against Japan.

The State Department and its Russian specialists also objected to cooperation because of their suspicions about Stalin's intentions. They had never comletely laid aside Stanley Hornbeck's warning of 1935 that the Kremlin favored "a war between Japan and the United States ... on the theory that these two combatants would weaken each other and thus relieve the Soviet Union of its fears of Japan ... [and] of the leading capitalist state, the United States."[39] Later in October, Secretary Hull, William Phillips, Assistant Secretary Hugh Wilson, and Ambassador Bullitt (now ambassador to France) argued that sanctions against Japan might lead to retaliation and "if effective and Japan were completely downed China would merely fall a prey to Russian anarchy and we would have the whole job to do over again and a worse one." Maxwell Hamilton of the Division of Far Eastern Affairs recommended, as part of a general settlement, the creation of a buffer state in Inner Mongolia, under nominal Chinese control, "to prevent the infiltration of communism from the Soviet Union into China."[40]

The State Department's objections had substantial merit but did not override the potential benefits of cooperation, at least in the Far East. Although Stalin, like Roosevelt, probably wanted to avoid any action that might seriously risk war with Japan, he did engage in massive military confrontations with Tokyo along the Manchurian borders in 1938–39. Undoubtedly the Kremlin would have appreciated the benefits of an American-Japanese war, as would have the Chinese, in both the Nationalist and Communist movements. But Stalin could not fabricate a Japanese-American war. This would have required, from the perspective of Pearl Harbor, a European war, major American economic sanctions, and months of argument within the Japanese government.

During October, 1937, when the Nine Power Conference on the Sino-Japanese war was held in Brussels, Roosevelt deferred to the State Department. His instructions to Norman Davis, head of the American delegation, did not refer to the Soviet Union, and he warned Davis to move cautiously and to check any attempt by London to push Washington "out in front as the leader." When the Soviet charge, Constantin Oumansky, asked Sumner Welles on October 2 if America would support economic and military sanctions against Japan, Welles said that America would follow "the terms of the existing neutrality legislation, on taking no sides in the present conflict."

The State Department also tried unsuccessfully to keep Moscow away from the conference. At a preliminary meeting in Paris, Bullitt, Davis, Stanley Hornbeck, and Pierrepont Moffat concluded that "Russia's role at Brussels would be to embarrass all the great powers in turn and if possible to prevent an agreement, at least until Japan had come to the end of her resources." At the conference, Davis and especially Moffat, a staunch isolationist, rejected Litvinov's feelers.[41] Despite his considerable flattery of Litvinov, Davis antagonized the commissar by recommending that the Soviet Union not participate because it was not one of the members of the Nine Power Treaty. Davis also declared that without support from the American public the United States would not take any action against Japan.[42] Secretary Hull also remained skeptical about the Kremlin. On November 15, Dodd told Hull about Roosevelt's agreement with his proposal that "Russia ought to be asked to join a 'solid front'" of the democracies against Germany and Japan. Hull immediately tried to counter Dodd's idea by warning Roosevelt that Washington could not get very "far in combating Nazism merely by falling back in company with the Soviet."[43]

The *Panay* crisis, which followed Japan's bombing of this American gunboat near Nanking on December 12, finally moved Roosevelt to act. During the conference in Brussels, he had rejected a navy proposal for staff talks with London and a British suggestion for a joint display of naval force in the Far East. Now Roosevelt proposed to the British ambassador, Sir Ronald Lindsay, secret naval staff talks and a quarantine blockade of Japan, running along a line from Hawaii to the Philippines and on to Hong Kong, to cut off Japan from raw materials the next time she committed an aggression. The president sent Captain Royal E. Ingersoll, director of the navy's War Plans Division, to London for the staff talks and for development of the plans for the blockade, and authorized several naval maneuvers, such as the dispatch of three cruisers to Singapore and the transfer of the fleet to the Pacific. Roosevelt also revived his earlier proposal of a general peace conference to help mold American opinion. Although Chamberlain rejected the last proposal, Roosevelt remained hopeful about the naval blockade until Anthony Eden, the British foreign minister, resigned in February, 1938. Ultimately Ingersoll obtained only an informal understanding that the two navies would work together in case of war in the Pacific.[44]

More cautiously, Roosevelt also asked Ambassador Davies to approach the Kremlin. Roosevelt proposed a liaison in the Far East to exchange data concerning the "military and naval situations of the United States and the Soviet Union vis-à-vis Japan and the general Far Eastern and Pacific problem." Although Roosevelt ruled out a pact or secret alliance, he believed an exchange of information "might be of substantial value in the future by reason of similarity of purposes and necessities even though each power were pursuing separate and independent courses." Finally, Roosevelt warned Davies to keep this matter strictly confidential even from the Moscow embassy and the State Department.[45]

Roosevelt also requested the State Department to make another attempt to clear up minor irritants in Soviet-American relations. Hull and Messersmith, who urged Hull to send a special emissary to Moscow to find out the "force that *may* be there [Moscow] and how it *may* be used," favored this move. Moffat and Kennan, however, were skeptical. On January 13, Hull asked the Soviet Union to clear up Washington's complaints, which included the debt issue and harrassment of the Moscow embassy.[46]

The Kremlin rebuffed Hull's complaints, except those about the debt, but tried to force Roosevelt's hand. When Davies described Roosevelt's secret proposal to Litvinov, the Soviet official said he would inform Stalin, although he preferred a definite pact that would prevent an embarrassing disclosure by anti-Soviet officials in Washington. Shortly after this meeting, Troyanovsky asked Hull for a conference to work out collective action against aggression—a proposal very similar to Roosevelt's recent offer to London. The State Department brusquely rejected the Soviet proposal. Litvinov's "idea has no merit but the question was in what form should it be rejected," Moffat noted in his diary.[47] Roosevelt also preferred to move warily and privately with the Kremlin, especially after a leak to the press in January about Ingersoll's mission in London stirred up isolationists in Congress. Consequently, Washington made no formal reply.

Stalin made a favorable reply to Roosevelt's proposal when he strolled into Davies' meeting with Molotov on June 5, 1938. Stalin approved the military liaison as long as Washington would keep it secret. Davies suggested that only the president, Hull, Welles, and a few military officials would know about the consultations. Stalin also offered to pay $50 million for the Kerensky debt in exchange for a ten-year credit of $150 million. On June 8 and 9 Davies continued discussions with Molotov in an attempt to get the Kremlin to pay interest on the debt; instead, Molotov raised the required credit to $200 million. Davies left Moscow hoping that at least the military liaison would work out.[48]

Roosevelt and Hull welcomed the Soviet reply, but the president suddenly backed away from the military liaison. To Ambassador Troyanovsky, who "bubbled over with enthusiasm" about Stalin's meeting with Davies, Hull expressed interest in a rapprochement and asked Moscow to drop its involvement with Communist movements. Roosevelt instructed Davies to negotiate the debt issue along the lines of Molotov's proposal, but the discussions soon collapsed. In the end, the president never replied to Stalin about the military liaison, despite encouragement by Davies from his new post in Brussels.[49]

The return to the debt issue was symptomatic of Roosevelt's problems. Whenever he made a step toward the Soviet Union, he quickly found himself—partly because of the State Department's opposition—enmeshed in old problems of little relevance to the current situation. Roosevelt probably hoped that a favorable debt settlement, like a general conference with London, would help to prepare America for the revelation of the secret proposals he had made to both countries. But Americans had become very critical of Stalin's totalitarianism, and such preparation would not have been enough. Without properly testing and preparing Americans for limited cooperation with Moscow in the Far East, Roosevelt almost inevitably undermined his approach before he even made it. He could not tolerate the possibility of a leak to the press about the military liaison; yet ultimately he would have to make these diplomatic moves public, if he wanted to move beyond secret discussions. He abandoned his own proposal to the Kremlin so quickly that it seems perhaps unwise to have made it in the first place. Instead of approaching Stalin at this time, Roosevelt should have prepared the public for a new policy and developed an alliance with Great Britain—which would have been difficult enough, considering Chamberlain's movement toward unilateral appeasement in Europe. The impact of Roosevelt's behavior was probably unfavorable, reinforcing Stalin's doubts about the reliability and consistency of Roosevelt's diplomacy. Moreover, the Kremlin subsequently adopted an almost completely unilateral policy in the Far East.

Roosevelt did not significantly alter Washington's policies toward Hitler or Japan in 1938–39. When Hitler subjugated Austria and Czechoslovakia, the White House only expressed doubts about Chamberlain's policy of appeasement. The president did approve French purchases of airplanes from American firms for defense against Hitler, although he tried to keep this arrangement secret from the press and Congress. Washington also continued its largely ineffective policy of limited pressure upon Japan, granting an Export-Import credit to China and issuing, in response to congressional pressure, the required six-month notice for abrogation of the American-Japanese commercial treaty.[50] When Roosevelt attempted to modify America's neutrality legislation in the spring and summer of 1939, especially by repeal of the arms embargo, congressional isolationists defeated his efforts.

Ambassador Troyanovsky reported to Moscow that, despite an erosion of isolationist sentiment in the United States, there would be little change in policy until after the November congressional elections; he recommended a Soviet policy of restraint with respect to the United States.[51] In turn, the president also let Soviet-American relations slide; he did not appoint a successor to Davies until the summer of 1939. In June, Secretary Morgenthau, with Roosevelt's and Hull's approval, asked if the Kremlin wanted to have "another go at debt negotiations." Constantin Oumansky's noncommittal reply indicated that the Kremlin had lost interest in this irritating issue. Ambassador Oumansky, the Kremlin's replacement for Troyanovsky, irritated Washington officials. According to Hull, Oumansky, who had served as counselor of the Soviet embassy since 1936, "was insulting in his manner and speech and had an infallible faculty for antagonizing those of us with whom he came in contact. Overbearing, he made demands for concessions as if they were a natural right, and protested our acts as if they were heinous offenses."[52]

The massive battles between Moscow and Tokyo along the Manchurian borders in the summers of 1938 and 1939 also may have reinforced Washington's reluctance to approach the Soviet Union in the Far East. The Moscow and Tokyo embassies, which expected both sides to limit the conflict, interpreted the Kremlin's actions as a warning to Germany and Japan and at the same time an effort to disrupt Japan's military activity in China. Washington evaded any involvement in the fracas, but at the same time profited, if only in the short run, from Japan's difficulties.[53]

When Great Britain and France tried to negotiate an anti-Hitler pact with the Soviet Union in the spring and summer of 1939, Roosevelt avoided the negotiations until July. In March, he told Adolf Berle, an assistant secretary in the State Department, that he expected Hitler to "go eastward" and "not make any agreement with Stalin."[54] After receiving detailed information about the Western talks with Moscow as well as the German discussions with Soviet officials, Roosevelt decided to send a message to Stalin. The president told Ambassador Oumansky that, without accepting any responsibility for British policies, he favored an alliance between the Kremlin and London. He also asked Oumansky and the new ambassador to the Soviet Union, Laurence Steinhardt, "to tell Stalin that if his Government joined up with Hitler, it was as certain as night followed day that as soon as Hitler had conquered France, he would turn on Russia, and that it would be the Soviets' turn next."[55]

Roosevelt's indecisiveness in 1939 as well as his warning to Stalin reflected the general mood of American spokesmen. Although most observers were not very enthusiastic about a Western alliance with the Kremlin, they gradually recognized that it was vital for an effective anti-Hitler coalition. When London initiated discussions with the Soviet Union in April, most journals either approved the British move or did not oppose it, despite reservations about Stalin's policy. The strongest support for inclusion of Moscow in an anti-Hitler front came from liberal journals and newspapers oriented toward foreign affairs. Nevertheless, except for the Nation's suggestion that Moscow and Washington "might still avert war if they worked closely together," liberal commentators generally did not recommend American involvement in the negotiations. Only the New York Times and the Washington Post suggested that the United States support the anti-Hitler coalition with at least economic aid.[56]

Many journals expressed doubts about the Kremlin's intentions, including uncertainty over whether Moscow would join an alliance or just sit on the sidelines. The *New York Herald Tribune* summarized these suspicions: "... the one strongest Soviet interest in the whole situation is not to stop Hitler but to see the axis and the democracies kill each other off ... and that makes the Soviets a more dubious ally than ever." If this strategy worked, the *Philadelphia Inquirer* warned, Stalin, "like a ravenous buzzard could swoop down and gobble what was left.[57] When Stalin removed Litvinov in May, he increased the concern of the press about his intentions.

A surprising number of editors considered a third alternative, a Nazi-Soviet agreement, to be a likely result. William Henry Chamberlin and the *Saturday Evening Post*, which published Walter G. Krivitsky's influential articles about Stalin's desire for cooperation with Hitler, were among those who agreed that Stalin, exploiting his advantageous position, was negotiating for the best deal with the Western powers or with Berlin.[58] The perception of a fundamental similarity between Stalinism and Nazism bolstered this viewpoint. The *Washington Post*, for example, referred to a "similarity so profound in the glorification of the state and the submergence of the individual as to make the difference in the two systems seem secondary." Even the *St. Louis Post-Dispatch* admitted that it would not be surprised by a Hitler-Stalin deal "for at heart their systems are alike."[59]

The specter of a Nazi-Soviet pact, as well as the growing threat of a European war over Hitler's pressure on Poland, brought increased support for a Western alliance with Stalin. Even the doubters, like the *New York Herald Tribune*, shifted to support an alliance of the Western powers with Moscow to maintain the stability of Europe "by balancing totalitarian Russia against the totalitarian axis."[60] However, the press did not advocate American involvement in the negotiations. The few journals that referred to Washington's position recommended that the White House steer clear of the deceptive, self-interested maneuverings in Europe.[61]

Roosevelt could have used this increasing approval by the press of a Western alliance with Stalin to win support for an American endorsement. However, he avoided a challenge to isolationist sentiment, particularly during his attempt in 1939 to modify the restrictive neutrality legislation. A stronger, more determined president might have more directly attacked isolationist sentiment as well as opposition to cooperation with the Soviet Union. Presidents generally have avoided this kind of major confrontation with the public.

The unsuccessful results of Roosevelt's attempt to reorient relations with Moscow toward limited cooperation reflected not only his lack of determination, but also the insuperable obstacles he faced. If Americans had found out about his secret proposal to Stalin, the president would have been in serious trouble, considering the strength of isolationist sentiment and the news media's critical perspective on the Soviet Union. He also encountered stubborn opposition from the State Department on almost every issue. Davies and Welles backed White House proposals, but Hull and most of the top echelon, despite the president's reorganization of the department, consistently opposed him. Even when Hull and Robert Kelley endorsed the Kremlin's efforts to purchase naval vessels, Roosevelt could not persuade the Navy Department to carry out official policy. Despite the Kremlin's advocacy of cooperation and acceptance of Roosevelt's secret proposal, Stalin's purge made it very difficult for the president to circumvent the estrangement in Soviet-American relations. Consequently, Roosevelt maneuvered within severe restraints without the necessary support for a successful reorientation.

8

Stalin Moves West

During the sweltering August days of 1939, President Roosevelt escaped from the White House for a cruise aboard the presidential yacht. As the president enjoyed his brief respite from the heat and the pressures of his office, Stalin and Hitler arranged an abrupt end to his vacation with the Nazi-Soviet Nonaggression Pact of August 23, 1939. When the news of the pact reached Roosevelt, he immediately ordered the yacht to head for the New Jersey shore and returned by train to the White House, where he soon learned that Stalin's rapprochement with Hitler would add new irritants, most notably Soviet territorial expansion, to the already strained relationship between Moscow and Washington.

Americans criticized Stalin and the British for the nonaggression pact. "The British dallied and they dawdled. They faltered and equivocated. They debated, hedged and quibbled," complained the *Philadelphia Inquirer.*[1] Some commentators criticized Stalin for "selling out" to Hitler in an "unusually cynical" way and emotionally blasted Stalin's maneuvers as "treachery on the grand scale." Within two days, the *Philadelphia Inquirer* shifted its criticism from London to Moscow, denouncing the pact as "conceived in duplicity and born in Godlessness and dishonor."[2] The pact had the most devastating impact on liberal commentators like Louis

Fischer and the *Nation*, who considered the agreement a "totally indefen-sible" betrayal of the anti-Fascist forces.[3]

Before the pact, the most important difference between Berlin and Moscow, according to the press, had been foreign policy. Now this distinction eroded quickly; twenty-five of thirty-five newspapers (see Table 8) noted similar systems. Columnists William Henry Chamberlin and Mark Sullivan approved Eugene Lyons' conclusion that the pact "exposed Hitler's Brown Bolshevism and Stalin's Red Fascism as aspects of the same totalitarian idea."[4] Stalin and Hitler themselves were also increasingly perceived as similar; ". . . they are alike as two peas in a pod," commented the *Omaha Morning World-Herald*. Other journals referred to them as "brother dictators, swindlers of the same breed," with an identical desire to destroy the civilization of the Western democracies. Even journals that still pointed to ideological differences stressed the similarity in Stalin's and Hitler's methods and objectives.[5] This similarity also fostered predictions that the partnership would not endure. "Two such experts in treachery as Hitler and Stalin," pointed out the *Pittsburgh Post-Gazette*, "will no doubt end up by cheating each other and so bring well-deserved disaster upon themselves."[6]

The expectation of eventual Nazi-Soviet conflict prompted twenty of thirty-five newspapers (see Table 5) to argue that Moscow's central concern was security, emphasizing the Soviet Union's desire to concen-trate on the border war with Japan and avoid a military conflict with Hitler over Poland. Moderate, conservative (see Table 6), and liberal newspa-pers endorsed the security theory.[7] "Stalin intends to play the limited game of temporary isolation for all it is worth," stated the *Des Moines Register*, "figuring that he can retain his power in Russia and achieve the nationalistic ends of Russia or the Socialist ends of Communism or both more safely that way."[8] Several moderate and conservative journals, however, suspected that the pact might contain a secret agreement to divide up the buffer states between Germany and the Soviet Union. "Russia is revealed as an aggressive imperialist power," remarked the *Kansas City Star*, "which may be in collusion wih Germany for the eventual partition of Poland and the seizure of the Baltic states."[9] A few conservative spokesmen considered the pact an ominous sign of Stalin's desires to spread Communism. Influential columnists Eugene Lyons and Mark Sullivan, for example, expected Stalin to encourage a European war, sit on the sidelines until the combatants exhausted each other, and then spread Communism upon the ruins. "Safe in his lair, he [Stalin] may behold the soul-warming spectacle of his enemies destroying each other," warned the *Omaha Morning World-Herald,* "then ... he may emerge in safety to glut his appetite, vulture-like, on the carcass of what once was European civilization."[10]

Stalin's next move, a September 16 armistice with Japan in the Manchurian border conflict, seemed to confirm the defensive interpretation, but the press found little comfort in this development. Although uncertain about the permanence and implications of the truce, commentators worried about its potential results, such as an end of Soviet aid to China and a nonaggression pact in the Far East which would unite the totalitarian powers.[11]

On September 17, the Red army invaded eastern Poland, in accordance with the secret protocol of the Nazi-Soviet pact. Those journals which had criticized London more than Moscow now turned angrily against Stalin. The *Cincinnati Enquirer* argued that the Soviet move proved that Moscow's "anti-fascist talk of recent years was a farce, and that its zeal for the defense of Poland was a sham."[12] Even liberal spokesmen, though somewhat sympathetic toward Soviet defense requirements against Hitler, moved closer to forthright denunciations of Stalin as an imperialistic dictator.[13] Emotional epithets and animalistic metaphors emerged in descriptions of the Kremlin. Stalin "will play the noble role of hyena to the German lion," remarked the *New York Times,* and many editorial cartoons depicted Moscow as a wolf or bear picking the bones of the Polish carcass.[14]

As Stalin joined Hitler as an aggressor and violator of treaties, twenty-one major newspapers commented on the similar diplomatic methods used by Berlin and Moscow, and ten reemphasized the identical nature of Nazism and Stalinism (see Table 8). Moscow's "invasion of Poland, and the shotgun methods it is using to extend its hegemony in the Baltic states are conclusive enough," remarked the *Minneapolis Tribune.* Even journals which noted some differences, primarily in ideology, stressed the similarities. "Communazism" seemed an appropriate new word, according to the *Christian Science Monitor,* to describe the "unholy alliance between the brown bolshevism of Adolf Hitler and the red fascism of Joseph Stalin."[15]

Stalin's new maneuvers caused a dramatic change of emphasis in the news media's assessment of his objectives. Whereas twenty of thirty-five newspapers stressed the security orientation of Stalin's pact with Hitler, twenty-two considered the Soviet invasion of Poland primarily an effort to acquire territory and only two continued to emphasize security (see Table 5). However, seven conservative and one moderate newspaper (see Tables 5 and 6) considered the expansion of Communism into

Poland more central to Stalin's calculations. Differing degrees of foreign-affairs orientation in these journals had little bearing on their responses (see Table 7). An increasing number of American observers recognized the complexity of Stalin's calculations and the possibility of concurrent objectives. Soviet expansion into Poland, for example, enabled Stalin to improve his defense position vis-à-vis Hitler, regain territory lost in 1919, and extend Stalinism into new territory. On the one hand, the swiftness of Poland's collapse and the eastward march of the Nazis seemed sufficient motivation for the Red army to act. On the other hand, there was considerable uncertainty about Moscow's final aims: Would the Soviet Union stay out of the war, or had Stalin turned back to Czarist imperialism? Would Stalin cooperate with Hitler in order to destroy democracy or would the Kremlin wait for Fascism and democracy to destroy each other and then spread Communism in Europe?[16]

The *Atlanta Constitution,* the *Baltimore Sun,* and the *Washington Post* agreed with *Time's* conclusion that the invasion of Poland "looked more like a step in a program of world distribution whose outlines were consciously obscured, whose possibilities were unknown, perhaps even to the partners in the enterprise."[17] A number of moderate and conservative editors touched on all three potential objectives, recognizing that the Kremlin was regaining old territory and improving its security but suspecting that Stalin had larger ambitions. The *Cincinnati Enquirer,* for example, initially reacted to Stalin's move as "an appallingly ruthless way to prostrate Middle and Western Europe and prepare the ground for Communism." But nine days later this newspaper suggested that "the obvious aims of Russia are not dictated by Communist ideology, but by Russian national aggrandizement."[18] A few editors, however, confidently announced that Stalin had abandoned Communism and resurrected Czarist imperialism in a new, more virulent form. Moscow "confronts Europe merely as another imperial power," the *Hartford Courant* asserted, "that plays the game of *realpolitik* with unscrupulous cunning." In announcing the "Death of Communism," the *Chicago Daily News* added its accord with the idea that Russia "stands revealed as just another vulgar imperialism, ruled by a despot."[19] Conservative commentators often dismissed too quickly much of the ambiguity surrounding Stalin's objectives and assumed that the Kremlin only wanted to exploit the war to spread Communism. The *San Francisco Chronicle* stressed the ideological focus of Stalin's "sideline operation, waiting for nations bled white to collapse in a Communist tailspin and so be brought under the Comintern automatically."[20]

Between September 28 and October 10, the Soviet Union forced

Estonia, Latvia, and Lithuania to sign mutual assistance pacts and secret agreements which gave Moscow naval, air, and army bases in each country, leaving them with only nominal independence. Reports also reached the American news media concerning Soviet pressure on Turkey and Rumania. Although these moves did not significantly alter the media's focus on three Soviet objectives, American commentators increasingly recognized the possibility of concurrent objectives. Even liberal journals, who still emphasized the defensive thrust of Stalin's moves, referred to the *Nation*'s suggestion of a "new form of communist imperialism" or the *New Republic*'s conclusion that Stalin was "playing the imperialist game as shrewdly as any."[21] Although a few conservative editors continued to endorse the *Philadelphia Inquirer*'s assertion that "Stalin is out to gain the world for Communism,"[22] most observers, such as columnists Dorothy Thompson and Walter Lippmann, emphasized Stalin's aggressive adoption of Czarist imperialism, the opportunistic grabbing of spoils along the lines of traditional Russian ambitions. On September 29, the *Cleveland Plain Dealer* noted Stalin's acquisition of defense outposts in the Baltics, on the next day reported that Moscow's "aim is to secure her own position and spread the world revolution," and on October 9 concluded that Stalin was realizing the dreams of the Czars and preparing against the Nazi menace. If the latter failed to materialize, the Cleveland newspaper pointed out, the "Russians have strengthened their position to carry far afield their campaign for aggrandizement under the slogans of the world revolution."[23]

Although some observers expected the Nazi-Soviet alliance to continue indefinitely with commercial and diplomatic if not military cooperation, more of them doubted that the relationship would last very long. Hitler undoubtedly resented Stalin's success, the press believed, especially since the Kremlin was dominating the borderlands between Germany and Russia and the invasion routes into the Soviet Union. The *Washington Post* captured best the general sentiment when it described the arrangement as "outwardly strong but inwardly rotten; superficially impressive but fundamentally treacherous."[24]

This expectation of Nazi-Soviet conflict reduced the general concern about Soviet expansion, although a few journals advocated allied peace negotiations with Hitler in order to contain Stalin. Most commentators probably shared the *National Republic*'s "hope that if the war must continue ... Communism and Nazism will be wiped out."[25] More significantly, Stalin's maneuvers widened the division of opinion among Americans about the appropriate American response to the war. Isolationists agreed with the *Los Angeles Times'* conclusion that the "Russian intervention has apparently strengthened American determination to stay out of the war, no matter what happens, short of an actual attack on us."[26] On the other hand, journals which welcomed the confrontation of totalitarian powers versus democracies argued that Soviet expansion illustrated the folly of the isolationist view. They favored the sale of arms to the allies in order to influence what Walter Lippmann called the real issue of the war: "what shall be the boundary of Europe against the expanding invasion of Russian imperial Bolshevism."[27]

Soviet expansion not only antagonized Americans but also contributed to a renewed anti-Communist offensive within the United States. The Dies committee charged that the "New Deal was hand in glove with the Communist Party." Other organizations, like the American Federation of Labor, launched their own purge of Communists within their membership. Even the American Civil Liberties Union, which had defended the civil liberties of Communists in the thirties, expelled Elizabeth Gurley Flynn for being a Communist.[28]

Roosevelt could not ignore the substantial impact of the Dies committee, although it turned up very little evidence of Communist influence in his administration. In February, 1939, the American Institute of Public Opinion asked what should be the most important activity of the Dies committee; 42 percent recommended a study of war propaganda, while 32 percent and 26 percent, respectively, favored an investigation of Nazi and Communist activities. In response to the same question in December, 1939, 70 percent called for a probe of Communist activities.[29] For the first time the Dies committee received extensive approval from the press, particularly from conservative journals which had criticized the committee's methods in the past.

The reaction of Americans to Stalin's expansion set the limits within which Washington made its official response. With the erosion of the distinction between Stalin's and Hitler's foreign policies, a critical consensus against the Kremlin emerged, ruling out any official recognition of the Kremlin's conquest. Yet observers did not pressure the White House for direct action against Moscow, such as a break in relations, and made only limited suggestions for indirect measures to check Soviet expansion.

Washington's response to Stalin's actions, about which it had received advance warning from the Moscow embassy, did differ from the actions taken against Hitler (for example, an arms embargo placed on Germany and the allies). Secretary Hull wanted to invoke the embargo section of the neutrality act against Moscow but resisted temptation; instead, he tried to appease critics of Moscow with a public statement. "The main difficulty confronting us," one official noted in his diary, "is that Russia's action in Poland is so similar to Japan's action in occupying Chinese territory that it will be hard to explain why we consider one a belligerent and not the other." The State Department also ignored the Kremlin's move into the Baltic states.[30]

Washington's restraint reflected not only an awareness of the public mood and of complex political questions involving the European and Far Eastern situations but also preoccupation with other matters. Roosevelt preferred to let Soviet-American relations drift. After announcing America's official neutrality toward the war, the president spent most of the fall of 1939 building up the unity of the American republics and battling isolationists in Congress for repeal of the arms embargo. On November 4, 1939, Roosevelt signed a new neutrality act that replaced the arms embargo with "cash and carry." Belligerent powers could purchase arms if they paid for them and took them away in their own ships. Congress and the president again affirmed their desire to stay out of the war; nonetheless, "cash and carry" represented the first, halting step toward American aid to the allies against Hitler.

The degree of cooperation or conflict in Nazi-Soviet relations was becoming increasingly important. If Stalin joined Hitler in an attack against the Western democracies, the future would be very bleak. Assistant Secretary Adolf Berle summed up Washington's initial conclusion after a meeting in Hull's office on September 3. "The ultimate issue," Berle noted in his diary, was an inevitable conflict between America and "a Russo-German domination bent on dominating the world." Although Berle felt that the "Russian-German domination would be huge, impressive and in appearance terribly powerful," he hoped that Washington could avoid a confrontation, because, "winning or losing, that combination must eventually break up."[31]

The Kremlin's move into Poland and Ambassador Steinhardt's reports, however, prompted some officials to question their initial assumption. According to Steinhardt, the Nazi-Soviet bloc was an "unholy alliance." The ambassador did not expect Moscow "to take an active part in the war," but he did believe that the Kremlin would "... do everything within her power to assist her partner," including the purchase of war materials for Hitler from neutral countries like America. The Ribbentrop-Molotov agreement of September 28, which revised the Polish boundary and initiated a new period of political, naval, and economic cooperation, seemed to Steinhardt "further indication of far-reaching cooperation" that might extend to the Balkans and the Far East. In short, though he did not reject the possibility of future Nazi-Soviet conflict, Steinhardt reported evidence of an extended period of cooperation for the immediate future.[32]

In his memoirs, Secretary Hull states that he and Roosevelt expected a Nazi-Soviet conflict in the immediate future. Yet the secretary's remarks to Assistant Secretary Breckinridge Long, perhaps his closest confidant in the department, revealed a somewhat different view. On September 2, Hull told Long that "Hitler will divide Poland with Russia and between them they will put the screws on Roumania, Bulgaria, probably Yugoslavia, Greece, and certainly Turkey." He worried about the possibility of a Nazi-Soviet hegemony which would cripple American trade, spreading into the Far East "after Russia eliminates Japan."[33] Roosevelt was also apprehensive about a continuation of Nazi-Soviet cooperation. "It would be logical to suppose that Stalin and Hitler would not get over-extended," the president remarked to Berle on September 22, "but ... in view of the kind of people they were ... they would keep going while the going was good." Roosevelt feared that the "next thing would be a drive at the west," and the "real objective would be to get into the Atlantic."[34]

Some diplomats shared the fear of conservatives that until the democracies and Hitler exhausted each other, Moscow would only nibble from the sidelines, but in the end would intervene and establish a Communist dictatorship through Europe. Pierrepont Moffat, William Bullitt, Long, and Hugh R. Wilson, then a special assistant in the State Department, strongly agreed on this point. In October, Long singled out Russia as "the only winner in a prolonged war." According to Long, Stalin "would like to see each side destroy the other, or so weaken themselves and each other that they could no longer resist the influences of Communism."[35]

Roosevelt brushed aside this fear, despite his concern about the Kremlin's intentions. Since at least 1937 Roosevelt had correctly perceived that Hitler, not Stalin, represented the most important immediate threat to Europe and America—in particular, Hitler's total unreliability, his desire to dominate Europe, and his wish for a showdown with the United States.[36] Between 1939 and 1941, the president checkmated German naval strategy by acquiring control of the Atlantic outposts (Greenland and Iceland) and the naval approaches to the United States. Roosevelt should have given more consideration to the fears of Bullitt and Long for long-range strategy, but in the short run he had to focus on Hitler.

Yet everyone favored a cautious response to Stalin's expansion, if for different reasons. Long and Wilson, for example, wanted Moscow and

Berlin to stay apart; a settlement in Europe would then bring out the basic antagonism between them. Long hoped that Roosevelt's support of London and Paris would not encourage continuation of "a war which would mean the victory of Communism in Europe and confront us with our eventual enemy—Russia." Wilson went further: "A cessation of hostilities in the West to allow Germany to take care of the Russian encroachment," he confided to a friend, would further the "ends of civilization."[37]

Roosevelt and the State Department, however, rejected any settlement that would either recognize Germany's conquests or turn Hitler against the Soviet Union. When Hitler and Stalin launched a peace campaign in September and November, Washington responded very cautiously, rejecting any approval of Hitler's conquests. Roosevelt and Hull were not at all certain about Stalin's intentions, although they hoped he would not join Hitler in an attack against Great Britain and France. Hull, who rarely favored a bold move on any issue outside of tariffs, probably urged Roosevelt simply to not recognize Stalin's conquests and to sit tight. The president "does not believe that Russia will send troops to fight France," Secretary Harold Ickes remarked after a luncheon with Roosevelt on October 14, "but he is worried about Russia's attitude toward Finland and the Scandinavian countries." As long as Stalin did not threaten Great Britain and France, Roosevelt would neither condone Soviet actions nor make a significant commitment against Stalin.[38]

The Far Eastern situation reinforced Washington's reluctance to agitate over Stalin's expansion. After the outbreak of war in Europe, the United States continued its twofold response to Japan's expansion in China. Hull, who directed Washington's Far Eastern policies, stubbornly refused to recognize Tokyo's conquests but at the same time opposed any effort to cut off Japan's access to American resources, which facilitated Japan's expansion. On September 16, 1939, Japan obtained an uneasy truce with the Soviet Union in their conflict along the Manchurian border. This announcement, as well as the start of Soviet-Japanese trade negotiations, forced Washington to reconsider the possiblility of a Soviet-Japanese rapprochement similar to the recent Nazi-Soviet pact.

"I can't for the life of me see any possibility of a real Soviet-Japanese rapprochement because far too many fundamental differences exist . . . ," Ambassador Grew wrote to Roosevelt, "but strange things are happening in the world today." A few days after the armistice, Assistant Secretary Long hopefully noticed a "few rifts in the cloud . . . it seems that Japan and Russia are not in accord." The Moscow and Tokyo embassies, moreover, expected the Kremlin to continue its aid to China, a serious block to any Soviet-Japanese detente.[39] Hull and Welles vigorously denied any chance of an accord because they wanted to evade pressure from London and Tokyo for concessions to Japan. On November 21, Welles told Lord Lothian, the British ambassador, that Japan would not turn to the south, since Tokyo knew "perfectly well that Russian policy in the Far East was inevitably antagonistic to Japanese policy and...that no reliance could be placed by Japan upon any agreement" with Moscow. Later in November Hull gave the Japanese ambassador a similar warning. When the British persisted, Welles argued very strongly that "we should not compromise our principles or surrender any of our material interest in an attempt to dissuade Japan from reaching an accord with the Soviet Union."[40]

When Ambassador Anthony Biddle wrote to the president that "Japan and Russia understand each other clearly: Russia is in the process ... of helping herself to Europe; Japan, of helping herself to China," Roosevelt replied that this tacit cooperation troubled him and Welles.[41] Yet Washington's concern about a Soviet-Japanese agreement was not strong enough to prompt any concessions to Japan on the China issue or any encouragement of Japan to attack the Soviet Union during Moscow's preoccupation with expansion in Europe. Both alternatives would have provoked heavy criticism from the press and from interest groups such as the American Committee for Non-Participation in Japanese Aggression. They also offended Secretary Hull's moralistic stance toward Japan and Washington's principle of opposing war in general in the Pacific. Since Japan was bogged down in China after more than two years of war, concessions at this time did not seem necessary. Furthermore, the Soviet Union's position was too fluid and indefinite for a major move against Moscow in the Far East; an effort to encourage a Japanese invasion of Siberia might, from Washington's perspective, prompt Stalin to solidify his alliance with Hitler and delay the expected clash between Hitler and Stalin. In addition, the Soviet Union could offer Japan more than Washington could, because of its aid to China and its influence with the Chinese Communists.

Roosevelt decided on a more cautious and limited response. In December he asked Secretary Morgenthau and the State Department to encourage China to "continue to play with Russia. To keep Russia and Japan apart."[42] Although he found less similarity in the interests of the Soviet Union and the United States in the Far East than there had been in 1938, he still hoped that Stalin would continue his aid to China and keep away from Japan. The president was beginning to link the European and the Far Eastern situations in his policy toward Moscow. A mild response to Stalin's moves in Europe might help in the Far East, and a cautious approach to the Soviet-Chinese-Japanese triangle could possibly influence Stalin's policy in Europe, though neither Roosevelt nor the State Department directly stated this intention.

Roosevelt's strategy of neither opposing nor recognizing Soviet expansion became more difficult when Washington received repeated warnings that Finland was the Kremlin's next objective. Moscow's pressure on Finland reflected defense considerations and a desire to regain former Russian territory. For example, the Gulf of Finland exposed Leningrad to direct attack. As early as April, 1938, the Kremlin offered to give Finland economic and military assistance against Hitler and, in July, asked Finland to fortify the strategic Aland Islands off the southwest corner of Finland and to give Moscow a base on the island of Suursaari in the Gulf of Finland. When Hitler launched his peace offensive in September, 1939, Moscow increased its demands upon Finland, perhaps fearing that peace might come before the Kremlin had Finland safely within its sphere of influence, as called for in the Nazi-Soviet pact. Stalin asked for the port of Hanko on the southwest tip of Finland, other islands, and a mutual assistance pact. In return, the Kremlin offered territory in nonstrategic areas. Finland stubbornly rejected the Kremlin's offers.[43] Long, Hull, and Roosevelt expressed concern over this matter, but Ambassador Steinhardt predicted that Stalin would not use force on Finland.[44]

The Soviet Union further antagonized Washington with the *City of Flint* affair. On October 9, 1939, a German battleship captured the *City of Flint*, a merchant ship under American registry, and took it to Murmansk, a Soviet port. Despite Washington's many protests, Soviet officials refused to release the American crew or permit the Moscow embassy to contact the crew. Hull kept returning to the issue, Moffat noted in his diary, and became "madder and madder all the time."[45]

Washington tried to avoid frequent requests from Finland and other Scandinavian countries for American intervention with Moscow. The Kremlin gave little consideration to American feelings, Hull and Moffat argued, and the president felt that "his influence" with Stalin "was just about zero."[46] Hull and Roosevelt also probably wanted to avoid any move that would perturb the isolationists in Congress, during the battle for repeal of the arms embargo. However, the president realized that his cautious approach toward Soviet expansion had satisfied spokesmen thus far, but any Soviet aggression against Finland would prompt demands for American action. Perhaps to protect himself against future criticism, he decided to approach Moscow, although he "did not believe his representations would do any good." He asked Ambassador Steinhardt to express to the Kremlin his "earnest hope that the Soviet Union will make no demands that would destroy Finland's independence."[47]

Roosevelt's cautious response to Soviet expansion was the best available alternative for American policy in 1939. Since Americans would have vigorously criticized any recognition of Moscow's annexations but did not desire, with any consensus or enthusiasm, direct or indirect actions against Moscow, Roosevelt had few alternatives besides non-recognition. Washington could not have gained anything from recognition at that time; moreover, if a Nazi-Soviet conflict occurred in the future, Moscow might lose all of its recent acquisitions. The circumstances of Nazi-Soviet cooperation as well as the course of Stalin's moves precluded any intervention either by Washington or by London and Paris. This general acquiescence may have encouraged Stalin to use force on Finland, but it was almost impossible for Roosevelt to head off this development. It was difficult enough for him to persuade isolationists in Congress to approve repeal of the arms embargo. Without a direct promise of American arms and even troops to Finland, he probably could not have convinced Stalin to reduce his demands on Finland.

Roosevelt's strategy of avoiding any action that might push Stalin closer to Hitler and Japan in the Far East did not prevent further deterioration in Soviet-American relations. Despite the fact that Stalin primarily sought territory lost in World War I, officials feared his opportunism and his ultimate desire to spread Communism. Stalin's methods brought an even greater emotional denunciation from Amercan commentators who opposed the spread of totalitarian "Red Fascism" across Western Europe. Consequently, Roosevelt's cautious policy rested upon a very fragile base that Stalin could destroy if he unleashed the Red army on Finland.

9

The Soviet-Finnish War

On November 30, 1939, the Soviet Union abruptly broke off negotiations with the Helsinki government. After recognizing a puppet regime headed by Otto W. Kuusinen, a veteran Finnish Communist, Stalin sent the Red army into Finland, announcing that Moscow would "liberate" the Finnish people. The Soviet attack challenged President Roosevelt's assumptions about Soviet policy, and the State Department briefly gave serious consideration to a return to nonrecognition.

Stalin's decision to use force in Finland provoked an overwhelming emotional denunciation from American observers. The accumulation of hostile feelings toward Soviet expansion since the start of the war erupted without restraint. The disparity in size, political systems, and past behavior of Helsinki and Moscow also influenced the response. Finland, which had made yearly payments on its small debt of $9 million, became the symbol of everything good, "the Gibraltar of Christianity"; Moscow became the direct opposite, "a modern anti-Christ" and a "bloodstained gangster," portrayed as a rapacious bear in many newspaper cartoons.

Most journals bitterly denounced the Soviet Union, regardless of their views on domestic politics and America's stance toward the European war. Republican newspapers, for example, generally agreed with the *Philadelphia Inquirer's* reaction that "Comrade Stalin, high priest of

Godlessness and terror, has more than out-Hitlered Hitler at his own diabolic game"; Stalin's action represented the final repudiation of "Russian Communism in its naked viciousness and its sickening depravity."[1] Independent and Democratic papers fully concurred with this emotional denunciation. "Now the calculated immorality, the sickening hypocrisy, and the complete ruthlessness of Stalin and his associates are revealed," announced the *Washington Post*.[2] Even liberal spokesmen abandoned any effort to defend Stalin and critically compared his actions with Fascist aggressions.[3]

The Red army's invasion of Finland brought an increased emphasis on Stalin's Communist imperialism by the news media. None of the thirty-five newspapers surveyed in Table 5 suggested that security concerns were central to the Kremlin's decision to initiate the Soviet-Finnish War. Instead, most of them cited Stalin's desire to gain territorial spoils or to spread Communism or both, with moderate journals favoring the former and conservative editors the latter (see Table 6).

Some American commentators recognized the immediate strategic interests that governed the Kremlin's negotiations with Finland leading up to the outbreak of war. Walter Lippmann, *Time*, and liberal journals pointed out that Stalin was trying to improve the defense of Leningrad with demands on Finland for a mutual assistance pact, Soviet bases, and boundary revisions. Yet even these observers believed that Stalin had moved beyond preparation for the eventual war with Hitler to what the *Christian Century* called "communist imperialism."[4]

Twenty-nine of thirty-five newspapers (see Table 5) endorsed the interpretation of Communist imperialism with varying emphasis. Almost a third of these twenty-nine newspapers believed with the Louisville *Courier-Journal* that Stalin "is following in the footsteps of the imperialists of the Czarist regime," without much ideological interest.[5] Another third of the journals noted concurrent objectives—the simultaneous acquisition of territory and spread of Communism—and revealed some uncertainty about their relative importance. On December 2, the moderate *Cincinnati Enquirer* referred to the "westward march of Bolshevism" but by December 16 had concluded that Stalin had attacked Finland for "purely strategic objectives, advertising to the world that Russia's Communism is only the mask for a new imperialism."[6] A third group of conservative journals and columnists like Mark Sullivan believed that world revolution remained the polestar of Stalin's calculations, despite a change in tactics from propaganda to "seizing violently any handy pieces of the earth while the world is too busy otherwise to stop him."[7]

With no dissent, editors now identified Stalin's methods in Finland with Hitler's tactics against Czechoslovakia and Poland. "There are the same stupid lies, the same outrageous demands, the same preposterous pretense of fear of attack—and the same surprise invasion, bombing, burning and slaughtering," concluded the *New York Herald Tribune*. The "Monster of Moscow" was a "brutal barbarian, like the Beast of Berlin," suggested the *Charlotte Observer*, and the *Chicago Daily News* denounced the dictators as "linked fast together in common bonds of treachery, deceit, oppression, robbery, murder and cowardly assault."[8]

Although the press generally favored private and official aid to Finland as long as there was little risk of direct involvement in the war, the issue of diplomatic reprisals against the Kremlin precipitated disagreement. Most commentators endorsed the expulsion of Moscow from the League of Nations as a necessary moral act but doubted that a moral condemnation of the Kremlin would have any practical effect on Soviet policy. Consequently, many editors called for the League powers to fulfill their moral obligation by providing effective military aid to Finland.[9]

The issue of moral significance versus practical effect also dominated the argument over whether Washington should withdraw recognition from the Soviet Union. For the first time since 1933 the press extensively debated this issue. Several conservative journals advocated a break in relations because of the immorality of official relations with a "gangster nation" like the Soviet Union. According to these observers, recognition had not provided any benefits, the Kremlin had violated its pledges, and a break now would help to curb Soviet subversive activities.[10] Most editors, however, opposed a break in relations for several practical reasons. "Breaking off relations would not make Soviet policy any less treacherous, blood-thirsty, cruel and slippery. It would not shame Russia into abandoning the savage assault upon weaker, neutral neighbors," argued the *San Francisco Chronicle*, nor would it "...put a stop to the subversive activities directed against the United States." These spokesmen wisely realized that recognition provided several benefits to Washington, such as an avenue to work out problems, to protest Soviet actions, and to watch Soviet movements closely.[11]

The Soviet-Finnish war also elicited a strong emotional response from Congress, organized groups, and the general public. Congressmen referred to "Muscovite barbarism," the "butchery of Stalin," and the "fiendish Molotovs and the scoundrelly murderous Stalins." On December 3, Rep. John W. McCormack, a Democrat from Massachusetts, asked for the recall of Ambassador Steinhardt. Shortly afterward, Republican Sen.

Arthur Vandenberg of Michigan, a leading candidate for the 1940 presidential nomination, asked for a return to nonrecognition. The House also debated a resolution to prevent the appropriation of any funds for the Moscow embassy. Even the members who opposed this bill, which was defeated, ninety-five to thirty-eight, admitted their disgust with Moscow. "I loathe Russia, I despise Stalin, I spew at Molotov, I spit upon this man Litvinov," exclaimed Rep. Emmanuel Cellar of New York, who voted against the resolution because the White House opposed it.[12]

"The whole of the United States is not only horrified but thoroughly angry," President Roosevelt wrote to Ambassador Grew. This reaction ensured that Roosevelt could no longer ignore the Kremlin's expansion while trying to focus America's attention on the threat of Hitler. Public criticism and official action would be necessary to appease public sentiment and protect the administration against partisan Republican attack. The concern of the press over Stalin's appetite for more territory and the similarity of Stalin and Hitler may also have reinforced Roosevelt's own doubts about the distinctions he had drawn between Stalin and Hitler. "I wonder what the next Russian plan is," Roosevelt remarked to an American diplomat. Later, in December, the president indicated his concern about Nazi-Soviet cooperation, although he mentioned two schools of thought about the degree of cooperation or conflict in Nazi-Soviet relations. If "Germany and Russia win the war or force a peace favorable to them, the situation of your civilization and mine is indeed in peril," he confided to an influential journalist.[13]

The general public expressed strong support for Finland. In a Gallup poll taken on December 31, 1939, 88 percent indicated sympathy for Finland. Many Americans backed their sympathy with private aid to Helsinki. The Finnish Relief Fund, directed by Herbert Hoover, obtained about $3 million for Finland from state and local groups, organized labor, and the religious community. General John O'Ryan's Fighting Funds for Finland organization also collected contributions for military supplies. However, there was disagreement on the issue of official aid to Finland. On February 6, 1940, the American Institute of Public Opinion asked if Congress should lend money to Finland for nonmilitary supplies. Only 58 percent of those polled said yes; of this group, 60 percent opposed a loan for military materials. In a Gallup poll three days later, 74 percent favored Great Britain's sending arms to Finland, but 50 percent of this group opposed a commitment of British troops. Later in February 97 percent replied negatively when asked if Washington should declare war on Russia and send the army and navy to help Finland.[14]

The president understood the reservations that were being expressed. Neither the press, Congress, nor the general public advocated official aid to Finland that might risk American involvement in the war. Moreover, the press rejected a break in relations with Moscow—despite the moral appeal of such a move—as an impractical gesture. Within the administration, a struggle between advocates of aid to Finland (led by Sumner Welles and Secretary Morgenthau) and supporters of Secretary Hull (who feared criticism from isolationists and Republicans over any significant official involvement) reinforced Roosevelt's tendency to improvise cautiously.

The conflict within the administration initially centered on the issue of a formal break with Moscow. Sumner Welles, who had supported Roosevelt's effort to improve relations with Moscow in 1937–38, urged a break in order to deter not only Moscow but also Berlin and Tokyo. Secretary Hull, the paragon of caution, disagreed. "We would be riding high on the tide of popular emotion, [and]...the action would be exceedingly popular at the time," Hull replied to Welles, "but that tide would recede and we would be left 'holding the bag'." Undoubtedly Hull also recognized that a break with Moscow would open the door to public pressure for similar steps against Germany and Japan. Pierrepont Moffat, Loy Henderson, and Ambassador Steinhardt supported Hull. "I was in favor of giving Russia a pretty heavy jolt," Moffat told Welles, "but I was not sure that this [a break in relations] was the best means to do it." Russian specialists opposed a break because they did not think it would have any significant effect on Soviet policy. "Since I am not surprised at what has taken place," Loy Henderson wrote to a friend, "I am not engulfed in this feeling of hysteria." Ambassador Steinhardt also dismissed the idea of a break in relations as an "idle gesture." "One might just as well strike an elephant with a feather," Steinhardt wrote to Henderson, "as to believe that the Kremlin is responsive to gestures."[15]

Although Roosevelt stayed out of the debate, his views probably guided the State Department's decision to shelve this question temporarily. The president obviously did not want to discard a policy pursued since 1933, particularly since doing so would strengthen the Republicans' consistently recurring criticism of recognition. The Republican National Committee, for example, immediately responded to the Soviet-Finnish war with a call for a return to nonrecognition. Roosevelt realized the value of the Moscow embassy as an observation post and an avenue of communication with the Kremlin, although he suggested to Hull and Welles that they could inform the Soviet ambassador that the "President honestly wonders whether the Soviet Government considers it worthwhile to continue diplomatic relations." Hull politely brushed aside congressional demands for a break, hoping to avoid either a public debate with critics like Senator Vandenberg or a public defense of formal relations with Moscow. The State Department did not rule out this step for the future; as Henderson advised Hull, events "may cause us to sever...relations."[16]

Instead of a break in relations, Roosevelt and Hull turned to public denunciations of the Kremlin and a moral embargo, initially against the export of airplanes to Moscow and later expanded to include aluminum, molybdenum, and technical information on gasoline production. This did not satisfy some officials in the administration. Secretary Morgenthau persuaded Roosevelt to ask Congress to refund a recent Finnish payment on its debt. Morgenthau also urged the president to arrange a credit with the Reconstruction Finance Corporation for Finnish purchases of agricultural supplies and nonmilitary manufactured goods. "I don't know where we could spend $50 million to better advantage than to give it to the Finns to fight our battle to keep them fellows from getting to the Atlantic," Morgenthau exclaimed to his staff, "because once they get to the Atlantic, God help England and then we are in the soup."[17]

Under Secretary Welles and other officials also persuaded Roosevelt to take further measures. With the president's permission, the State Department ordered the Maritime Commission to withhold any tankers carrying oil shipments to Moscow, encouraged American engineers in the Soviet Union to return home, and supported—against the objections of Moffat and Henderson—American companies who wanted to break contracts with the Kremlin. When Soviet officials complained and intensified their harrassment of the Moscow embassy, Roosevelt approved a firm response of "match[ing] every Soviet annoyance by a similar annoyance here against them."[18]

The press applauded Roosevelt's steps against Moscow. Even isolationist journals either approved or refrained from criticizing the White House's actions. The *Boston Evening Transcript*, for example, commended Roosevelt's measures, although worried about the ability of Americans to keep a "cool head" and stay out of the European war.[19] Only a few editors criticized the White House for making gestures rather than providing military arms. "It is idle to suppose that we can save either Finland or civilization from Stalinism," complained the *New York Herald Tribune*, "with moral indignation and a few pennies worth of credit."[20]

Finland's surprising resistance against the Red army inspired serious consideration of further official aid to Finland, especially a loan for the purchase of munitions. By the middle of December many journals favored the release of military supplies to Finland in order to keep Stalin out of Scandinavia and possibly disrupt Nazi-Soviet cooperation. Isolationists, however, opposed this step because it might eventually lead to involvement in the European war. "We are not suggesting that Americans should deny Finland their sympathy or the aid they can and should extend as neutrals," the *Detroit News* explained defensively, but "...the mind should keep command...of the course emotion might otherwise lay out for us." Those who took this position were uncomfortable about it, however, and urged the Leagaue of Nations to aid Finland—particularly London and Paris, who had acquired the chief obligation to stop the westward march of Stalin.[21]

The division within the press coincided with a similar split in the Roosevelt administration. Ambassador Steinhardt shifted to the side of Welles and Morgenthau and urged Washington to aid Finland. Steinhardt predicted that the Red army would wear down Finland's resistance unless Helsinki received major assistance, which "might complicate Stalin's internal and external situation to such an extent as to endanger the present regime."[22] Steinhardt also disagreed with the Washington officials who favored a mild response based on assumptions of Nazi-Soviet conflict. "The Soviet Government is leaning heavily on the German alliance and apparently looks to the Germans to pull them through," Steinhardt wrote to Henderson. Although he admitted that eventually Berlin and Moscow would quarrel, the ambassador suggested that for the immediate future Washington should expect the "kind of cooperation that gangsters give one another while the job is being 'pulled'." He felt that aid to Finland would "split the unholy alliance" but did not explain how this would happen. Perhaps he hoped that a firm rebuff to Moscow in Finland would compel the Kremlin, nursing its wounds, to abstain from further cooperation with Hitler. Washington's response to the Kremlin's harassment of the Moscow embassy also disappointed the ambassador. "Thus far there has been a good deal of barking from Washington in the form of public announcements," Steinhardt complained to Henderson, "but very little biting."[23]

Other administration officials also continued to encourage a stronger American response to the Soviet invasion. From his post in Paris, Ambassador Bullitt asked Washington to support the movement to expel Moscow from the League of Nations. Under Secretary Welles not only approved a Latin American proposal for a joint denunciation of the

Kremlin but also, with the support of Secretary Morgenthau, urged the president to provide financial aid and sell surplus weapons to Finland.[24]

Secretary Hull successfully checked all such attempts. In reply to Bullitt's request, Hull rejected any American involvement because of possible domestic criticism, and he pigeonholed the Latin American plan. When Roosevelt indicated support for the shipment of a small quantity of arms including airplanes, artillery and ammunition to Finland, the secretary vigorously opposed this step. With the aid of Secretary of War Harry Woodring, an isolationist, and a War Department that was reluctant to relinquish any arms, Hull blocked repeated efforts by the White House in January and February to release several howitzers and field guns to Finland. The secretary even delayed Roosevelt's proposal of indirect aid to Finland through the sale of arms to Sweden for Finland's use until after the Red army had broken through Finland's defense. When Finland made a desperate request for airplanes early in March, Roosevelt gave his approval if "it did not mean too much hot water" with either isolationists in Congress or, perhaps, Hull. The scarcity of surplus airplanes, however, scuttled this maneuver.[25]

According to Secretary Hull, his and Roosevelt's restraint followed from their desire to avoid any action that might push Stalin further into Hitler's arms. Perhaps this motivation had some influence on their calculations, especially if they ignored Steinhardt's accurate reports of Nazi-Soviet cooperation over Finland. During December, Roosevelt was encouraging China to help keep the Soviet Union away from Japan, and he may have considered the impact of any steps against Stalin in this Far Eastern context. But Hull's caution came primarily from his fear of criticism by isolationists in Congress and Republicans.[26]

When Roosevelt considered an official loan to Finland at the end of December, Hull repeatedly urged him to be careful. As the secretary explained the situation to Moffat, Republicans and isolationists, wounded over the recent repeal of the arms embargo, lurked in the corridors of Congress ready to blast any executive initiative on Finland as a step toward war. Hull and Roosevelt were also apprehensive about Republican exploitation of the Finland issue, most notably the favorable publicity Herbert Hoover received for his leadership of private aid to Finland. Instead of trying to compete with the Republicans, Hull and Assistant Secretary Long preferred to let the Republicans "get out in front," and for the administration to "sit by and let them do it ... [for] if we took any action as a Government ... it might be later construed as a violation of neutrality and we might be held politically accountable for it."[27]

Hull successfully persuaded Roosevelt to let Congress handle the issue of aid to Finland. When Sen. Prentiss Brown, a Michigan isolationist, introduced a bill to double the capitalization of the Export-Import Bank to $200 million in order to facilitate a loan to Finland for nonmilitary goods, Roosevelt gave only a lukewarm endorsement on January 16 and allowed the issue to drift. On February 9, in response to a press question, the president emphasized Congress's responsibility: "I sent a message up there and they are still talking about it. And it has been, what? Three weeks nearly—it has been just about a month." Although a few senators favored credits for war materials, most Democrats and Republicans avoided discussing this proposal. A few isolationists like Arthur Capper and Patrick McCarran opposed the bill as a step toward war, despite effusive expressions of love for Finland and hate toward the Kremlin. On February 13, forty-nine senators voted for the bill and twenty-seven opposed it. The House approved a similar proposal on February 28, after rejecting an attempt to remove the prohibition on military supplies.[28]

The reaction of the press to Congress's belated response to Finland's plight illustrated the advantages of Hull's cautious approach. The loan issue splintered editorial opinion into five different viewpoints. A few journals fully approved a loan to Finland. Others expressed concern over a violation of the spirit, if not the strict letter of the neutrality legislation. A small segment of the press favored a loan for military goods and aimed some criticism at the White House. Roosevelt "has evidently decided not to venture out on any limb for the sake of Finland," protested the *Washington Post*, and the Republican *New York Herald Tribune* sarcastically wondered "how long the foreign policy of the United States can be safely left ... to the unlovely combination of hypocrisy and timidity here starkly exemplified."[29] Some isolationist newspapers expressed relief that the White House had not included munitions, while others more forthrightly opposed an official loan to Finland.[30] When Congress finally approved a loan for Finland, many journals did not bother to comment. Congress, moreover, attracted most of the criticism for this late and limited response.[31]

Behind the posture of sympathetic neutrality, Washington tried unsuccessfully to initiate and influence a Soviet-Finnish peace settlement. Late in January the administration privately encouraged negotiations for an armistice, but Molotov rejected this approach. After a breakthrough by the Red army in February and reports of a British and French plan to attack the Soviet oil fields in the Caucasus and intervene in Finland with an expeditionary force, Stalin offered peace terms to Finland. Hull sent word to Molotov that "our public opinion would be deeply impressed were the Soviet government to take a generous attitude toward Finland." The secretary also hinted that the moral embargo against the Soviet Union might be relaxed "depending on the degree of moderation and generosity arrived at in the Finnish settlement." When Ambassador Steinhardt suggested that the Finnish delegates stay at his residence, Hull quickly warned him to urge favorable terms but not to act as an intermediary.[32]

Stalin, however, ignored these gestures from Washington. To the demands of November, 1939, he added the Karelian Isthmus and part of the Rybachi Peninsula (including a port at Petsamo), as well as access to strategic minerals. The settlement left Finland essentially defenseless before the Red army. Yet Stalin gained few strategic benefits from a big military effort that involved extensive losses in arms, men, and, most of all, prestige. The reaction of American spokesmen to the settlement indicated how much prestige the Soviet Union had lost.

"The Finns, fighting for civilization and democracy against the Soviet hordes, have lost to an overwhelming foe," announced the *San Francisco Chronicle*. Almost all journals praised Finland and denounced Moscow. The *New York Times* typified the general reaction: "... like a bloated monster the Russian army now sits on a corner of Finnish soil bringing the odor of corruption and death to everything that it touches."[33] The Soviet Union's loss of military preeminence also received extensive coverage, emphasizing the inadequacies of the Red army: the impact of the purge on its leadership; its poor planning, logistics, and transportation; and its general lack of offensive capability.[34] The press speculated about Stalin's intentions now that he was free of the Soviet-Finnish war. Some feared an increase in Nazi-Soviet cooperation or further Soviet expansion, either into Scandinavia or against Rumania in the Balkans. Many continued to debate whether Stalin aimed at nationalistic strategic objectives or the spread of Communist revolution.[35]

The lack of criticism directed at Washington again illustrated the advantages of Roosevelt's and Hull's caution. Only a few newspapers, such as the *Chicago Tribune* and the *New York Herald Tribune*, suggested that the response of Roosevelt and Congress was not something "of which the country can be proud." Instead the press criticized Great Britain and France for their failure to provide effective aid to Finland. A few of the isolationist journals not only approved Washington's stance but also expressed hope that the fate of Finland would increase America's determination to keep clear of Europe's "old struggle for the balance of power."[36]

The terms of the peace settlement did not change Washington's circumspect attitude. Roosevelt publicly praised the stubborn resistance of the Finnish people but avoided any direct criticism of the Kremlin. When Congress approved a resolution for the recall of Ambassador Steinhardt, Secretary Hull adroitly replied that Washington needed a channel through which to express its opposition to Soviet acts and policies, such as the attack on Finland. Hull, however, revealed his feelings about Moscow when Soviet Ambassador Constantin Oumansky made a complaint about alleged discrimination against the Soviet Union. "Russia knew just what had happened, from the break of the debt and propaganda obligations down to recent occurrences," Hull admonished Oumansky. Washington did "not know what new policy or step Russia may take any time," Hull continued, for Moscow "... plunged into fighting with Finland to the surprise of all of us."[37]

A number of issues from the Soviet-Finnish war continued to embitter official relations in the spring of 1940, notably the moral embargo, the Maritime Commission's refusal to charter tonnage in Pacific ports for Soviet shipments and the Wright Aeronautical Company's cancellation of visits by Soviet engineers. The State Department favored a continuation of the moral embargo in order to curb Soviet purchases, since many officials feared that some of the Kremlin's purchases of metals, machinery, and petroleum products either went directly to Germany or replaced Soviet goods shipped to Berlin. The Wright incident exhibited the State Department's preference for a strictly legal rejection of Oumansky's complaints. On April 9, Pierrepont Moffat pointed out to the Soviet ambassador that Moscow's original contract with the Wright firm gave Washington the right to end visits by Soviet engineers—neglecting to add that naval officials and the Military Intelligence Division of the War Department opposed visits because they believed that the engineers engaged in espionage.[38]

Although the administration objected to the methods of the Dies committee's continuing search for Communist agents, concern about Soviet espionage increased in May, 1940, when it was discovered that two clerks in the London embassy had kept copies of confidential messages in their rooms. Officials feared that Stalin and Hitler had received enough data from these clerks to decipher Washington's secret codes.[39] Hull submitted a bill to Congress in May that called for the registration of all aliens and the deportation of those who had entered illegally. The Smith Act, or Alien Registration Act, passed by Congress in June, required three-and-a-half million aliens to be registered and fingerprinted at local post offices. This act also provided for the deportation of alien criminals and subversives. In September, Congress required, by the Voorhis Act, the registration of all organizations subject to foreign control.[40]

Washington's accelerated defense preparations in the spring of 1940 added a new layer of antagonism between Moscow and Washington. In May, Roosevelt instructed the secretary of the navy to requisition machine tools. The order primarily affected machines for the production of heavy ordnance and aircraft that American firms were producing for foreign governments, especially Japan and the Soviet Union. The requisition created a conflict between Washington's military preparations and the Kremlin's orders for American machinery. The White House, which could neither satisfy the Kremlin's orders nor obtain any political advantages by providing machine tools to Stalin, did not manage this conflict very smoothly. Hull and other officials, for example, neglected to state clearly that orders by Great Britain would receive priority second only to American orders. After Ambassador Oumansky complained about this discrimination against Soviet orders, a State Department official asked the Treasury and the Navy Department to requisition from Allied orders a "few non-consequential items such as grindstones," in order to weaken Oumansky's accusations.[41]

The Navy Department also got into a bitter dispute with Amtorg over the requisitions. Under the Export Control Act of July 2, 1940, the navy had the authority to requisition—but until October 10 could not purchase—goods taken over from foreign concerns. Consequently, the navy withheld export licenses to Amtorg for machine tools already purchased from American firms. When Loy Henderson reviewed the impasse on July 26, he found increasing "Soviet irritation with us."[42]

He had received four heated calls from Oumansky during the first week of June, when American customs officials forced the unloading of requisitioned tools from aboard the Soviet steamship Rodina. Another incident occurred in July when the Maritime Commission ordered the steamer Wildwood, bound for Vladivostok with machinery and other goods, to turn around in the middle of the Pacific and return for a requisition.[43]

Moscow's continued cooperation with Hitler heightened the tension in Washington's relationship with the Kremlin. Since the nonaggression pact of 1939, Nazi-Soviet relations "have grown steadily closer," reported Ambassador Steinhardt in April. Although Hitler and Stalin pursued their own interests, Steinhardt noted an "element of stability" in their relations since "they do not transcend the limits of mutual self-interest." The ambassador expected Stalin to side with Hitler as long as he feared the German army. The Kremlin "is pursuing a cautious and opportunist policy," he concluded, "and for the moment is quite content to endeavor to avoid ... participation ... in the war while acquiring such positive benefits to the future defense of the Soviet Union as may be possible under the circumstances."[44] Steinhardt retained this view of Soviet policy, without major modification, until April, 1941.

The State Department accepted Steinhardt's analysis. Many officials probably shared Assistant Secretary Berle's feeling that Washington should express its disgust with the "whole farce of Russia insisting that she be treated in all aspects as a friendly nation while she left-handedly carries on a campaign hostile" to America. Hull indirectly communicated this point to Oumansky on June 12, 1940, telling the Soviet ambassador that Washington "would be glad whenever Russia should see fit to return to a set of policies that would make possible the fuller development of ... cooperation in every practicable way."[45]

Despite the diplomatic friction generated by the Soviet-Finnish war, Roosevelt and Hull successfully weathered the emotional storm it stirred up. By taking a cautious approach, they avoided a number of diplomatic and domestic problems. A return to nonrecognition of Moscow would have satisfied conservative critics of the Roosevelt administration, a small segment of the press, and some officials like Sumner Welles, but it would have had little impact on the Soviet-Finnish war and, in the long run, would have forced Roosevelt into another recognition debate when strategic considerations made recognition a necessity in 1941. Under the prodding of Hull, Roosevelt also kept the Republicans from using the Finland issue to gain partisan advantages and deflected any significant criticism from isolationists; by relegating to Congress the question of aid to Finland, for example, he effectively neutralized and redirected the criticism of these two groups. Roosevelt also kept the general focus of American policy on Hitler as the most important threat to American interests, despite the emotional reaction of Americans to Stalin's movements.

The use of caution also produced some unfavorable results. By providing Finland with a maximum of emotional rhetoric and a bare minimum of material aid, Roosevelt placed himself in a rather unheroic posture. Although Washington lacked a significant amount of surplus arms and ammunitition to send to Finland, a decision to provide arms—which Roosevelt seemed to favor against the stubborn opposition of Hull— might have had several beneficial effects. It would have set a precedent which the administration could have used in assisting London and Paris against Hitler. A vigorous effort by the president, exploiting the emotional sympathy for Finland which affected even the isolationists in Congress, would have had a good chance of success. Aid to Finland presumably would have had little impact on Hitler but Stalin might have acquired some respect for Roosevelt's determination and toughness. Instead, from the Kremlin's perspective, the president probably continued to appear indecisive and fairly unimportant with respect to the European situation. Washington's firm rejection of Oumansky's complaints did not counterbalance this impression, particularly since Hitler's conquest of France in May, 1940, induced Washington to change its attitude toward Moscow.

10

Trying to Keep Stalin on the Fence: The Welles-Oumansky Talks

When Nazi Germany defeated France and seemed to have Great Britain within its reach, Washington had to reconsider its policies. Hitler had become a serious threat to the security of the United States. German naval strategists had initiated plans for the acquisition of bases in the Atlantic because of Hitler's recurring interest in a military showdown with the United States. By wiping out French military power and weakening Great Britain, Germany had also opened the door to the south for Japan. Tokyo was moving gradually into the power vacuum in the French colony of Indochina; by September Japanese troops would arrive in northern Indochina.

Under these circumstances, Washington's hostility and unyielding rejection of Soviet complaints began to diminish. Roosevelt and the leaders of the State Department decided to approach the Kremlin again, despite the skepticism of some officials about the likelihood of any change in Soviet policy. Without expecting any immediate shifts in Stalin's position, Roosevelt, Hull, and Welles wanted to encourage any signs of Soviet opposition to Hitler and to deter Stalin from any alliance with Japan. New discussions with Ambassador Oumansky established a different framework and tone in official relations. "I began to wonder whether some change" in Soviet-American relations "could not be brought about," Under Secretary Sumner Welles wrote in his memoirs.

Washington officials hoped, Loy Henderson wrote to Ambassador Steinhardt, that a few concessions to Stalin might prevent him from "entering into certain commitments with Japan and Germany which would result in the strengthening of the latter two countries and in rendering more difficult the carrying out of our policies." Stanley Hornbeck, the State Department's specialist on Far Eastern affairs, pointed to similar if more limited objectives when he frequently recommended an effort to "court" Moscow, "using somewhat softer tones than we have used of late in talking with the Russians and at least intimating in contacts with the Soviet Government that amicable relations between the two countries are not impossible and might be to the advantage of both."[1]

Roosevelt and the top echelon of the State Department approved the new approach, but without much enthusiasm. They did not expect an imminent break in Nazi-Soviet collaboration. When Secretary Ickes asked Roosevelt on June 5 if Russia might switch to the Allied side, Roosevelt said that "Stalin is becoming worried" but would not change course. "Russia is getting tougher and tougher with us," he told Ickes. Steinhardt is "under very strict surveillance. He is watched day and night and is even followed into public toilets."[2] Hull and Welles, moreover, refused to support a proposal for cooperation against Hitler offered by the British to Stalin. Welles argued that only major concessions on issues like the moral embargo and requisition of machine tools, which Washington was unwilling to make, would help the British in this case. When Stalin rejected the proposal, saying that he hoped to postpone a conflict with Berlin through cooperation with Hitler, the Moscow embassy interpreted Stalin's remark as a "very frank and realistic statement of the attitude of the Soviet Government."[3]

Washington may also have avoided involvement in the British demarche because the Moscow embassy had warned the State Department about the likelihood of Soviet moves in Eastern Europe in May and early June. On June 15 and 16, the Kremlin completed its absorption of the Baltic states by establishing pro-Soviet governments and shortly afterward incorporated them into the Soviet Union. Then, supported by Germany and Italy, the Kremlin seized Bessarabia and Northern Bukovina from Rumania. The Moscow embassy was also concerned about the possibility of further Soviet aggression against Finland and Iran.

Roosevelt and the State Department initially avoided any response to Stalin's expansion, perhaps waiting to measure the public reaction and to see if the Kremlin had further plans. When Secretary Morgenthau advocated an immediate extension of currency and assets controls to the Baltic states, the State Department delayed such action. To a Treasury official, Assistant Secretary Berle admitted that in principle Washington should freeze Baltic assets. However, "you might make a distinction [between Hitler's and Stalin's expansion]," Berle argued rather disingenuously, because "...there was some semblance of agreement here, ... and after all we don't want to do anything that might hurt this Russian move against Germany." When the Treasury official informed Morgenthau of Berle's remarks, Morgenthau replied: "They [Berle's remarks] are pro-Russia today. . . . Well, my compliments to Mr. Berle and tell him that I can't see a damn bit of difference."[4]

The reaction of American observers to Stalin's latest expansion indicated that nonrecognition would be the most prudent official response. Although an increasing number of newspapers and organizations accepted Roosevelt's policy of aid to the Allies, they rejected any distinction between Hitler's and Stalin's expansion. The Committee to Defend America by Aiding the Allies and the Century Group, which advocated, respectively, aid to Great Britain and American belligerency, were hostile toward the Soviet Union.[5] Most journals emphasized the defensive orientation behind Stalin's moves and doubted that Stalin would directly join the Allies against Hitler. "As long as Hitler is strong, Stalin cannot afford to displease the Nazis," suggested the New York Herald Tribune, "and he must move cautiously for fear of hastening a German attack which he must already dread." Many newspapers expected Stalin to avoid any confrontation with Hitler while concentrating on his defenses against a German invasion.[6]

Few Americans advocated any response beyond nonrecognition, but an undercurrent of suspicion and hostility toward the Kremlin prevailed. The Soviet Union may have aimed at security, Raymond Gram Swing announced on June 17, but the "Kremlin cannot evade being called the midwives of German victory." Commentators suspected that behind the Soviet acquisitions lurked either the influence of Nazi-Soviet cooperation or Stalin's continuing desire to spread Communism upon an exhausted Europe. They also continued to denounce the similarity between Stalin's and Hitler's tactics. As the New Orleans Times-Picayune pointed out, "Stalin paid Hitler the compliment of copying Hitlerian methods and strategy, grabbing when he covets while the grabbing is good without notice and regardless of his agreements." Consequently, Soviet policy had become the "rankest kind of imperialism," according to a former defender of Soviet policy, the Cleveland Plain Dealer—a policy of helping Hitler crush Europe while picking up pieces of territory and preparing for the eventual showdown between the totalitarian allies.[7]

Official recognition of Soviet expansion was an unattractive alternative for several reasons. Since Washington did not expect any significant change in Soviet policy, there was little reason to risk a strongly critical reaction from the press by making concessions to Stalin. The political advantages of delay also appealed to some officials. On July 15, Loy Henderson advocated a policy of postponement: "Our failure to recognize Soviet conquests, just now, although not pleasant to the Soviet Government, may possibly place another card in our hands when... a conference regarding the future of Europe takes place."[8] Henderson's advice was realistic for 1940 (although the military situation eventually undermined this position). The Kremlin was offering little in return for recognition of its expansion; in the future, Stalin might be pushed out of Eastern Europe or forced to make genuine concessions for recognition of his sphere of control.

After Moscow's puppet governments in the Baltic states voted to join the Soviet Union in July, Washington froze Baltic assets, primarily currency and ships in American ports, and reaffirmed recognition of Baltic representatives in Washington. Hull and Welles publicly criticized the Soviet Union. After referring caustically to the "devious processes" used to subvert the Baltic states, Welles on July 23 announced America's opposition "to predatory activities, no matter whether they are carried out by the use of force or by the threat of force." While Washington hoped for "an improvement in American-Soviet relations," Welles told the Moscow embassy, "we had to protest."[9]

Four days later, on July 27, Welles suggested to Ambassador Oumansky that they review all of the problems in Soviet-American relations. When Oumansky responded with an objection to the freeze of Baltic assets, Welles replied that Washington had to "protest against acts of aggression of this character." Instead of expansion which "necessarily must result in a deterioration of relations," Welles warned Oumansky, the Kremlin should "logically" want friendly relations with America "from which it never had and never would have anything to fear."[10]

The negotiations soon slipped into a pattern. Ambassador Oumansky demanded the release of Baltic assets and machinery requisitioned by the War Department. Each small concession from Welles, such as the release of a few machine tools, prompted Oumansky to push harder. Instead of making concessions upon a quid pro quo basis, Welles obtained tankers for the Soviet Union at Pacific ports. When the under secretary offered to review the moral embargo and grant export licenses for Soviet machinery not needed by the War Department, the Soviet ambassador refused to release machinery already requisitioned. Instead, Oumansky demanded irrevocable export licenses, abolition of the moral embargo, and visiting privileges for Soviet engineers.

Welles and Oumansky also engaged in a unique, one-sided discussion about Soviet-American cooperation. After criticizing Soviet expansion, the under secretary remarked on August 7 that Washington and Moscow had "no occasion whatsoever for any conflict of interest." The international situation had changed, Oumansky replied, but not Soviet policy. Welles persisted. Washington and Moscow "should work together more closely during these troublesome periods," he suggested. Oumansky continued to back away. "Mr. Welles was making statements of real importance and looking ahead," remarked the Soviet ambassador, who preferred to discuss specific issues.[11]

An impasse quickly developed. For example, Welles tied the removal of the moral embargo to a general settlement of outstanding issues; he also indicated that Moscow would have to halt its expansion. In addition, America's defensive buildup and aid to Great Britain required more and more of the machinery ordered by Moscow. Naval officials, who suspected that Soviet engineers would give information about the Wright Aeronautical plant to "certain subversive elements," resisted Henderson's request for a "friendly gesture" such as allowing Soviet engineers "a little more leeway in the plant." Welles did persuade Roosevelt not to retaliate against Soviet consulates in America when Moscow closed American consulates in the Baltic states. The Kremlin, however, ignored Washington's protests against the detention of American citizens and expropriation of American interests in Poland, the Baltic states, and Bessarabia. When Oumansky on August 15 asked for permission to take over the Baltic consulates in America, the under secretary, a master of understatement, replied that "there were some problems between the two countries which it might not be possible to solve for the present."[12]

The impasse continued until changes in the European and Far Eastern situations brought a few gestures from each side. On July 21, Hitler made the decision to attack the Soviet Union and immediately began military preparations. He also encroached upon Finland and Rumania, which Moscow considered part of its sphere according to the Nazi-Soviet agreements of 1939. As part of a rapprochement with Finland, Berlin signed a trade agreement and in September negotiated a transit agreement for German troops. Rumania received a guarantee of its territory from Berlin, and a German division soon arrived, ostensibly for training purposes. On September 27 Germany, Italy, and Japan signed the Tripartite Pact, which included mutual recognition of "new orders" in Europe and Asia and an agreement to support each other against an American attack. Hitler's actions, taken after only perfunctory consultation with Moscow, provoked the first serious rift in Nazi-Soviet relations since the pact of 1939.[13]

The Moscow embassy noted the tension between Berlin and Moscow but expected Stalin to avoid a break with Hitler. When Germany intruded into the Soviet sphere in Finland and Rumania, chargé Walter Thurston and Ambassador Steinhardt, who returned to Moscow in August, emphasized the timidity of Moscow's response. According to Thurston, "fear of involvement in the European war" and a desire to expand with minimum effort governed Soviet policy. Steinhardt expected Stalin to remain passively faithful to Hitler, despite his fears about Hitler's intentions. The Kremlin also "might not be adverse to a bilateral agreement with Japan," Steinhardt warned Washington.[14]

The State Department agreed with the Moscow embassy. Loy Henderson, for example, felt that Stalin's policies were "consistent and in conformity with" the Nazi-Soviet pact, despite Hitler's violations. After a chat with Hull on October 8, Assistant Secretary Long wrote in his diary that the Soviet Union "would do whatever is best to save her own skin for the time being."[15]

A major intelligence coup, however, bolstered Washington's belief in an eventual Nazi-Soviet clash. Starting in August, the State Department received crucial data from Samuel E. Woods, commercial attaché in the Berlin embassy. An anti-Nazi German with contacts in the government slipped confidential information about plans for an invasion of the Soviet Union to Woods in a motion picture theater.[16] This information probably reinforced Roosevelt's and Welles' desire to reduce the friction in Soviet-American relations. They could not simply sit back and wait for Hitler to invade the Soviet Union; indeed, Stalin might change Hitler's plans through concessions or a general appeasement. Without expecting Stalin to make a dramatic switch to the Allied side, Roosevelt and Welles probably hoped that a few concessions to Moscow would help to restrain Stalin from full cooperation with Hitler.

The Far Eastern situation had a similar impact. On June 10 Moscow and Tokyo made a boundary agreement that contributed to the end of border hostilities, and throughout the summer and fall of 1940 American officials remained apprehensive about a general Soviet-Japanese rapprochement. In July Secretary Morgenthau considered proposing a triangular trade exchange among China, the Soviet Union, and the United States in response to Roosevelt's desire to "do something to keep Russia on the fence" in the Far East. Morgenthau put this idea aside when Welles reminded him how upset Moscow was over Washington's position on the Baltic states.[17] However, in September the situation drastically changed. After Tokyo sent troops into Indochina on September 23 and signed the Tripartite Pact, Washington responded with a loan to China and an embargo on Japanese purchases of iron and steel scrap. Japan's moves made Soviet neutrality in the Far East or cooperation with Washington in an anti-Japanese front even more important.

Morgenthau then revived his trade plan. With Roosevelt's approval, he asked Ambassador Oumansky on September 20 if Moscow would ship raw materials to Washington for cash. Washington would make a loan to China, which then could purchase more military material from the Soviet Union. After consultation with the Kremlin, Oumansky told Morgenthau that Moscow would sell raw materials to Washington but would not link this with its aid to China. On September 27 the cabinet debated Morgenthau's plan. According to Secretary Stimson, discussion revolved around the question of "whether we could not woo Russia a little." Stimson, who felt that the Kremlin's "interests ran parallel with ours" in the Pacific, favored another offer to Moscow through Chiang Kai-shek in China. When Moscow turned down this proposal, Roosevelt predicted that the Kremlin would persist in its "Mugwump policy of sitting on the fence." A continuation of Soviet aid to China heightened Washington's hopes for continuing Soviet-Japanese friction.[18]

Hull strongly opposed the trade plan, warning Morgenthau on September 20 that the Russians would not increase aid to China, for "they are utterly as unreliable as Jesse James." Hull's and Welles' opposition, however, represented a disagreement over timing and personal prerogatives more than over policy. Moreover, they disliked any interference in their negotiations with Oumansky. Hull, who always resented Morgenthau's ventures into foreign policy, was "all wrought up and provoked again. He said that continual interference within the sphere of his own function greatly irritated him," Long wrote in his diary after another Hull-Morgenthau meeting on September 25.[19] The secretary also felt that a triangular exchange in addition to the embargo and the loan to China might precipitate an armed clash with Japan. Neither he nor Welles completely distrusted the Soviet Union. If the Kremlin withdrew its association with Germany and Japan, Hull and Welles were ready to make concessions.

They moved in this direction in October. After Ambassador Oumansky accepted the navy's requisition of Soviet orders, Welles said that Moscow would receive more machine tools in the future, in addition to shipments held back by the navy since the spring of 1940. (The demands of American defense, however, increased the rejection of Soviet orders from 30 to 50 percent in October.) Hull went further: "If Russia should show a real disposition to move in our common direction with respect to the Axis countries," he told the British ambassador on October 14, then Washington would adopt a flexible, quid pro quo approach to the Baltic assets, a primary concern of Moscow. He asked Steinhardt to convey this intention, in a more oblique manner, to Molotov. Hull realized, however, that Washington could offer very little beyond this. "Russia is trembling in the balance under pressure from Germany who can give her ample quid pro quo which we can't answer," Secretary Stimson concluded, after a meeting with Hull on October 23.[20]

Washington may have stopped short of more concessions to Moscow because of concern about the domestic reaction. Although the Welles-Oumansky discussions and the October concessions attracted little attention, there was a certain amount of criticism, especially from conservative commentators. According to the National Republic, any effort to cooperate with Stalin would end up in "enthroning the bloody, unscrupulous system of ungodly Communist totalitarianism" upon Europe. Eugene Lyons argued that Stalin would not break with Hitler "because of our gestures of appeasement"—that only pressure by Hitler could split the alliance. "The periodical 'wooing' of Russia is a waste of affection," Lyons concluded. More significantly, the United States News reported on November 1 that 80 percent of the press believed that courting Moscow would not bring any benefits. "Have we forgotten Russia's war against Finland, her gobbling the Baltic states, her annexation of Bessarabia," complained the Roanoke World-News, a Democratic journal.[21]

The press expected Stalin to stay with Hitler, despite the friction in Nazi-Soviet relations. When Premier Molotov visited Berlin in November, editors suspected a new deal between Hitler and Stalin, as well as a Soviet-Japanese alliance. The latter possibility was particularly disturbing, since, as the Seattle Post-Intelligencer pointed out, it "would bring the facts of the totalitarian threat home to our region with a vengeance."[22] The uneventful conference in Berlin and the continuing Nazi-Soviet friction in the Balkans reduced this concern. Most journals agreed with the *Cincinnati Enquirer's* conclusion that "Russia at long last is swinging away from passive support of German expansion." But they expected Stalin, fearful of Hitler's intentions and of the German army, reluctantly to accept German domination of the Balkans.[23]

Officials in the Division of European Affairs and the Moscow embassy agreed with this assessment of Soviet policy and resisted Welles' conciliatory approach. Loy Henderson's experience in negotiations with Moscow since 1934 prompted him to favor strict reciprocity. "In the past," Henderson complained to a friend, "... we have always laid low and lost everything that we had or was owed to us." He did support Welles' negotiations, although with "grave doubts that our policy of so-called appeasement will get us any place."[24] Ambassador Steinhardt, who was not consulted about the new approach while he was in Washington in May and June, agreed with Henderson. When Molotov refused to discuss American complaints, rejected another British overture, and visited Berlin, Steinhardt became convinced that Stalin would cling to Hitler—although he underestimated the friction in Nazi-Soviet relations. "Greater rather than a lesser degree of Soviet-German collaboration must be anticipated in the immediate future," the ambassador informed Washington. "Unilateral concessions not only would be futile but would tend to impair" American prestige, he cautioned Hull.[25] Soviet-Japanese discussions in December, which took place because the Kremlin refused to stop its assistance to China, reinforced Steinhardt's skepticism about the value of concessions. The ambassador felt that Moscow wanted an agreement and would exploit American-Japanese tension to obtain concessions from Tokyo.[26]

On November 26, 1940, the Division of European Affairs tried to restrain Welles before his next meeting with Oumansky, showing him excerpts from a warning from Ambassador Steinhardt that the Kremlin's objective in the Far East "must be war between the United States and Japan." Steinhardt also complained about concessions to Oumansky. "I assume that the 'higher ups' regarded international 'policies' as more important than profitable results," he curtly remarked, "and are still fooling themselves into believing that the Soviet Government responds to kindness or evidences of good will." Only force and bartering, Steinhardt argued in December, would make Moscow reciprocate with more than the "encouragement of wishful thinking."[27]

Welles and Hull accepted Steinhardt's analysis of Soviet policy but disregarded his warnings—perhaps because the confidential information they had received about German military preparations made them see value in exploiting Nazi-Soviet friction. In addition, Soviet-Japanese negotiations probably increased their fear that the United States might end up standing alone against Japan. Welles and Hull favored the removal of the moral embargo imposed during the Soviet-Finnish war. Welles felt that Oumansky's statements about a similarity of interest in the Far East and a continuation of Soviet aid to China were "of the utmost importance and...most gratifying." After the Kremlin released 100 American citizens from its occupied territories and granted permission for an American consulate-general at Vladivostok, Hull concluded that Moscow, "for the present at least, is assuming a more reasonable attitude."[28]

On January 8, 1941, Welles offered Oumansky a private cancellation of the embargo in return for a general settlement of outstanding issues, a course that Roosevelt felt was desirable. In reply, the Soviet ambassador asked for a publicized removal of the embargo, separate from other issues. He also warned Welles that "a real adjustment of Soviet-American relations" would come only after Washington turned over the Baltic assets and withdrew recognition of the Baltic representatives. The under secretary immediately accepted Oumansky's position on the embargo. With Hull's approval, Welles asked Roosevelt's endorsement of a public statement about the embargo in order to remove the moral stigma from Soviet trade. "On the whole, our negotiations with the Soviet Union have progressed favorably...," Welles wrote, with some exaggeration, "and the more friendly relationship which is beginning to exist is unquestionably of real advantage...insofar as the Far Eastern situation is concerned."[29]

After obtaining a favorable reply from Roosevelt, Welles publicly announced the end of the moral embargo on January 23—more a symbolic gesture than a major concession. Hull reassured Steinhardt that all articles covered by the moral embargo fell within Washington's export controls. Since the national defense program consumed increasing amounts of raw materials and production facilities, Washington's gesture did not enable the Kremlin to actually purchase more machinery.[30]

Nevertheless, the removal of the embargo was assailed by domestic critics. Rep. George Tinkham of Massachusetts and Sen. Charles Tobey of New Hampshire charged the White House with appeasement of "homicidal, communistic Soviet Russia." With similar bluntness, the Dies committee attacked the administration. Although newspaper editors recognized that the removal was only a gesture, they still disliked the implications of appeasement. Very few agreed with the *Cincinnati Enquirer* that "more friendly relations…might be a means of dissuading Japan from any reckless venture."[31]

"Now the United States is embarked on another of its efforts to woo the Bolsheviks from their alliance with the Nazis," announced the Louisville *Courier-Journal*, arguing that it would not work, because "Russia today is the great war profiteer.… It can hardly be brought off by the lifting of a meaningless 'moral embargo'." Many observers believed that Stalin was unreliable and would ship anything he purchased in the United States to Berlin. More emotionally, the *Pittsburgh Post-Gazette* complained that the removal "seems to mean that this country has forgotten and forgiven the unwarranted aggression on Finland, and the brutal seizure of the Baltic countries." Most commentators, including the liberal *New Republic*, agreed with the *Philadelphia Inquirer*'s warning to Roosevelt: "If we must play expedient politics with Moscow, let us face all the facts and act with all caution. Let us not rely upon unreliability. Let us not put our faith where there is no faith. Let us not place America in any danger of being a sucker for Stalin."[32]

The public reaction was particularly important because, during January and February of 1941, congressional critics were challenging Roosevelt's policy toward Moscow. The challenge arose indirectly over the Lend-Lease Bill that Roosevelt submitted to Congress in January. Section 3(a)(1) of the bill authorized the president to provide aid to any country whose defense he considered vital to the United States. The question of possible aid to the Soviet Union stayed in the background during the formulation of the bill. Roosevelt and other administration officials wanted to aid Great Britain and other countries opposing Hitler, and they wanted extensive powers of discretion in order to avoid continuous referrals to Congress.

An early draft proposal of the bill, submitted to the president on January 6, listed possible recipients of aid but omitted Moscow. Democratic spokesmen in Congress also urged Roosevelt to exclude the Kremlin, in order to undermine one of the opposition's arguments against Lend-Lease. However, the president submitted the bill to Congress without the names of any countries. Confidential information from Berlin indicated that Hitler would soon attack the Soviet Union, perhaps in the spring, and Roosevelt wanted maximum flexibility to meet this potential situation. More immediately, a specific exclusion of Moscow from any future assistance would have contradicted Welles' policy toward Moscow, which indicated that Washington realistically considered any potential opponent of Hitler to be a potential recipient of aid.[33]

The opponents of Lend-Lease raised the possibility of aid to the Soviet Union as a major argument against the bill. Using the repeal of the moral embargo as an indication of Roosevelt's intentions, Rep. Karl Mundt of South Dakota and Sen. Hiram Johnson of California demanded the exclusion of Moscow in order to prevent any secret deals with Stalin. On February 7 Rep. George Tinkham introduced an amendment to this effect, and Sen. Robert Reynolds did the same in the Senate on March 3. The administration wisely responded to this tactic with silence. Secretaries Hull and Morgenthau, for example, refused to discuss the Soviet Union during congressional hearings, instead focusing upon the importance of Great Britain to America's security. Shortly before the vote on Tinkham's amendment, Luther A. Johnson of Texas, who directed the bill in the House, stated the administration's position. "Is it prudent, is it statesmanlike to slap Russia in the face when at this time she is not a part of the Axis Powers that have threatened us?" Johnson asked. The House defeated Tinkham's amendment, 94 to 185. On March 7 the Senate rejected Reynolds' amendment, with 35 senators favoring it and 56 opposed.[34]

Roosevelt's signing of the Lend-Lease Bill on March 11 represented a major victory for his general foreign policy and a smaller one with respect to the Soviet Union. Tactically, the administration had defeated the opposition by keeping the debate focused on aid to London. The press, for example, had largely ignored the Soviet Union in the extensive editorial response to the Lend-Lease issue. Roosevelt had again illustrated his astute sense of political timing and skillful legislative tactics.

However, the emergence of the Soviet issue in Congress and the critical reaction to the repeal of the moral embargo probably reinforced Roosevelt's and the State Department's decision to move cautiously in dealing with the Soviet Union in the spring of 1941. Washington avoided further concessions to Moscow. When Oumansky continued to complain that London received preferential treatment of its orders, Welles replied that "if the Soviet Union were now resisting aggression," it would receive similar favors. He also pressed Oumansky about Soviet economic assistance to Germany until the Soviet ambassador publicly denied that any Soviet imports from America went to Hitler. Furthermore, Welles told Oumansky on February 27 that "problems relating to the Baltic states should be considered to be in the class of unsolvable problems."[35]

By the end of February Welles and Hull had returned to their original approach. They talked about cooperation with Moscow, opposed any steps against the Soviet Union, but rejected any major concessions. Hull rejected Secretary Morgenthau's proposal for a general freeze of European assets in February by arguing that it would drive Moscow into the arms of Japan. When London switched to a hard line toward Moscow, Hull denied a British request that Washington further curb its exports to the Soviet Union, overstating the degree of Stalin's opposition to Germany and Japan. The secretary told the British ambassador that Welles' negotiations had removed "many small grievances...so...there would be less occasion for Soviet officials to feel unkindly toward this Government."[36]

"We are trying to encourage [the Kremlin] to nag Japan [and] Hitler," Secretary Hull told journalist Raymond Clapper on March 5. Late in January the State Department had received from Sam Woods a copy of Hitler's Directive No. 21, which summarized German military plans for an invasion of the Soviet Union. Steinhardt opposed disclosure of this information to the Kremlin; he felt that if the Kremlin accepted the report or reached the same conclusion on the basis of its own intelligence, it would try to make an agreement with Japan, occupy Finland, demand concessions from Washington, and appease Hitler in order to stall the attack. These objections, which accurately anticipated many of Stalin's maneuvers, did not prevent Welles from passing the information to Oumansky on March 1. "Oumansky turned very white," the under secretary observed, remained silent briefly, and then thanked him. On March 20 Oumansky asked if Washington had received more information about German plans. Having received another document from Woods that "envisages very definitely war against Russia," Welles replied affirmatively.[37]

Nazi-Soviet tension over German expansion in Eastern Europe finally induced Ambassador Steinhardt to modify some of his views. The Kremlin protested Germany's occupation of Bulgaria on March 1 and encouraged Yugoslavia's opposition to Hitler. After an anti-Nazi coup in Yugoslavia on March 25, the Kremlin signed a treaty of friendship with the new government on April 5. However, when the Nazi army invaded Yugoslavia the next morning, Moscow made only verbal protests. As Steinhardt pointed out, Stalin wanted other countries to oppose Hitler in order to postpone an attack on the Soviet Union. He also expected the Kremlin to continue its economic assistance to Germany and "will be careful to avoid any action which would be likely to provoke a German attack." Yet by April 12 Steinhardt admitted that the "long anticipated change in the relationship between the Soviet Union and Germany is in [the] process of taking place, although this fact need not...mean that an immediate clash...must occur."[38]

Washington did not make any concessions to Moscow, however. When Oumansky asked for more machine tools, Welles reminded him of Soviet economic assistance to Hitler. Welles agreed with the Soviet ambassador's remark that Soviet and American attitudes toward Yugoslavia were similar, but he remained silent when Oumansky suggested that they make their views identical on the Baltic issue.[39]

Welles did warn Oumansky against a Soviet-Japanese rapprochement when Yosuke Matsuoka, Tokyo's foreign minister, visited Berlin and Moscow in March. After a conference on March 20, the under secretary asked Oumansky to stay for a private chat. He recommended that Moscow and Washington leave "Japan in a state of complete uncertainty" about their intentions, observing that "the Soviet Union and the United States were equally interested in the maintenance of peace in the Pacific." Oumansky replied that he privately shared Welles' opinion.[40]

Stalin and Matsuoka ultimately ignored Washington and signed a pact of neutrality on April 13. Trying to conceal his disappointment, Hull told the press on April 14, "The agreement would seem to be descriptive of a situation which has in effect existed...for some time past," and American policy "of course remains unchanged." But Bertram D. Hulen, the *New York Times* correspondent at the State Department, noted intense disappointment among American officials, many of whom may have agreed with Stanley Hornbeck's assessment that the "Soviet Union wants Japan to go southward—and would like to see Japan embroiled with the United States." Although Stalin probably viewed this alternative favorably, he seemed more immediately interested in the protection of his eastern front, weakened by the necessity of moving troops to the western border; for example, he ordered a quiet partial mobilization in April, as more and more evidence of a German invasion accumulated.[41] The Soviet-Japanese agreement guaranteed very little to either side, and Moscow continued its aid to China. Nevertheless, the pact signaled a partial defeat for Washington's attempt to keep Stalin away from Japan, and some American observers viewed it as further evidence of the futility and danger involved in the Welles-Oumansky talks.

"For weeks Washington has been playing ring-around-a-rosy with the Soviet trying to gain its good will for any eventuality in the Orient," commented the *Cleveland Plain Dealer*. "This should be the final lesson in the futility of dealing with aggressors."[42] It seemed to many observers that the agreement duplicated the Nazi-Soviet pact of 1939, this time with Moscow giving tacit approval to Japan for expansion to the south and conflict with the United States. "Russia is making herself the accomplice before the fact for further Japanese aggression in Asia," complained the *Washington Post* and broadcasters H. V. Kaltenborn and Raymond Gram Swing. A majority of editors agreed with the *New York Times'* conclusion that the pact provided ample evidence of the "futility of any Washington policy of appeasing Stalin."[43]

Some newspapers concurred with Hull's opinion that the significance of the pact could be overrated. The New Orleans *Times-Picayune* and the *Los Angeles Times* argued that immediate self-interest—not any formal pacts, which would be discarded without hesitation—guided both Soviet and Japanese policy. Reports of the continuation of Soviet aid to China bolstered this assessment. Very few editors, however, expected Stalin to take a firmer stance against German expansion in the Balkans after reducing the tension with Japan. "Any belief that the agreement implies a tougher Russian attitude toward the Nazis," the *Cincinnati Enquirer* pronounced, "is wishful thinking."[44] Stalin soon confirmed this conclusion. The Kremlin's protests over the Nazi acquisition of Bulgaria and Yugoslavia were viewed as evidence of a fearful but passive Soviet policy. As the *Baltimore Sun* pointed out, Russia "is seeing possible allies killed off and its windows on the world closed, one by one."[45]

Stalin accepted a settlement of a boundary dispute favorable to Berlin on April 15, 1941. In May he withdrew recognition of a number of anti-Nazi governments-in-exile. The Kremlin also continued its shipments of crucial strategic materials to Hitler until the German attack on June 22, 1941. Soviet defense preparations—most notably, the preparation of a new defense line in the Baltics, the dispersal of the armaments industry, and the mass mobilization of industry—were neglected by Stalin. Without ruling out the possibility of conflict, Stalin seemed to hope for negotiations with Hitler and avoided any action that might upset him—such as a full military alert—until the night before the German attack.[46]

"Any time Hitler says boo to Stalin, the bear will run in the direction Hitler points," columnist Paul Mallon remarked. *Newsweek* referred to Stalin's "hasty appeasement," and Joseph Alsop and Robert Kinter suggested that "it is a foregone conclusion here that Soviet Russia will become a full-fledged member of the Axis, in fact and probably in name."[47] Even when reports of German troop movements circulated in June, most journals interpreted this as a pressure tactic by Hitler that would work. The *Hartford Courant*, for example, predicted that Stalin would probably go "unreservedly into the service of Germany." Even the *New Republic* expected Stalin to become a full partner with Hitler, "for communism and nazism are alike as two peas in their means."[48]

Stalin's appeasement of Hitler provided additional ammunition for critics to use against the Welles-Oumansky talks. Washington should "realize that when it pets and babies Communist Russia by granting it trade and other concessions it is coddling a deadly viper," admonishd the *Philadelphia Inquirer*. When an inaccurate report that Washington had stopped all exports of machinery to Moscow appeared early in May, a number of editors applauded, expressing the hope that the Roosevelt administration had learned a lesson. "The United States thus admits," reported the Louisville *Courier-Journal*, "that its efforts to win the Bolshevik State away from the Nazi nation have been utterly futile." The *Pittsburgh Post-Gazette* agreed: "We lifted the 'moral embargo' earlier this year, and got soundly slapped by the Soviets in return."[49]

The Moscow embassy and the State Department concurred with the press's prediction that Stalin would appease Hitler in order to avoid the likelihood of defeat. Ambassador Steinhardt expected the Soviet regime to collapse under a Nazi attack, and "many unbiased observers" in Moscow felt that "military resistance could be crushed within a few weeks."[50] Washington officials expected Germany to defeat the Red army within three months. The assistant chief of staff of the Military Intelligence Division described Russia as a power "only because of its bulk. In its inherent inefficiency it is a menace to all."[51] The State Department also discarded Welles' conciliatory attitude toward Soviet complaints, presuming that Stalin would appease Hitler regardless of any Washington concessions. When Ambassador Oumansky raised all of the old issues on May 14, Hull vigorously rejected his complaints. In June, Washington declared two Soviet military attachés persona non grata and froze all assets of European countries, including the Soviet Union.[52]

Hull, Welles, and the Division of European Affairs recommended that Washington respond very cautiously to a Nazi-Soviet clash, remaining within the guidelines of Welles' negotiations with Moscow since July, 1940, and "making no approaches to the Soviet Government." Any demarches from Moscow, moreover, should be handled "with reserve" in order to make sure that the Kremlin "is not engaging merely in maneuvers for the purpose of obtaining unilaterally concessions and advantages for itself." Finally, Washington should demand strict reciprocity and make "no sacrifices in principle in order to improve relations."[53]

On June 15, 1941, Welles expanded Washington's position in a conversation with the British ambassador, Lord Halifax. Washington might give Moscow some economic assistance, Welles remarked, depending upon considerations of national defense, aid to Great Britain, and Japan's reaction to a German invasion of the Soviet Union. If Japan attacked the

Soviet Union, any Washington aid to Stalin "would necessarily be contingent upon what we considered the best interests of the United States" with respect to Japanese relations. When Lord Halifax hinted that London might recognize Stalin's conquest of the Baltic states, Welles urged him to reconsider the "moral issues involved." The under secretary felt that there was no "logical distinction" between recognition of Moscow's "brutal" conquests and Hitler's expansion, and that London would gain few practical benefits by recognizing Moscow's "loot."[54]

Ambassador Steinhardt "wholeheartedly" agreed with Washington for the first time since Welles had begun his discussions with Oumansky. Steinhardt especially liked the firmness of Washington's planned response, which reflected a somewhat harsher tone than Welles' and Hull's earlier remarks to Oumansky. The ambassador pointed out that he had advocated this "for quite some time" as the best way "to maintain our prestige in Moscow." The Kremlin's "psychology recognizes only firmness, power and force," he wrote to Hull, "and reflects primitive instincts and reactions entirely devoid of the restraints of civilization." A firm policy would become very important, Steinhardt concluded, when Stalin turned to Washington "in an endeavor to escape the consequences of having precipitated the European war and of its aggressive exploitation thereof."[55]

On June 21 Ray Atherton and Loy Henderson refined the State Department's guidelines in a memorandum to Welles. If Stalin requested assistance against a German invasion, they recommended that Washington "relax restrictions on exports to the Soviet Union," provide whatever military supplies "we could afford to spare," but "make no commitment" that would prevent a refusal "to recognize a refugee Soviet Government ... in case the Soviet Union should be defeated." Finally, Atherton and Henderson strongly advised that "we should steadfastly adhere to the line" that the Soviet Union's resistance to Germany "does not mean that it is defending, struggling for, or adhering to, the principles in international relations which we are supporting."[56]

These guidelines represented a fairly realistic response, although they underestimated the strategic benefits in Europe and the Far East that Washington would gain from Soviet resistance to Hitler. State Department officials favored material aid to Moscow, despite their obvious hostility toward the Kremlin. On the other hand, Welles and Henderson recognized the moral and pragmatic objections to recognition of Stalin's expansion since 1939. Such recognition would have little effect, pro or con, on Stalin's defense against the German army. The unfavorable reaction of the press and some Congressmen to the repeal of the moral embargo and to the Welles-Oumansky talks in general also made any general concession too risky. The most serious weakness of the State Department's policy lay in its references to a refugee Soviet government and its general expectation that the Red army would resist Hitler for only three months. Within this framework, there was little motivation for bargaining with Moscow over American aid and even less reason to worry about limiting Soviet expansion in central Europe at the expense of a defeated Germany.

President Roosevelt, who had stayed in the background during Welles' negotiations, had approved those negotiations. With the collapse of France and the imminent defeat of Great Britain, Roosevelt had had to reopen discussions with Moscow in order to probe Soviet intentions toward Hitler and try to deter Stalin from a rapprochement with Tokyo. By allowing Welles to handle the negotiations, the president had kept them out of the 1940 election campaign. Undoubtedly the criticism of the talks that emerged in the winter and spring of 1941, as well as the issue of the Soviet Union in the Lend-Lease battle in Congress, had reinforced Roosevelt's inclinaton to approach the issue of aid to the Soviet Union cautiously. Nevertheless, the president indicated that he might not follow the new guidelines drafted by Henderson and Steinhardt, and Hull encouraged him in this direction. After Prime Minister Winston Churchill wrote Roosevelt on June 14 about his intention to "give all encouragement and any help we can spare to the Russians," Roosevelt asked Ambassador John Winant to tell Churchill that he would endorse any statement "welcoming Russia as an ally." On June 22, after the German attack, Hull telephoned Roosevelt and Welles, pleading that "we must give Russia all aid to the hilt. We have repeatedly said we will give all the help we can to any nation resisting the Axis."[57]

The Soviet-American rapprochement which followed the German invasion represented the culmination of the Roosevelt administration's decision in July, 1940, to initiate discussions with Oumansky in Moscow. The discussions had removed very few points of friction. Welles and Hull had hoped that Stalin would move away from Hitler and from Japan, but the Kremlin had stayed with Hitler until the bitter end and had signed a neutrality pact with Tokyo. Thus, the discussions had provided few benefits beyond valuable learning experience about the means and ends of Stalin's foreign policy.

Ambassador Steinhardt and Loy Henderson, who disliked Welles' approach, had correctly evaluated the dynamics and direction of Soviet policy since 1939. They had understood the Kremlin's policy to revolve around Stalin's desire to expand in the wake of Hitler's triumphs. When Hitler had turned his attention to the East, they had perceived the fearful passivity of the Kremlin's response. Negotiations with Moscow had bolstered their interest in a firm policy, based on reciprocity and an understanding of the different interests and principles held by Washington and Moscow. Under the pressure of a two-front war, the Roosevelt administration seemed almost to forget those differences, and gradually deserted a firm approach. Hull's and Welles' discussions with Ambassador Oumansky had augured this development. Both officials had tended to favor small concessions to Moscow, sometimes ignoring Steinhardt's objections. When the Kremlin had offered a gesture—usually a routine action rather than a concession—Hull and Welles had read too much into it, especially with respect to the Far East. On an issue of principle like the Baltic states, Hull and Welles had wavered between a quid pro quo approach and postponement for the future. Washington had tried to resolve conflicts of interest through compromise and had put off the difficult political questions that Moscow had continually raised.

Whether or not Washington followed a firm policy or one of minor concessions from July, 1940, to June, 1941, made little difference in the short run. But the Welles-Oumansky negotiations established the framework and tone of the discussions that followed Hitler's invasion of the Soviet Union.

11

Lend-Lease to the Soviet Union

Early on the morning of June 23, 1941, Sumner Welles released an official statement about the Nazi-Soviet war. Religious oppression and "other principles and doctrines of communistic dictatorship are as intolerable and as alien" to America, Welles remarked, "as are the principles and doctrines of Nazi dictatorship." Yet the most immediate threat to American interests, Welles announced, was Nazi aggression, and "any rallying of the forces opposing Hitlerism, from whatever source these forces may spring, will . . . redound to the benefit of our own defense and security." At a press conference the next day, Roosevelt indicated his approval of Welles' statement and added that "of course we are going to give all the aid we possibly can to Russia," although Great Britain would have priority on American aid. When asked if the Soviet Union would receive Lend-Lease, Roosevelt replied, "I don't know," and brushed aside other questions.[1]

Welles and Roosevelt broke no new ground with these announcements. Since the outbreak of the war in 1939, the White House and the State Department had favored aid to any forces opposing Hitler. Soviet resistance to Germany would provide Washington with many military and political benefits. Consequently, aid to the Soviet Union fitted, at least theoretically, into the framework of established American policy. But a number of practical problems—notably, doubts about the Red army's capabilities and the American people's lack of enthusiasm—prompted Roosevelt to approach the matter of Lend-Lease very cautiously. Although the issues had changed since 1933, Roosevelt's Lend-Lease decision was strikingly similar to his handling of recognition. Again he used individuals like his chief aide, Harry Hopkins, to speed up the process. Roosevelt also tested American opinion with trial balloons, tried to disarm opponents of aid, and refused to extend Lend-Lease until Congress and the news media indicated their approval. Roosevelt reaffirmed his virtuosity in winning congressional and public approval for what was initially a controversial issue, turning it into a consensus—a noncontroversial question—and overwhelming the opposition. But he also revealed his weaknesses as a negotiator with Moscow when he and the State Department neglected to bargain with Stalin for Soviet concessions in return for Lend-Lease.

The statements quoted above represented the administration's first trial balloon, and the general response of American observers justified Washington's caution. In Congress, anti-Communist fire-eaters like Hamilton Fish had a field day. Fish predicted that Roosevelt would "turn the lend-lease bill into a Lenin-lease bill and send our money and defense articles to Soviet Russia in the name of four freedoms." Some isolationists, though they hoped that Stalin and Hitler would destroy each other, felt that assistance to Moscow was morally out of the question. "The war party can hardly ask the people of America to take up arms behind the red flag of Stalin," the isolationist organization America First protested. Former president Herbert Hoover also criticized aid to Stalin and "his militant Communist conspiracy."[2]

Initially, the *Cleveland Plain Dealer* opposed the use of any American tax dollars to "save the Communists from taking a licking," and recommended sending only a regiment of American Communists, fellow travelers, and defense strikers. Within four days, however, the *Plain Dealer* reluctantly accepted Washington's position, postulating that the "question of helping Russia is largely academic" because of the likelihood of a Soviet defeat or a deal with Hitler.[3] Most commentators agreed with this assessment. The Committee to Defend America by Aiding the Allies and the conservative *National Republic* unwillingly supported but continued to criticize aid to Moscow. Eugene Lyons and William Henry Chamberlin did not expect the Kremlin to hold out very long against Hitler's attack and largely discounted the likelihood of a Soviet victory.[4] Even if Stalin won, the *Chicago Daily News* argued, the United States had to stop Hitler first, despite the general acknowledgment that Stalin "differs from Hitler as an international menace only in degree and efficiency."[5]

Most observers preferred to avoid extensive discussion of the question of aid to Stalin. Instead, they welcomed the Nazi-Soviet war as an opportunity for the United States to accelerate its defense buildup and aid to London. Many editors approved Welles' emphasis on Germany as the most important threat to America and rejected the isolationist argument that Washington could sit back and let the totalitarian dictators destroy each other. They also presented a number of reasons why aid to the Soviet Union should not be an important issue: a lack of surplus supplies, available shipping facilities, and time to get any arms to Moscow before the expected German victory. "Ever since the Russo-German war began," the *Washington Post* complained, "we have been talking about aid to Russia and in the process asking many confusing, unnecessary and academic questions."[6] Many journals still recommended against Lend-Lease aid to Moscow and continued to warn Washington to be very careful with the unreliable Kremlin.[7]

This reluctant approval of aid to Moscow conformed with the State Department's recommendation of a reserved response to the Nazi-Soviet conflict within the guidelines of the Division of European Affairs memoranda. Acting Secretary Welles cautioned the British ambassador against a formal alliance with Moscow: "The wise policy," Welles advised Lord Halifax, was "a policy of expediency," of limited aid, until the situation in Europe and the Far East became clearer.[8]

The State Department and the Moscow embassy questioned Moscow's ability to withstand the Nazi blitzkrieg. Moscow's previous difficulties in the Soviet-Finnish war seemed to provide ample evidence of Soviet weakness. Stalin's purge had weakened the economy, liquidated military leaders, and created a reservoir of discontent that, if handled skillfully by Hitler, would turn against the Kremlin. As the German army broke through the Kremlin's frontier defenses, Ambassador Steinhardt and military attaché Major Ivan D. Yeaton emphasized the imminent prospect of a Soviet defeat. "I anticipate that the Soviet government will shortly leave Moscow," Steinhardt informed Washington on June 26; two days later he predicted that the German army would enter Moscow within sixty days or "much earlier." Yeaton and the War Department were even gloomier than Steinhardt, who expected the Red army to keep fighting as it retreated to the Urals. Secretaries Knox and Stimson felt that Hitler would conquer Russia within one to three months.[9]

Only a few officials expected Moscow to check the Nazi attack. Joseph Davies, who had emphasized the Kremlin's strength during his tenure in Moscow, predicted that the "resistance of the Red Army would amaze and surprise the world." But even Davies felt that Hitler would overcome Moscow and the Ukraine before he was stopped. Roosevelt and Harry Hopkins shared some of Davies' optimism, although they wanted proof of the Red army's endurance before Washington made a major commitment.[10]

Suspicions about the Kremlin's political goals made the State Department very wary. Since 1933, American officials had assumed that the Kremlin's long-range objective was the expansion of Communism. Its activities after 1939, though inspired more by an opportunistic desire to regain former territory than by ideology, seemed to confirm this assumption. When Stalin took possession of the Baltic states and eastern Poland, he installed the apparatus—secret police, puppet regimes, and collectivization—that would consolidate his control. Like the Soviet takeover of Eastern Europe that would occur after the war, Stalin's expansion and use of familiar methods looked like a major step toward world revolution. After June, 1941, the Kremlin continued to press Washington for recognition of its post-1939 expansion. With remarkable sangfroid, the Kremlin demanded acceptance of its control of the Baltic states and talked about postwar territorial and political agreements even as German panzer divisions sliced through the Red army.

On July 2, Ambassador Oumansky resumed his campaign on this issue when he took his old adversary, Loy Henderson, out to dinner at a small restaurant near Washington. After a round of cordial exchanges, Oumansky requested that Washington remove its freeze on Baltic assets, notably ships with a Baltic registry. Henderson replied that recognition of "any Soviet interest in the Baltic ships would necessarily imply recognition of Soviet conquests in Eastern Europe, particularly in the Baltic" and asked Oumansky to take up all political questions through official channels in the future.[11] Shortly after this discussion, Assistant Secretary Adolf A. Berle wrote to J. Edgar Hoover, director of the Federal Bureau of Investigation: "Considerations of expediency have led the Russian policy from one of hostility to the United States to one of friendship." Since Soviet policy might reverse itself "without previous warning," he asked Hoover to continue a close surveillance of Soviet agents. At the end of July, Berle recommended, with the approval of Welles, Henderson, and Secretary Stimson, that Washington not release any military secrets to the Kremlin. "At least for the time being we are not too clear about the Russian policy," Berle concluded.[12]

However, the military and political advantages that America gained from giving aid to the Soviet Union were obvious. The longer the Kremlin occupied Hitler's attention, the more time Washington would have to rearm Great Britain and to build up its own defenses for the eventual showdown with Hitler. In May, Hitler again returned to the idea of acquiring bases in the Atlantic, such as the Azores, and remarked that he hoped for a quick defeat of the Soviet Union as a stepping-stone to the final confrontation with the United States.[13]

The Kremlin's requests for massive assistance—especially for aircraft, antiaircraft guns, gasoline, and lubricants—impressed Washington officials who had initially believed that the Soviet Union would either collapse or make a deal with Hitler. By July, 1941, Ambassador Steinhardt, modifying his original views, could see little Soviet interest in a settlement with Hitler. Although he gave credit to the Red army for holding up the German army, Steinhardt suggested in August that "American and British support will have a very important bearing in strengthening their morale and in shaping Stalin's policy." At the end of August the ambassador commented on the failure of the German blitzkreig as the Red army continued to "give battle on a front of over 1500 miles."[14]

Despite the State Department's insistence in June on strict reciprocity in any new exchanges with Moscow, the department opposed the use of American aid as a bargaining counter in negotiations with Stalin. When London and the Polish government-in-exile indicated an interest in a settlement that would recognize a limited Soviet sphere of influence in Eastern Europe, the department firmly opposed such a step. U.S. officials still expected the Red army to collapse eventually before Hitler's onslaught and could see little advantage in negotiations with Moscow on territorial issues. They preferred to let political questions ride, perhaps hoping that at the end of the war the Stalinist regime, if it still existed, would accept a considerable reduction of its 1941 boundaries.

Roosevelt concurred with the State Department, although his viewpoint was somewhat different. The president agreed with his advisors' prediction that America's bargaining position with Stalin would improve considerably with time. Roosevelt feared that any pressure on Stalin would discourage Soviet resistance to Germany and possibly push the Kremlin into another agreement with Hitler. Roosevelt also worried about the domestic repercussions of a political concession to Stalin's firm demands for his 1941 boundaries. Any recognition of the Kremlin's expansion would result in heavy criticism from Congress and the public. The president may also have remembered that he had not been very successful in the negotiations of 1933 and that he had lost much of his maneuverability as a result of his tactics. He characteristically preferred to postpone political questions until events gave him more leverage with Americans and with Stalin, hoping that the military situation and U.S. aid to the Kremlin would make future alternatives more attractive than present ones.[15]

The strategy of postponement was a realistic response to the unstable military situation of 1941. Even George Kennan did not advocate negotiations to prevent Soviet domination of Eastern Europe. At most, Kennan worried about the suitability of extending moral, political, or ideological support to the Soviet war effort when "Soviet Russia could more soundly be regarded as a 'fellow traveler' in the accepted Moscow sense, rather than as a political associate."[16]

As the Red army slowed the blitzkrieg in the summer of 1941, Roosevelt and his Soviet experts in the State Department should have demanded concessions for Lend-Lease. If the unexpected happened and the Red army not only stopped Hitler but pushed him back, Washington would be committed to assisting this effort without exercising much influence on the eventual objectives of the Red army. However, any Washington interest in negotiations was arrested by Stalin's firm demands for recognition of his 1941 boundaries.

It is true that negotiations in 1941 would have antagonized some Americans, would probably not have budged the Kremlin from its position, and would not have prevented an expansion of Soviet influence and control in Eastern Europe under the impact of the war. Yet an effort to bargain with Stalin might have yielded some protection against Soviet domination of Eastern Europe or at least have provided a useful gauge of Stalin's intentions and the feasibility of Soviet-American cooperation. More concretely, an exchange for Lend-Lease—such as a Soviet promise to withdraw the Red army from Eastern Europe after the war—would have placed relations with Stalin on a basis of reciprocity instead of unilateral American concessions. A more astute, firmer approach to the Kremlin would have impressed Stalin and would have placed political questions in a more appropriate central position.

The Nazi-Soviet conflict also prompted Washington to review the Far Eastern situation. Initially, Sumner Welles asked London to avoid any alliance with Moscow "because of the Japanese angle of the problem." A Soviet-Japanese clash, which Welles and the Division of Far Eastern Affairs expected, seemed to offer short-range benefits to America. In the thirties, many officials had believed that Moscow wanted to precipitate a

Japanese-American conflict in order to deflect Japan's challenge to Soviet territory. Now was Washington's chance to turn the tables. If Tokyo invaded Siberia, the Japanese advance on Indochina and beyond would halt. Washington would gain precious time to bolster its defenses without having to make any concessions to Japan.[17]

This approach, however, contradicted Washington's policy of aid to Moscow against Hitler. If Japan attacked the Soviet Union, the Kremlin's resistance to the German army would clearly suffer, since Stalin would have to stop moving combat-tested troops from the Far East to his western front. The State Department realized that the short-range advantages of a Soviet-Japanese clash were not worth the risk of a German victory. The Division of Far Eastern Affairs also pointed out that this approach would violate America's "fundamental purpose ... to maintain and to preserve peace in the entire Pacific area" and recommended instead that "our interest in defeating the forces of aggression as a whole" required an attempt to immobilize Japan, preventing a Tokyo move against either Siberia or Dutch and British possessions in the South Pacific.[18]

Roosevelt and the State Department followed this strategy, melding the European and Far Eastern strains of their Russian policy. In July, when a Japanese attack against the Soviet Union was rumored to be imminent, Roosevelt sent a direct warning to the Japanese premier, Prince Konoye, asking for assurance that the "reports ... are not based upon fact."[19] In September, Washington rejected any concessions to Japan, partly because officials feared that this might discourage Stalin or encourage a Japanese attack on Siberia. An agreement with Tokyo, Stanley Hornbeck warned, "would give a terrific jolt to the Chinese and the Dutch and the Russians and even the British." Hornbeck also felt that it would increase the chance of Japan "attacking the Soviet Union."[20] This exaggerated the impact of Washington's actions on the Red army's resistance to Germany. The effort to prevent a Tokyo move on Siberia was astute, but Washington should not have permitted it to increase the likelihood of Japanese-American conflict.

The strategic benefits of continuing Soviet resistance to Hitler not only guided the course of Washington's aid to Stalin but also presented Roosevelt with a persuasive argument by which to mobilize public approval for Lend-Lease to Moscow. Surveys taken by the American Institute of Public Opinion indicated that American opinion was extremely volatile, full of emotional hostility against Stalin but also fearful of Hitler and open to persuasion. Although 54 percent opposed military aid to Moscow compared to 34 percent in favor, 72 percent hoped for a Russian victory over Hitler.[21]

Roosevelt skillfully exploited American fears about Hitler. He and other officials played up the value of Soviet opposition to Germany. In July and August, Postmaster-General Frank C. Walker and Associate Justice Frank Murphy publicly deplored the "over-shadowing menace" of Hitler. By August Washington's rhetoric and the Red army's continuing resistance had shifted the general public's views somewhat. In an August poll, 70 percent favored the sale of war supplies to Stalin; in September, 49 percent approved credits, although 44 percent were still opposed. Even some of the groups that had objected to Roosevelt's Russian policy since 1933 reduced their criticism. On August 8 William Green, president of the American Federation of Labor, came out for aid to Moscow; the American Legion also defeated a resolution opposing Lend-Lease to Stalin. *America* and *Commonweal* reluctantly accepted aid to the Kremlin, but the *National Republic* continued its opposition.[22]

Editorial support of aid to the Kremlin also increased. The most pronounced change appeared in endorsements by leading conservative Republican newspapers, notably the *San Francisco Chronicle,* the *New York Herald Tribune,* and the *Hartford Courant.* Assailing senators who still opposed aid to Moscow, the *Chronicle* chided, "We should stop snapping at the tail of the Red Bear and instead help grab the Nazi monster by the throat."[23] Roosevelt also picked up stronger support from independent and Democratic papers like the *Cleveland Plain Dealer,* which argued that "every tank, every plane, every shell that can possibly be spared must be shipped" to the Red army.[24]

As public support increased, Roosevelt outmaneuvered congressional critics. Whenever the press questioned him about possible Lend-Lease aid, Roosevelt evaded their questions. Late in June isolationists tried to force the issue by asking the House of Representatives to rule out any future Lend-Lease to Moscow. Instead of taking up the challenge, Roosevelt guided these proposals to a quiet demise in committee rooms. Since aid to the Soviet Union progressed very slowly because of a severe shortage of supplies as well as other problems, the president could postpone facing the issue. He did order the State Department and other officials to promise more assistance to Moscow, using various financial subterfuges like deferred gold transfers to cover the expense. At the same time, Roosevelt enlisted Harry Hopkins and Averell Harriman, head of Lend-Lease operations in London, to convey to Stalin his determination to support the Soviet Union, during their trips to Moscow in July and August.[25]

By October Roosevelt could not postpone much longer a decision about Lend-Lease. However, he had one more maneuver up his sleeve. During September and October, Congress debated a second appropriation bill for the Lend-Lease program. Instead of introducing the Soviet issue into the debate, Roosevelt waited, ready to exploit any weakness shown by his critics. On September 24, Hamilton Fish and other Russophobes in the House of Representatives introduced an amendment excluding the Soviet Union from Lend-Lease. Spokesmen for the administration, emphasizing the importance of the Russian front, asked that the president be left free to pursue various options. The House Appropriations Committee not only opposed the amendment but expressed approval of Lend-Lease for Moscow. The House rejected the exclusion amendment by a vote of 162 to 21. Roosevelt's opponents in the Senate, recognizing their defeat, did not even attempt a similar amendment.[26]

On November 7, only ten days before the eighth anniversary of recognition, President Roosevelt extended Lend-Lease assistance to the Soviet Union. The reaction of the press indicated the extent of the President's triumph. By delaying a decision on Lend-Lease until events and the administration's efforts had shifted domestic opinion, Roosevelt turned a controversial, potentially explosive issue into a consensus question that attracted little editorial criticism. A few journals, such as the *Chicago Tribune* and Hearst's *Los Angeles Examiner,* still opposed Roosevelt. But most papers, regardless of party loyalties and political outlook, approved his decision. Lend-Lease to Stalin "adds up in common sense and practical defensive strategy," concluded the *Charlotte Observer.*[27]

Approval of Lend-Lease as a necessary expedient did not change the continuing hostility of Americans toward Stalin and his system, despite some admiration for the Red army's resistance to Hitler. Religious leaders and the press, for example, rejected Roosevelt's effort to spruce up the Kremlin's image in the fall of 1941. The president asked Ambassador Oumansky and Stalin to make some statements about freedom of religion in the Soviet Union. When the press questioned him about the Soviet constitution's plank on religion, Roosevelt lamely replied: "Well, I haven't learned it by heart sufficiently to quote—I might be off a little bit, but anyway: Freedom of conscience ... and freedom of religion." Even interventionist spokesmen blasted this feeble whitewash attempt.[28] "There is no call to press [Stalin's] pants, put bear grease on his hair and invite him into the parlor," complained the *Omaha Morning World-Herald,* for "he's a hard man to get rid of, once he's over the threshold."[29]

Roosevelt's decision to extend Lend-Lease to Stalin marked an extension of his Russian policy since 1939, rather than departure from it. The wartime alliance between Washington and Moscow which followed Japan's attack upon Pearl Harbor on December 7, 1941, also resulted from the basic assumptions of 1939 about the primacy of the Nazi threat and the benefits of Soviet opposition. In fact, since 1933 the president, if not the State Department, had looked toward the Soviet Union as a source of cooperation in the event of trouble in Europe and the Far East.

As America entered the war in December, Roosevelt did not have the time nor even perhaps the desire to review the largely unsuccessful Russian policy he had pursued since 1933. Had he done so, he would have been forced to recognize that few of the hopes of 1933 had been fulfilled. For example, the president, as well as many exporters, had hoped that recognition would pave the way for an extremely beneficial export trade with the Soviet Union. But the Russian market, which the interested exporters had described as almost limitless, remained very small. The Kremlin strove for self-sufficiency, though it continued to purchase American machinery—almost $80 million worth in 1938, the last year of normal trading. However, this represented only a very small part of America's total exports of slightly over $3 billion for that year. Western European countries and Canada remained America's best markets, not the Soviet Union.

Roosevelt's attempts to cooperate with the Soviet Union on diplomatic issues had also been dashed by 1941. The president's initial tactics contributed to his failure. By surrounding recognition with specific agreements in order to satisfy the State Department and domestic pressure groups, Roosevelt reduced his flexibility in dealing with Moscow. When the debt negotiations failed and the Kremlin overtly violated its agreement on noninterference in American affairs, the president lost maneuverability over even more important issues, such as Japanese expansion.

Until June, 1940, the president had faced stubborn resistance from the State Department and the Moscow embassy whenever he advanced a proposal for cooperation with Moscow. Without directly opposing Roosevelt on issues like recognition or cooperation in 1938–39, most officials strongly questioned Moscow's reliability and raised a variety of bureaucratic and political obstacles. Like many others, Secretary Cordell Hull was very wary of the Soviet Union. Repeatedly deferring to congressional isolationists, and often concealing his personal objections behind theirs, Hull consistently discouraged Roosevelt's attempts in 1937–38 to cooperate with Moscow and London against Japan and Germany. On the other hand, Hull did oppose a formal break with Moscow over the Russo-Finnish war, and he supported Under Secretary Sumner Welles' negotiations with Ambassador Oumansky after June, 1940. The under secretary fluctuated more than Hull did with respect to relations with Moscow. In 1937, Welles backed Roosevelt's efforts to cooperate with Moscow in the Far East, yet he vigorously pushed for a return to non-recognition after the Soviet attack upon Finland. He shifted his position again in July, 1940, when he initiated negotiations with Oumansky.

A shuffling of personnel in the top echelon of the State Department probably would not have much reduced this distrust of the Kremlin. The reorganization of the State Department in 1937, for example, did not substantially change the department's outlook on the Kremlin, despite the removal of Robert Kelley. Most ambassadors and career officers felt that the Soviet Union, despite its defensive tactics in its diplomacy, "never departed from the ultimate aim to enlarge ... [its] domain and to include under the Soviet system additional peoples and territories."[30] Only a few—like George S. Messersmith, who recognized the magnitude of Germany's and Japan's threat to American interests and values—consistently supported Roosevelt's attempts to work with the Kremlin. Even if Roosevelt had placed more of these officials in the top echelon, as he did with Messersmith in 1937, they could hardly have erased the suspicions directed at the Soviet Union.

These suspicions were advanced most persistently by the State Department's Russian specialists, who included some of Washington's most perceptive and conscientious career officers. Although they could not openly oppose the president, Robert Kelley, Loy Henderson, George Kennan, and Charles Bohlen provided very little encouragement for his Russian policy, from recognition through the decision to extend Lend-Lease. Though they tried to be objective, the Soviet specialists were convinced that Stalin's rhetoric about cooperation with the Western democracies against Hitler and Japan concealed an enduring interest in the expansion of Communism as well as a somewhat favorable attitude toward a European war and an American-Japanese clash. Their close observation of Stalin's domestic policies, most notably the Moscow trials and the general purge, intensified their belief that friendly relations with Stalin were impossible.

Roosevelt's appointments to the Moscow embassy, which reflected his varying intentions in 1933, 1936, and 1939, did not surmount the State Department's opposition to cooperation. William Bullitt, for example, despite his initial sympathy for Soviet foreign policy, became increasingly hostile—largely because of personal disappointment rather than a shift in Soviet policy. In 1936, the president sought a more optimistic approach to Moscow and appointed Joseph Davies, who strived for cooperation without much success. When Roosevelt began to avoid the Kremlin in 1939, he sent Laurence Steinhardt to Moscow with no more ambitious purpose than to keep communications open. Steinhardt fitted Washington's needs very well until Roosevelt, Hull, and Welles began trying to use minor concessions to keep Stalin away from Japan and to encourage a Soviet break with Hitler. Steinhardt opposed this activity, and his accurate reports about Stalin's immediate aims checked any illusions in Washington about Soviet policy.

After recognition, the temper of American opinion almost precluded any breakthrough for Roosevelt's Russian policy. By 1935 American isolationism had forced the president to move very slowly in dealing with the Kremlin as well as with Great Britain. The unfavorable reaction of the press and organized groups to the unsuccessful debt negotiations and Moscow's violation of its agreement about propaganda reinforced this trend. American commentators did respond favorably to Stalin's diplomacy, emphasizing Moscow's defensive stance and the erosion of Soviet interest in world revolution. However, Stalin's trials and purge gradually undermined the press's favorable assessment of Soviet diplomacy. Starting in 1935, American observers, led by conservative spokesmen, began to emphasize the similarities between Nazism and Stalinism. At first Soviet foreign policy remained a positive contrast, but under the impact of Stalin's expansion, this distinction disappeared. Emotional condemnations of Hitler and Stalin and their seemingly identical systems featured the popular phrase "red Fascism and brown Bolshevism." There was a return to editorial emphasis on Stalin's desire to spread Communism upon an exhausted Europe after first subjugating Eastern Europe.

The changes in American attitudes had both immediate and long-range impact on relations with the Soviet Union. In the short run, Stalin's increasingly unfavorable image intensified the estrangement in official relations after 1935. Although American hostility toward the Kremlin was diminished and somewhat submerged by the wartime alliance, it revived after the defeat of Germany, in response to Stalin's hegemony in Eastern Europe. After having helped to defeat Hitler and Nazism, Americans angrily watched Stalin and Communism replace them. It was easy to misconstrue Stalin's postwar expansion as a threat identical to Nazism.

Roosevelt paid close attention to the shifts in American opinion. To develop support for his major demarches, for recognition, and for Lend-

Lease, he used similar tactics: waiting for the course of events and his own manipulative devices to prepare the ground for public approval before he committed himself publicly to a new policy. By arranging for officials and private groups to push recognition and Lend-Lease for over six months while the White House floated occasional trial balloons, he made both decisions seem inevitable before he announced them. The president also suppressed antagonistic groups several times in the years after 1933. He silenced the American Federation of Labor and Catholic spokesmen before recognition, rejected their demands for a break in relations in 1935, and subdued critics during the Russo-Finnish war by tossing the question of aid to Finland into Congress's lap.

Roosevelt's greatest skill as a diplomat was his ability to lead American opinion without challenging it too much. But isolationism and opposition to cooperation with Stalin's totalitarian regime were insurmountable obstacles even for him. When he wanted to initiate cooperation with Stalin in 1937–38, he was doomed to limited, secret discussions on the Far East, from which he eventually retreated despite Stalin's approval. He also kept away from the Kremlin when elections approached in 1936, 1938, and 1940.

Roosevelt approached the Soviet Union in 1941 with a certain amount of wariness, though less than that of the State Department and many public spokesmen. He publicly stated that the Kremlin ruled Russia through a "dictatorship, as absolute as any other dictatorship in the world."[31] Yet he never fully understood the nature of Stalin's regime nor the implications regarding postwar cooperation with Stalin and a Soviet sphere of influence in Eastern Europe. Understandably, the president could not read all of the reports on Soviet domestic developments submitted by the Moscow embassy. Nevertheless, as the Soviet Union became more important in Washington's general diplomacy, he should have given more attention to his Soviet specialists and their assessments of Stalin and the Soviet system. Roosevelt unduly minimized the role of ideology in Soviet policy and too quickly brushed aside fears about Soviet designs on Eastern Europe. Unlike many officials, he felt that Stalin's dictatorship, though interested in territorial annexations, had abandoned the goal of spreading Communism, and he preferred to focus on Moscow's current aims and means.[32] "I do not think we need to worry about any possibility of Russian domination," he confided to a staunch critic of the Kremlin.

Like many advocates of recognition, Roosevelt never completely discarded his hopes about relations with Moscow. Specifically, he had hoped recognition would help to disarm mutual suspicions and would contribute to world peace. By 1941 events had undermined these expectations. However, he could not justify aid to the Soviet Union or opposition to Hitler and Japan as only a realistic expedient; instead, he returned to his earlier hope that by working together against Hitler, Washington, Moscow, and London would improve the future for all nations.

Moscow also lost many of the advantages it had hoped to gain from recognition, partly because of its own policies. Stalin had wanted to obtain long-term credits in order to facilitate purchases of American products. But his perfunctory attitude toward a debt settlement and his refusal to exclude America from the Comintern's propaganda activities ensured that Washington would not grant credits. More important, the Kremlin had encouraged Washington in 1933–34 and again in 1937–38 to cooperate against Hitler and Japan. Although American isolationism made this an unlikely prospect, the impact of Stalin's domestic tyranny on the United States—officials, news media, and public alike—rendered it virtually impossible. In addition, Stalin did not burn all of his bridges to Hitler, though until 1939 he made fewer overtures than either London or Paris. The Nazi-Soviet Nonaggression Pact and Soviet expansion in 1939–40 indicated that the Kremlin's territorial goals—though not limitless, as some critics suggested—would be pursued regardless of unfavorable repercussions on Soviet-American relations.

The first eight years of American relations with the Soviet Union did provide a few permanent benefits. The experiences of this period proved that diplomatic relations neither markedly increased foreign subversion, as many opponents of recognition had feared, nor induced Americans to accept the ideals of the Soviet Union, as some advocates had hoped. Washington gained a valuable observation post in the Soviet Union that not only provided reports about Soviet domestic developments but also contributed to the training of Soviet specialists like George Kennan and Charles Bohlen. When Roosevelt maneuvered to win public approval for Lend-Lease to the Soviet Union, recognition of Moscow was an accomplished fact. Instead of having to win two tricky battles—perhaps an impossible task, considering the nature of domestic opinion—Roosevelt was able to send some aid to Moscow, negotiate with the Kremlin, and muster public support.

President Roosevelt demonstrated a number of strengths as a diplomat in his direction of American-Soviet relations. Not only was he a superb leader of American opinion, but he also grasped—ahead of the State Department and his Soviet specialists—the importance of trying to cooperate with Stalin against Japan and Germany. However, the president did not grow very much in eight years, particularly in his weakest areas: negotiating with and understanding the Soviet Union. Instead of profiting from the advice of the Soviet specialists, who advocated a strategy of firmness with quid pro quo tactics, Roosevelt favored a compromise approach and avoided difficult negotiations. When he encountered resistance from Litvinov on the debt issue, he soon retreated, settling for a sloppy and somewhat misleading agreement which hindered relations following recognition. Faced with Soviet firmness on territorial issues in 1941, he again backed away. Moreover, the Soviet commissar was not impressed with Roosevelt's concern over the domestic political importance of a settlement in 1933 and his willingness to concede points to the commissar. Litvinov's recommendation, which the Kremlin never forgot, was to negotiate if possible with Roosevelt rather than with his subordinates.

Roosevelt's failure to work with his Soviet specialists was unfortunate, for they would have complemented each other very well. With his unmatched understanding of Soviet tactics and diplomatic agreements, Robert Kelley could have helped the president to negotiate a better settlement in 1933. Loy Henderson and George Kennan could have immensely enriched Roosevelt's understanding of Stalin and the Soviet system. Ambassador Steinhardt and the Moscow embassy staff made a cogent argument for firmness toward Stalin from 1939 to 1941 which might have encouraged Roosevelt to take a stronger line on the Soviet-Finnish war and Stalin's cooperation with Hitler. Finally, the Soviet specialists would have changed Roosevelt's image as a somewhat weak and vacillating compromiser, an image which Stalin exploited.

The State Department and the Russian specialists would also have profited much from Roosevelt's strengths. In spite of the doubts and institutional rigidity of his diplomats, the president recognized the advantages of recognition in 1933 and scrapped their ineffective policy. Their opposition to cooperation with the Kremlin might also have been reduced somewhat by his superior understanding of German and Japanese expansion.

Unfortunately, America's entry into the war did not improve communication between the president and his most astute Soviet specialists. As Roosevelt assumed control not only of general strategy toward the Soviet Union but also of negotiations at the major conferences with Stalin, his strengths and weaknesses as a diplomat remained the same. He recognized the importance of cooperation with Stalin and successfully guided

American opinion toward this end. But the gulf between Roosevelt and the embassy specialists widened over the president's exaggerated hopes for postwar cooperation and his lack of firmness in dealing with Stalin. The cold war was to be a part of the legacy of this failure by Roosevelt and his advisors to coordinate their views.

The first eight years of America's formal relations with the Soviet Union did not dissolve the hostilities and suspicions of the past. Ironically, recognition brought only a brief interlude of friendly relations, and officials on both sides soon returned to traditional suspicions and bitter disagreements. Estrangement pervaded official relations, and the reactions of American observers to Soviet policies intensified this estrangement. When another effort to cooperate with Moscow became expedient, beginning in 1940, Americans should have remembered the limits to cooperation with the Soviet Union.

Appendix

TABLE 1

Magazines Surveyed[a]

	Political Persuasion	1934 Circulation[b]	1941 Circulation[b]
America	C	NA	NA
American Mercury	C	33,316	50,494
Atlantic Monthly	M	99,439	105,925
Business Week	C	70,688	113,272
Catholic World	C	NA	NA
Christian Century	L	28,643 (1936)	29,177
Common Sense	L	NA	NA
The Commonweal	M	19,638	15,000
Foreign Affairs	M	10,000	15,515
Foreign Policy Association Bulletin	M	NA	NA
Fortune	C	75,597	155,623
Harper's Magazine	M	100,105	107,770
Life	M	78,727	2,860,484
Literary Digest	M	978,178	NA
Nation	L	36,092	37,005
National Republic	C	50,000	30,000
New Republic	L	25,000	31,120
Newsweek	M	47,767 (1935)	407,837
Reader's Digest	C	NA	NA
Saturday Evening Post	C	2,776,502	3,231,496
Soviet Russia Today	L	NA	NA
Time	M	428,950	777,688
U.S. News	C	34,500 (1935)	111,312

NA = Not available
L = Liberal
M = Moderate
C = Conservative

a. This list includes the leading news and opinion magazines, although several important ones such as *Collier's* were not available. Since over half of them did not have editorials, they were not included in tables in this volume. Those magazines without editorials were primarily useful for their feature articles or regular columnists.
b. Source: N. W. Ayer and Sons, *Directory of Newspapers and Periodicals* (Philadelphia, 1934, 1941).

TABLE 2

Newspapers Surveyed[a]

Newspaper	Announced Affiliation	1934 Circulation[b]	1941 Circulation[b]
Atlanta Constitution	Democrat	84,783	122,021
Baltimore Sun	Ind. Democrat	137,749	147,231
Boston Evening Transcript	Ind. Republican	34,996	18,452
Charlotte Observer	Independent	46,538	83,413
Chicago Daily News	Independent	399,795	461,701
Chicago Tribune	Ind. Republican	771,190	1,076,866
Christian Science Monitor	Non-Partisan	112,454	119,791
Cincinnati Enquirer	Democrat	81,364	122,672
Cleveland Plain Dealer	Ind. Democrat	182,748	227,657
Courier-Journal (Louisville)	Independent	97,719	116,399
Dallas Morning News	Ind. Democrat	77,344	102,522
Denver Post	Independent	137,744	156,800
Des Moines Register	Ind. Republican	118,310	169,725
Detroit News	Independent	249,770	340,022
Hartford Courant	Republican	36,307	43,062
Kansas City Star	Independent	293,936	311,985
Los Angeles Examiner	Independent	192,058	220,195
Los Angeles Times	Ind. Republican	177,903	215,137
Miami Herald	Ind. Democrat	37,650	72,490
Minneapolis Tribune	Republican	61,654	77,419
New York Herald Tribune	Ind. Republican	317,697	356,512
New York Times	Ind. Democrat	456,966	477,385
New York World-Telegram	Independent	395,689	434,603
Omaha Morning World-Herald	Independent	55,863	92,974
Philadelphia Inquirer	Independent	210,795	415,630
Pittsburgh Post-Gazette	Ind. Republican	173,060	235,839
Portland Oregonian	Ind. Republican	92,485	135,517
Richmond Times-Dispatch	Ind. Democrat	62,810	85,192
St. Louis Post-Dispatch	Ind. Democrat	222,123	240,533
San Francisco Chronicle	Republican	96,031	122,191
Seattle Post-Intelligencer	Independent	86,853	102,806
Seattle Times	Independent	89,750	103,434
Times-Picayune (New Orleans)	Ind. Democrat	94,401	123,799
Wall Street Journal	Independent	28,537	27,801
Washington Post	Independent	54,476	132,089

a. These newspapers were selected on the basis of geographical location, political outlook, and circulation figures. They represent a fairly accurate reflection of editorial opinion in the leading American papers. Research design was based on coverage of sigificant events and time periods.

b. N. W. Ayer and Sons, *Directory of Newspapers and Periodicals* (Philadelphia, 1934, 1941).

TABLE 3

Newspaper Classifications

Newspaper	Views on the Soviet Union[a]	Foreign Affairs Orientation[b]
Atlanta Constitution	Conservative	Moderate
Baltimore Sun	Moderate	Strong
Boston Evening Transcript	Conservative	Moderate
Charlotte Observer	Conservative	Little
Chicago Daily News	Moderate	Moderate
Chicago Tribune	Conservative	Moderate
Christian Science Monitor	Conservative	Strong
Cincinnati Enquirer	Moderate	Strong
Cleveland Plain Dealer	Conservative	Moderate
Courier-Journal (Louisville)	Moderate	Strong
Dallas Morning News	Moderate	Little
Denver Post	Conservative	Little
Des Moines Register	Moderate	Little
Detroit News	Conservative	Moderate
Hartford Courant	Moderate	Strong
Kansas City Star	Moderate	Little
Los Angeles Examiner	Conservative	Little
Los Angeles Times	Conservative	Moderate
Miami Herald	Conservative	Little
Minneapolis Tribune	Conservative	Little
New York Herald Tribune	Conservative	Strong
New York Times	Moderate	Strong
New York World-Telegram	Conservative	Little
Omaha Morning World-Herald	Moderate	Little
Philadelphia Inquirer	Conservative	Strong
Pittsburgh Post-Gazette	Conservative	Little
Portland Oregonian	Moderate	Moderate
Richmond Times-Dispatch	Moderate	Moderate
St. Louis Post-Dispatch	Moderate	Moderate
San Francisco Chronicle	Conservative	Moderate
Seattle Post-Intelligencer	Conservative	Little
Seattle Times	Conservative	Little
Times-Picayune (New Orleans)	Moderate	Little
Wall Street Journal	Conservative	Little
Washington Post	Moderate	Strong
Totals	Conservative 20 Moderate 15	Strong 9 Moderate 11 Little 15

a. This classification has more significance than the political affiliations or the general views of the newspapers on foreign affairs. The distinctions are based on each newspaper's views on the Soviet system, Stalin's diplomacy, and American Communism. None of the editors expressed views that could be classified as liberal, like the opinions of the *Nation* or *New Republic*.

b. This classification ranks the newspapers according to the degree of their interest in foreign affairs as indicated in the amount of coverage by their news stories, editorials, and featured columnists.

TABLE 4

Assessments of Soviet Foreign Policy Objectives
in 1933, 1934–35, and 1936–39

Newspaper	1933	1934–35	1936–39
Atlanta Constitution	SP	E	E
Baltimore Sun	SP	SP	SP
Boston Evening Transcript	E	E	E
Charlotte Observer	NC	E	E
Chicago Daily News	SP	SP	SP
Chicago Tribune	E	E	E
Christian Science Monitor	SP	SP	SP
Cincinnati Enquirer	SP	S	S
Cleveland Plain Dealer	SP	SP	SP
Courier-Journal (Louisville)	S	S	S
Dallas Morning News	SP	SP	SP
Denver Post	NC	E	E
Des Moines Register	NC	S	S
Detroit News	NC	SP	SP
Hartford Courant	S	S	S
Kansas City Star	S	S	S
Los Angeles Examiner	NC	E	E
Los Angeles Times	NC	E	E
Miami Herald	SP	E	E
Minneapolis Tribune	SP	SP	SP
New York Herald Tribune	SP	SP	SP
New York Times	SP	S	S
New York World-Telegram	NC	NC	E
Omaha Morning World-Herald	S	S	S
Philadelphia Inquirer	S	SP	SP
Pittsburgh Post-Gazette	NC	SP	E
Portland Oregonian	S	S	S
Richmond Times-Dispatch	NC	SP	SP
St. Louis Post-Dispatch	S	S	S
San Francisco Chronicle	NC	SP	SP
Seattle Post-Intelligencer	S	E	E
Seattle Times	E	E	E
Times-Picayune (New Orleans)	NC	SP	SP
Wall Street Journal	S	NC	SP
Washington Post	S	SP	SP
Totals			
S = Security	10	9	9
SP = Security primary, propaganda secondary	11	14	14
E = Expansion of Communism	3	10	12
NC = No comment	11	2	0

TABLE 5

Assessments of Soviet Foreign Policy Objectives
for Three Political Issues and in 1940−41

Newspaper	Nazi-Soviet Nonaggression Pact	Poland and Baltic states	Finland	1940−41
Atlanta Constitution	S	ET	EC	EC
Baltimore Sun	S	ET	ET	S
Boston Evening Transcript	EC	ET	EC	EC
Charlotte Observer	S	ET	EC	EC
Chicago Daily News	S	ET	ET	S
Chicago Tribune	EC	EC	EC	EC
Christian Science Monitor	S	ET	ET	S
Cincinnati Enquirer	S	ET	ET	S
Cleveland Plain Dealer	S	ET	ET	ET
Courier-Journal (Louisville)	NC	ET	ET	S
Dallas Morning News	S	ET	EC	S
Denver Post	S	ET	ET	S
Des Moines Register	S	NC	ET	S
Detroit News	S	EC	EC	S
Hartford Courant	S	ET	ET	ET
Kansas City Star	ET	ET	ET	EC
Los Angeles Examiner	NC	ET	ET	EC
Los Angeles Times	S	ET	ET	NC
Miami Herald	NC	EC	NC	NC
Minneapolis Tribune	S	ET	NC	NC
New York Herald Tribune	ET	ET	NC	S
New York Times	EC	ET	ET	S
New York World-Telegram	NC	NC	NC	EC
Omaha Morning World Telegram	ET	EC	EC	NC
Philadelphia Inquirer	NC	EC	EC	EC
Pittsburgh Post-Gazette	NC	EC	EC	S
Portland Oregonian	S	ET	ET	S
Richmond Times-Dispatch	S	S	ET	S
St. Louis Post-Dispatch	NC	ET	ET	S
San Francisco Chronicle	NC	EC	EC	NC
Seattle Post-Intelligencer	EC	EC	EC	EC
Seattle Times	S	ET	NC	EC
Times-Picayune (New Orleans)	S	S	ET	ET
Wall Street Journal	S	NC	NC	EC
Washington Post	S	ET	EC	S
Totals				
S = Security	20	2	0	16
EC = Expansion of Communism	4	8	12	11
ET = Expansion for territory	3	22	17	3
NC = No comment	8	3	6	5

TABLE 6

Assessments of Soviet Foreign Policy Objectives by Conservative and Moderate Newspapers

Assessment	1933	1934–35	1936–39	Nazi-Soviet Nonaggression Pact	Poland and Baltic states	Finland	1940–41
Conservatives (20 newspapers)							
Security	3	0	0	9	0	0	4
Security and propaganda	6	8	7	0	0	0	0
Expansion of Communism	3	10	13	4	7	11	10
Expansion for territory	0	0	0	1	11	4	1
No comment	8	2	0	6	2	5	5
Moderates (15 newspapers)							
Security	7	9	9	11	2	0	12
Security and propaganda	5	6	6	1	0	0	0
Expansion of Communism	0	0	0	2	1	3	1
Expansion for territory	0	0	0	1	11	12	2
No comment	3	0	0	0	1	0	0

TABLE 7

Assessments of Soviet Foreign Policy Objectives, by Degree of Interest in Foreign Affairs

Assessment	1933	1934–35	1936–39	Nazi-Soviet Nonaggression Pact	Poland and Baltic states	Finland	1940–41
Strong interest (9 newspapers)							
Security	4	4	4	5	0	0	8
Security and propaganda	5	5	5	0	0	0	0
Expansion of Communism	0	0	0	1	1	2	1
Expansion for territory	0	0	0	1	8	5	0
No comment	0	0	0	2	0	2	0
Moderate interest (11 newspapers)							
Security	2	2	2	7	1	0	5
Security and propaganda	3	5	5	0	0	0	0
Expansion of Communism	2	4	4	2	3	5	3
Expansion for territory	0	0	0	0	7	6	1
No comment	4	0	0	2	0	0	2
Little interest (15 newspapers)							
Security	4	3	3	8	1	0	3
Security and propaganda	3	4	4	0	0	0	0
Expansion of Communism	1	6	8	1	3	5	7
Expansion for territory	0	0	0	3	8	5	2
No comment	7	2	0	3	3	5	3

TABLE 8

Comparisons of Nazism and Stalinism

Newspaper	Kirov Affair (1934)	Stalin's Purge (1936–39)	Nazi-Soviet Nonaggression Pact (1939)	Soviet Expansion (1939–40)
Atlanta Constitution	DD	NC	SS	SM
Baltimore Sun	SM	SM	NC	SM
Boston Evening Transcript	DD	SM	NC	SS
Charlotte Observer	NC	SS	SS	SM
Chicago Daily News	NC	SM	NC	SM
Chicago Tribune	SS	SS	SS	SS
Christian Science Monitor	NC	SM	SS	SS
Cincinnati Enquirer	DD	NC	SS	SM
Cleveland Plain Dealer	DD	SM	SS	SM
Courier-Journal (Louisville)	NC	SM	SS	SM
Dallas Morning News	NC	SS	SS	SS
Denver Post	DD	SM	SS	SS
Des Moines Register	DD	SM	NC	SM
Detroit News	NC	NC	SS	NC
Hartford Courant	SM	NC	SS	SM
Kansas City Star	SM	SS	NC	SS
Los Angeles Examiner	NC	NC	NC	NC
Los Angeles Times	NC	NC	SS	NC
Miami Herald	DD	SS	NC	SM
Minneapolis Tribune	DD	SS	NC	SM
New York Herald Tribune	SM	SS	SS	SM
New York Times	SM	SM	SS	SS
New York World-Telegram	NC	SM	NC	SM
Omaha Morning World-Herald	SS	SS	SS	SM
Philadelphia Inquirer	SM	SS	SS	SM
Pittsburgh Post-Gazette	DD	SS	SS	SM
Portland Oregonian	DD	SS	SS	SS
Richmond Times-Dispatch	SM	NC	SS	SM
St. Louis Post-Dispatch	SM	SS	SS	SS
San Francisco Chronicle	NC	SM	SS	SS
Seattle Post-Intelligencer	NC	NC	SS	SM
Seattle Times	DD	SM	NC	SM
Times-Picayune (New Orleans)	NC	SS	SS	SM
Wall Street Journal	NC	NC	SS	NC
Washington Post	DD	SS	SS	SM
Totals				
DD = Dictatorship discussed (but no definite opinion)	12	0	0	0
SM = Similar methods (opinion expressed)	8	12	0	21
SS = Similar systems (opinion expressed)	2	14	25	10
NC = No comment	13	9	10	4

Notes

1. See Robert P. Browder, *The Origins of Soviet-American Diplomacy*, 3–24. The total Soviet debt of approximately $631 million included the financial obligations of the Tsarist regime, Washington's loan of $188 million to the provisional government of Russia, and the confiscated property, assets, and bank deposits of Americans.

2. See John Lewis Gaddis, *Russia, the Soviet Union, and the United States: An Interpretive History*, 57–85, for an excellent introduction. For conflicting assessments of the American intervention, see William A. Williams, *American-Russian Relations, 1781–1947*, 105–32; George F. Kennan, *Soviet-American Relations*; N. Gordon Levin, *Woodrow Wilson and World Politics: America's Response to War and Revolution*.

3. For Soviet-American relations in the twenties, see Gaddis, *Soviet Union*, 87–117; Peter G. Filene, *Americans and the Soviet Experiment, 1917–1933*, 65–155; Edward M. Bennett, *Recognition of Russia: An American Foreign Policy Dilemma*, 47–86.

4. See Floyd J. Fithian, "Soviet-American Economic Relations, 1918–1933: American Business in Russia During the Period of Nonrecognition," 184–389; Joan H. Wilson, *Ideology and Economics: U.S. Relations with the Soviet Union, 1918–1933*, 91–102.

5. Browder, *Soviet-American Diplomacy*, 29–38, 42–48; Wilson, *Ideology and Economics*, 104–9.

6. Gaddis, *Soviet Union*, 114–15; Joan H. Wilson, "American Business and the Recognition of the Soviet Union," 355–59.

7. Wilson, "American Business," 358; *Business Week*, April 19, 1933, 25; S. R. Bertron to Daniel Roper, July 13, 1933, File 448, Russia—Trade with U.S., Department of Commerce MSS, National Archives. Roper was secretary of commerce. See also Bertron to Louis Howe, September 12, 1933, President's Personal File 907, Roosevelt Papers,

Franklin D. Roosevelt Library (hereafter cited as P.P.F.). Howe was a devoted aide to Roosevelt.

8. See Wilson, "American Business," 359–60; American Foundation memorandum, Box 182, Poole Papers, State Historical Society of Wisconsin (hereafter cited as A.F.M.); Spencer Williams to Alexander Gumberg, May 15, Gumberg to Williams, November 8, 1933, Box 10B, 23, Gumberg Papers, State Historical Society of Wisconsin. Williams was the Chamber's representative in Moscow. The American Foundation was an independent organization that supported various public policies.

9. See New York Times, March 25 and 27, 1933; Frederick L. Schuman to Samuel Harper, February 4 and March 9, 1933, Letters 1933, Harper Papers, University of Chicago Library.

10. Cleveland Plain Dealer, October 22, 1933; Richmond Times-Dispatch, October 21, 1933; Atlanta Constitution, October 22, 1933; San Francisco Chronicle, October 21, 1933; Washington Post, October 20, 1933. See also Literary Digest, March 18, 1933, 8, and July 15, 1933, 8; Meno Lovenstein, American Opinion of Soviet Russia, 139–46.

11. See Filene, Soviet Experiment, 187–259; Soviet Russia Today 1, no. 12 (1933):14, no. 4 (1933):13, and no. 10 (1933):6; Frank A. Warren, III, Liberals and Communism: The "Red Decade" Revisited, 6–33, 63–88; R. Alan Lawson, The Failure of Independent Liberalism, 1930–1941, 72–73, 78–79. Soviet Russia Today was published by the Friends of the Soviet Union.

12. Davis to Robins, March 29, April 1 and 5, and August 9, 1933, Box 25, Robins Papers, State Historical Society of Wisconsin; Davis to Louis Howe, March 23, 1933, Official File 220 A, Russia Misc., Roosevelt Papers (hereafter cited as O.F.); Robins to Salmon O. Levinson, March 17, 1933, Robins to William Borah, August 8, 1933, Robins to Jane Addams, August 26, 1933, Box 25, Robins Papers; Robins to Gumberg, July 14, 16, and 17, 1933, Robins to Margaret Dreier Robins, May 4, 1933, Gumberg to Philip F. LaFollette, July 17, 1933, Box 10B, Gumberg Papers. See also William A. Williams, "Raymond Robins and Russian-American Relations, 1917–1938," 218–22.

13. National Republic 20, no. 11 (1933):26. See also America, April 22, 1933, 50–51; Congressional Record, 73rd Cong., 1st sess., May 18, 1933, 3682–83, for the Philadelphia Board of Trade. See also James Brown to Roosevelt, July 11, 1933, O.F. 220 A, Russia Misc., Roosevelt Papers. Brown directed the New York Chamber of Commerce.

14. National Republic, 21, no. 3 (1933):23; Fish address, February 25, 1933, and Walsh address, April 18, 1933, Congressional Record, 72nd Cong., 2nd sess., March 1, 1933, 5395, and 73rd Cong., 1st sess., April 21, 1933, 2100–2101. See also New York Times, January 30, February 21, 22, and 26, 1933; Ralph Easley's letters to Cordell Hull, Department of State File 811.00B/1467-1506, Department of State MSS, National Archives (hereafter cited as D.S.F.). Easley directed the National Civic Federation, a united front organization for anticommunist groups. See also Chicago Tribune, March 21, April 19, 1933; Boston Evening Transcript, October 21 and 26, 1933; Los Angeles Times, October 25, 1933.

15. Dallas Morning News, October 23, 1933; Philadelphia Inquirer, October 20, 1933; Kansas City Star, October 21, 1933; Courier-Journal (Louisville), October 22, 1933; Dulles to Ester E. Lape, March 16, 1933, Corres. II, 1933, Dulles Papers, Firestone Memorial Library; A.F.M., 38–40, 67, 71–72, 75, 89–91, 126–32, 141–46; Hartford Courant, October 22, 1933; San Francisco Chronicle, October 21, 1933; Boston Evening Transcript, October 21, 1933; Seattle-Post-Intelligencer, October 27, 1933; Los Angeles Times, October 25, 1933.

16. See 72nd Cong., 2nd sess., March 1, 1933, 5394–95; 73rd Cong., 1st sess., April 21, 1933, 2100; Commonweal, October 6, 1933, 526–28.

17. Fish folder, Box 156, Easley to Shepard, May 27, 1938, Box 215, and Amtorg Trading Company folder I, Box 155, National Civic Federation (N.C.F.) Papers, New York Public Library. Fish headed an investigation of subversive activities in 1930. See also New

York Times, April 9 and 16, 1933; *America,* February 18, 1933, 472; *National Republic* 20, no. 12 (1933):25–27, 32; Boxes 723 and 215, N.C.F. Papers; *Congressional Record,* 72nd Cong., 2nd sess., March 1, 1933, 5394–95; Demarest Lloyd to Roosevelt, May 17, 1933, P.P.F. 399, Roosevelt Papers; Fred D. Goddard to Roosevelt, November 4, 1933, D.S.F. 711.61/349. Lloyd and Goddard represented the American Coalition of Patriotic Societies and the American Legion, respectively.

18. *Congressional Record,* 72nd Cong., 2nd sess., March 1, 1933, 5396; *America,* October 7, 1933, 1–2; 73rd Cong., 1st sess., April 21, 1933, 2101. For similar criticism, see William Hand memorandum to Cordell Hull, March 28, 1933, Corres. II, Box 24, File 58, Hull Papers, Library of Congress; Rev. Hugh W. White to Hull, December 5, 1933, D.S.F. 861.01/2038.

19. See Adam B. Ulam, *Expansion and Coexistence: The History of Soviet Foreign Policy, 1917–1967,* 198–201; Browder, *Soviet-American Diplomacy,* 49–74; and Edward M. Bennett, "Franklin D. Roosevelt and Russian-American Relations, 1933–1939," 23–74.

20. R. W. to Hornbeck, March, 1932, Hornbeck memoranda, March 11, July 11, 1932, Box 61, Hornbeck Papers, Hoover Institution.

21. Stimson to Borah, September 8, 1932, in U.S., Department of State, *Foreign Relations of the United States: The Soviet Union, 1933–1939,* 2 (hereafter cited as *F.R.U.S.*); Browder, *Soviet-American Diplomacy,* 67–68; Bennett, *Recognition,* 73–79.

22. For this interpretation of Soviet policy, see the detailed analysis of Max Beloff, *The Foreign Policy of Soviet Russia, 1929–1941,* and the incisive analysis of Ulam, *Expansion and Coexistence,* 3–208. See also James E. McSherry, *Stalin, Hitler, and Europe,* for a conflicting evaluation, and B. Ponomaryov et al., *History of Soviet Foreign Policy 1917–1945,* for an unconvincing Soviet Marxist assessment.

23. *Philadelphia Inquirer,* October 20, 1933. See also *Los Angeles Times,* October 25, 1933; *Minneapolis Tribune,* October 22, 1933; *Kansas City Star,* October 21, 1933.

24. *Hartford Courant,* October 22, 1933; *Wall Street Journal,* November 7 and 20, 1933; *Washington Post,* November 8, 1933; *New York Times,* October 22, November 18, 1933.

25. *St. Louis Post-Dispatch,* October 22, 1933. See also *Times-Picayune* (New Orleans), October 23, 1933; *Chicago Daily News,* October 21, 1933; *Cleveland Plain Dealer,* October 21, 1933; *Christian Science Monitor,* October 21, 1933; *Portland Oregonian,* October 22, 1933; *Cincinnati Enquirer,* October 21, 1933.

26. *America,* August 5, 1933, 409–10; *National Republic* 20, no. 12 (1933):32; *Commonweal,* November 3, 1933, 5–6.

27. *Seattle Times,* November 7, 1933; *Boston Evening Transcript,* October 21, 1933; *Chicago Tribune,* October 25, November 20, 1933.

28. Castle to Fred L. Eberhardt, March 3, 1933, *F.R.U.S. Soviet Union,* 2.

29. See the October 30, 1933, press release of the American Foundation, which was based on their May survey, O.F. 220 Russia, Roosevelt Papers. A State Department survey obtained similar results: William Phillips to Roosevelt, October 19, 1933, O.F. 220 A, Russia Misc., Roosevelt Papers.

NOTES TO CHAPTER 2

1. *Soviet Russia Today* 1, no. 11 (1933):3.

2. Robert A. Divine, *Roosevelt and World War II,* 37. For Bullitt, who was visiting European countries in order to obtain information about debt settlements and other issues, see Robert E. Bowers, "Senator Arthur Robinson of Indiana Vindicated: William Bullitt's Secret Mission to Europe," *Indiana Magazine of History* 61, no. 3 (1965): 189–205. For Morgenthau, who became secretary of the treasury, see John M. Blum, *From The Morgenthau Diaries: Years of Crisis, 1928–1938,* 54–55.

3. For the preliminary discussions, see Robert P. Browder, *The Origins of Soviet-*

174   Notes to pages 12–16

American Diplomacy, 99–127; William A. Williams, American-Russian Relations, 1781–1947, 231–39; Beatrice Farnsworth, William C. Bullitt and the Soviet Union, 89–96; Robert E. Bowers, "American Diplomacy, the 1933 Wheat Conference, and Recognition of the Soviet Union," 39–53.

4. Blum, Years of Crisis, 54–55. For conflicting assessments of Roosevelt's motivation, see Williams, American-Russian Relations, 235–40, which emphasizes trade considerations. Browder, Soviet-American Diplomacy, 111, and Joan H. Wilson, Ideology and Economics: U.S. Relations with the Soviet Union, 1918–1933, 120–21, stress the Far Eastern situation. Farnsworth, Bullitt, 89–91, emphasizes the abnormality of non-recognition. Edward M. Bennett, Recognition of Russia: An American Foreign Policy Dilemma, 86, gives equal weight to all three factors.

5. Karl A. Bickel to Raymond Clapper, August 24, 1933, Personal File–Diaries 1933, 8, Clapper Papers, Library of Congress. According to William Phillips, a close friend of Roosevelt and under secretary of state in 1933, the futility of nonrecognition influenced the president more than other considerations (William Phillips, Ventures in Diplomacy, 156).

6. For a brief discussion of America's traditional policy of recognizing any government that controlled a state, see Bennett, Recognition, 1–14. Washington had not consistently followed this policy.

7. F.C.A. diary, May 9, 1933, Morgenthau Papers, Franklin D. Roosevelt Library. See also Wilson's excessive deemphasis of economic concerns in Roosevelt's calculations in Ideology and Economics, 124–28.

8. Morgenthau, with the assistance of intermediaries, negotiated with Amtorg, a trading company which was incorporated in New York but was actually a Soviet agency. See Blum, Years of Crisis, 54–55; New York Times, May 31, June 14, July 3, 4, and 9, 1933; Literary Digest, July 15, 1933, 9.

9. F.C.A. diary, September 26, October 23, 1933, Morgenthau Papers.

10. For Bullitt's, Morgenthau's, and Hull's views, see Browder, Soviet-American Diplomacy, 111–12; Cordell Hull, The Memoirs of Cordell Hull, 1:297, 304.

11. See Frank Freidel, Franklin D. Roosevelt: Launching the New Deal, 377–78, 390–407; Gerhard Weinberg, The Foreign Policy of Hitler's Germany: Diplomatic Revolution in Europe, 1933–1936, 133–45; Arnold A. Offner, "Appeasement Revisited: The United States, Great Britain, and Germany, 1933–1940," 373–78.

12. Litvinov to Soviet Foreign Affairs Ministry, November 8 and 17, 1933, in U.S.S.R., Soviet Ministry of Foreign Affairs, Dokumenty vneshnei politiki, SSSR, 16:609, 658–59. The Soviet documents contain a more detailed record of the negotiations than American sources, despite important omissions of some discussions between Litvinov and American officials. Several of the documents also have deletions that are not indicated or explained by the editors.

13. Henry L. Stimson diary, March 28, 1933, vol. 26, Stimson Papers, Yale University Library; Karl A. Bickel to Raymond Clapper, August 24, 1933, Personal File–Diaries 1933, 8, Clapper Papers. Bickel was president of the United Press Association and Clapper was a syndicated columnist. See Max Beloff, The Foreign Policy of Soviet Russia, 1:163–70; Freidel, Launching the New Deal, 121–23, 365–68, 455–56; Dorothy Borg, The United States and the Far Eastern Crisis of 1933–1938, 22–88.

14. Bullitt to Roosevelt, July 8, 1933, President's Secretary's File, London Economic Conference 1933, Box 52, Roosevelt Papers, Franklin D. Roosevelt Library (hereafter cited as P.S.F.); F.C.A. diary, September 23, 1933, Morgenthau Papers. In a letter to Browder, February 2, 1950, Bullitt did discount the influence of the Far Eastern situation (Browder, Soviet-American Diplomacy, 111).

15. Press conferences, April 14, May 16, July 5, 1933 (Edgar B. Nixon, ed., Franklin D. Roosevelt and Foreign Affairs, 1933–36, 1:55, 129, 278–79).

16. Bennett, Recognition, 111–12.

17. Erwin D. Cahnam, Christian Science Monitor, October 21, 1933, 1; U.S.,

Department of State, *Foreign Relations of the United States: The Soviet Union*, 17–18 (hereafter cited as *F.R.U.S.*).

18. See James MacGregor Burns, *Roosevelt: The Lion and the Fox*, 284; Freidel, *Launching the New Deal*, 274–75.

19. *Chicago Tribune*, October 25, 1933; *Los Angeles Times*, October 25, 1933. See also *Boston Evening Transcript*, October 21, 1933; *Seattle Times*, November 7, 1933.

20. *Hartford Courant*, October 22, 1933; *Cincinnati Enquirer*, October 21, 1933; *Seattle Post-Intelligencer*, October 27, 1933; *Chicago Daily News*, October 21, 1933; *Times-Picayune* (New Orleans), October 23, 1933; *St. Louis Post-Dispatch*, October 22, 1933; *Miami Herald*, October 24, 1933; *Cleveland Plain Dealer*, October 22, 1933; *Omaha Morning World-Herald*, October 23, 1933.

21. *New York Herald Tribune*, October 21, 1933; *Boston Evening Transcript*, October 21, 1933; *Chicago Tribune*, October 25, 1933; *Los Angeles Times*, October 25, 1933; *Seattle Times*, November 7, 1933.

22. See Brookhart to Sen. George Norris, October 27, 1933, Tray 8, Box 8, no. 18, Russia, 1931–35, Norris Papers, Library of Congress; Green memorandum to Roosevelt, November 10, 1933, Department of State File 811.00B/1478, Department of State MSS, National Archives (hereafter cited as D.S.F.); *New York Times*, October 21, 1933.

23. Louis J. Gallagher, *Edmund A. Walsh, S.J.: A Biography*, 93; Hooke to McIntyre, October 15, McIntyre memorandum to Roosevelt, October 30, Walsh to Roosevelt, November 4 and 7, Reverend Maurice S. Sheely to McIntyre, November 3, 1933, Official File 220 A, Russia Misc., Roosevelt Papers (hereafter cited as O.F.); *America*, November 4, 1933, 87; George Q. Flynn, *American Catholics and the Roosevelt Presidency, 1932–1936*, 134, 148–49.

24. Counselor Felix Cole to Hull, July 26, 1933, D.S.F. 661.115/511; Robert F. Kelley memorandum, November 1, 1933, D.S.F. 611.61/11; Department of Commerce Files 448 Russia–Trade with U.S., 221 Machinery–Russia, Department of Commerce MSS, National Archives. Commerce officials agreed with Kelley.

25. Hugh Gibson to Edward House, February 17, 1933, Corres. II, Box 35, File 65, Hull Papers, Library of Congress. Hull put red marks next to Gibson's quoted statement. Although Hull mentions his "open mind" toward recognition in his *Memoirs* (1:294), his statements and actions at the time suggested a more ambivalent attitude.

26. Kelley memorandum to Hull, October 27, 1933, D.S.F. 800.00B/227; Packer memorandum to Bullitt, August 31, 1933, D.S.F. 711.61/287/3/4. See also Kelley memoranda, July 27, September 25, 1933, *F.R.U.S. Soviet Union*, 6–11, 14. For the Russian section's views, see Felix Cole and Robert Skinner memoranda, January 20, April 12, 1933, D.S.F. 800.00B–Communist International/169; George F. Kennan, *Memoirs 1925–1950*, 49–57.

27. Johnson to Stanley K. Hornbeck, August 16, 1933, Personal Corres., 1933, 18, Johnson Papers, Library of Congress.

28. See memoranda to Hornbeck, March 21, 1933, Hornbeck to Hull, March 24, 1933, Box 61, Hornbeck Papers, Hoover Institution; Hull to Roosevelt, September 21, 1933, O.F. 779 Bullitt, Roosevelt Papers; Hull, *Memoirs*, 1:293–97; Phillips to Grew, October 21, 1933, *F.R.U.S. 1933*, 3:445; Phillips diary, December 26, 1933, Phillips Papers, Houghton Library; Moore to Dodd, December 26, 1933, Box 42, Dodd Papers, Library of Congress. Moore was a veteran Virginian politician.

29. Hornbeck memorandum, September 29, 1933, Box 143, Hornbeck Papers. Of course, Bullitt could have approached Hornbeck without Roosevelt's instructions or knowledge. But the sequence of Hull's letter, followed by Bullitt's conversations with Morgenthau and Hornbeck, raises the possibility that Roosevelt approved Bullitt's approach.

30. Kelley memorandum, July 27, Hull to Roosevelt, October 5, 1933, *F.R.U.S. Soviet Union*, 6–11, 16–19; Browder, *Soviet-American Diplomacy*, 105–7, 112–15.

31. See Robert E. Bowers, "Hull, Russian Subversion in Cuba, and Recognition of the U.S.S.R.," 542–55. Bowers overstates his argument that the State Department used the Cuban situation to sabotage recognition, for he has little direct evidence. This episode should be viewed in the larger context of the State Department's attitude toward recognition from March to November, 1933.

32. Hornbeck memoranda, October 11, 28, and 31, 1933, D.S.F. 761.94/638, and F.R.U.S. 1933, 2:801–2, and Box 61, Hornbeck Papers. For Grew's and Johnson's reports, see Grew telegrams to Hull, July 18, September 29, 1933, Grew dispatches to Phillips and Hull, October 6, and 20, 1933, F.R.U.S. 1933, 3:372–73, 412–16, 434–38, 445; Johnson to Hornbeck, August 16, 1933, Personal Corres., 1933, 18, Johnson Papers. Joseph Grew was ambassador to Japan.

33. Hull to Roosevelt, September 21 and 23, 1933, O.F. 779 Bullitt, Roosevelt Papers; F.R.U.S. Soviet Union, 12–13; Hull, Memoirs, 1:293–97; Moore memorandum to Hull, October 4, 1933, F.R.U.S. Soviet Union, 15. Hull submitted Moore's memorandum to Roosevelt. See also Phillips diary, October 31, 1933, Phillips Papers; Kelley to author, February 14, 1968.

34. Bullitt memorandum to Hull, October 4, 1933, F.R.U.S. Soviet Union, 16.

35. Hull, Memoirs, 1:300.

36. Litvinov to Soviet Foreign Affairs Ministry, November 8, 1933, Dokumenty vneshnei politiki, SSSR, 16:607–9; Hull, Memoirs, 1:299–301; F.C.A. diary, November 6, 1933, Morgenthau Papers; Phillips diary, November 7–10, 1933, Phillips Papers; Moore memorandum, November 9, 1933, Box 18, Robert Walton Moore Papers, Franklin D. Roosevelt Library.

37. Litvinov to Soviet Foreign Affairs Ministry, November 8, 1933, Dokumenty vneshnei politiki, SSSR, 16:609–10.

38. Phillips diary, November 10, 1933, Phillips Papers. For detailed descriptions of the negotiations and agreements, see Donald G. Bishop, The Roosevelt-Litvinov Agreements: The American View, 18–22, 29–41, 63–67, 90–94, 148–52, 179–88, 199–206, Browder, Soviet-American Diplomacy, 128–50.

39. Litvinov to Soviet Foreign Affairs Ministry, November 10, 1933, Dokumenty vneshnei politiki, SSSR, 16:621–22.

40. See F.R.U.S. Soviet Union, 28–33. Roosevelt made a reciprocal pledge within the limits of the Constitution.

41. Bullitt to Hull, November 9, 1935, F.R.U.S. Soviet Union, 265. Neither the American nor the Soviet documents provide any record of the Litvinov-Roosevelt discussion of this matter in 1933.

42. See Robert Kelley memorandum, October 25, 1933, F.R.U.S. Soviet Union, 23–24. By implication, Kelley suggested that Washington should keep the Tsarist debt and private claims out of the negotiations. See Phillips diary, November 11, 1933, Phillips Papers; Hull to Moore, November 13, 1933, Box 24, Robert Walton Moore Papers; Bullitt to Roosevelt, November 15, 1933, and Roosevelt and Litvinov memorandum, November 15, 1933, F.R.U.S. Soviet Union, 25–27. Roosevelt could deposit Soviet payments with the Treasury or assign various amounts to private claimants.

43. Litvinov to Soviet Foreign Affairs Ministry, November 15, 1933, Dokumenty vneshnei politiki, SSSR, 16:639. Litvinov also referred to a credit rather than a loan in his negotiations with Bullitt and Morgenthau in the week after recognition. See Litvinov to Soviet Foreign Affairs Ministry, November 18 and 22, 1933, ibid., 16:662–63, 675–76.

44. Litvinov to Soviet Foreign Affairs Ministry, November 17, 1933, ibid., 16:658–60. John L. Gaddis suggests that Roosevelt was "brainstorming" in this conversation, in Russia, the Soviet Union, and the United States: An Interpretive History, 123–25.

45. Roosevelt and Litvinov exchanged letters about the debt, noninterference, religious and legal rights for Americans in the Soviet Union, Soviet claims, and the meaning of economic espionage. See F.R.U.S. Soviet Union, 25–37.

46. See American-Russian Chamber of Commerce pamphlet, November 25, 1933, Box 23, Gumberg Papers, State Historical Society of Wisconsin; *Barron's*, November 27, 1933, 12; *Business Week*, November 18, 1933, 8–9; *New York Times*, November 18 and 19, 1933, January 2, 1934; *Cincinnati Enquirer*, November 22, 1933; *Baltimore Sun*, November 18, 1933; *Christian Science Monitor*, November 18, 1933; *Denver Post*, November 18, 1933.

47. *Baltimore Sun*, November 19, 1933; *Cleveland Plain Dealer*, November 18, 1933; *New York World-Telegram*, November 18, 1933; *Philadelphia Inquirer*, November 19, 1933; *Des Moines Register*, November 19, 1933; *Denver Post*, November 18, 1933.

48. *Dallas Morning News*, November 20, 1933; *Baltimore Sun*, November 18, 1933; *Detroit News*, November 20, 1933; *Richmond Times-Dispatch*, November 19, 1933; *Des Moines Register*, November 19, 1933; *Charlotte Observer*, November 18, 1933.

49. *Wall Street Journal*, November 20, 1933; *Commercial and Financial Chronicle*, November 25, 1933, 3724–25; *Seattle Post-Intelligencer*, November 23, 1933; *Richmond Times-Dispatch*, November 19, 1933; *Des Moines Register*, November 19, 1933; *St. Louis Post-Dispatch*, November 19, 1933; *Kansas City Star*, November 18, 1933.

50. *Chicago Daily News*, November 18, 1933; *Minneapolis Tribune*, November 20, 1933; *Philadelphia Inquirer*, November 18, 1933; *Hartford Courant*, November 18, 1933; *Portland Oregonian*, November 18, 1933; *San Francisco Chronicle*, November 18, 1933; *Christian Century*, November 29, 1933, 1494–95; *New Republic*, November 29, 1933, 61–62; *Nation*, November 29, 1933, 607; *Common Sense* 2, no. 6 (1933):4.

51. *America*, November 25, 1933, 172, and December 2, 1933, 193–94; *Commonweal*, November 24, 1933, 85–86, December 1, 1933, 115; Monsignor Robert F. Keegan to Roosevelt, November 18, Roosevelt to Keegan, November 22, 1933, President's Personal File, Cardinal Hayes, Roosevelt Papers; J.F.T. O'Connor to Roosevelt, December 13, 1933, O.F. 220 A, Roosevelt Papers.

52. *National Republic* 21, no. 8 (1933):12–13, 25. See also *New York Times*, November 18 and 19, 1933; *Chicago Tribune*, November 20, 1933; *Los Angeles Times*, November 18, 1933; *Boston Evening Transcript*, November 18, 1933.

53. Moffat diary, November 17 and 21, 1933, vol. 34, Moffat Papers, Houghton Library. Moffat was chief of the Division of Western European Affairs. See also Phillips diary, November 18, 1933, Phillips Papers; Hull telegram to Phillips, November 18, 1933, *F.R.U.S. Soviet Union*, 39; Moore radio address, November 22, 1933, D.S.F. 711.61/406.

54. Kennan, *Memoirs*, 56; *New York Times*, November 18, 1933; Browder, *Soviet-American Diplomacy*, 150; Litvinov to Soviet Foreign Affairs Ministry, November 18 and 22, 1933, *Dokumenty vneshnei politiki, SSSR* 16:662–63, 675–76.

55. Roosevelt address at Savannah, Georgia, November 18, 1933, in Samuel Rosenman, ed., *The Public Papers and Addresses of Franklin D. Roosevelt*, 2:492.

56. Litvinov to Soviet Foreign Affairs Ministry, November 18 and 20, 1933, *Dokumenty vneshnei politiki, SSSR*, 16:663, 666–67.

NOTES TO CHAPTER 3

1. Richard B. Scandrett, Jr., address, April 16, 1934, and Scandrett to Gumberg, January 31, 1934, Box 11, Gumberg Papers, State Historical Society of Wisconsin; U.S. Department of State File, Recognition Trade Flight/1-18, Department of State MSS, National Archives (hereafter cited as D.S.F.); Grigory I. Gokhman to Scandrett, May 18, and Scandrett to Gokhman, May 31, 1934, Box 11, Gumberg Papers. Gokhman was a secretary in the Soviet embassy.

2. See J. Chal Vinson, "War Debts and Peace Legislation: The Johnson Act of 1934," 206–22; Robert A. Divine, *The Illusion of Neutrality*, 1–121.

3. See R. Walton Moore to Sen. Joseph T. Robinson, January 27, 1934, in Edgar B. Nixon, ed., *Franklin D. Roosevelt and Foreign Affairs, 1933–1936*, 1:615–16; Vinson, "Johnson Act," 206–22; Frederick C. Adams, *Economic Diplomacy: The Export-Import Bank and American Foreign Policy, 1934–1939*, 1–71.

4. Phillips diary, November 20, December 10 and 11, 1933, Phillips Papers, Houghton Library; Moffat diary, December 10, 1933, vol. 34, Moffat Papers, Houghton Library. For Roosevelt's rejection, see Bullitt to Hull, March 13, 1934, in U.S., Department of State, *Foreign Relations of the United States 1934*, 3:74 (hereafter cited as *F.R.U.S.*). See also Grew to Hull, November 18, 1933, *F.R.U.S. 1933*, 3:463.

5. Johnson to Hornbeck, December 28, 1933, Personal Corres., 1933, 18, Johnson Papers, Columbia University Library; Grew diary, Nov. 18, 1933, Vol. 65, Grew Papers, Houghton Library; Division of Far Eastern Affairs memorandum, December 12, 1933, D.S.F. 711.61/365; Hull telegram to Grew, November 20, 1933, D.S.F. 711.94/872; Moore to Hull, December 29, 1933, Corres. II, Box 35, File 67, Hull Papers, Library of Congress; Kelley memorandum, January 16, 1934, D.S.F. 800.51 W 89 U.S.S.R./21/3/4; Phillips diary, December 26, 1933, Phillips Papers.

6. For American policy toward the Far East, see Borg, *The United States and the Far Eastern Crisis of 1933–1938*, 46–88; Stanley Hornbeck to Bullitt, January 11, 1934, Box 143, Hornbeck Papers, Hoover Institution.

7. Carr diary, no. 17, 1933, Carr Papers, Library of Congress. See also Cordell Hull, *Memoirs of Cordell Hull*, 1:302; William Phillips, *Ventures in Diplomacy*, 158; Moffat diary, November 17 and 18, 1933, vol. 34, Moffat Papers.

8. See Beatrice C. Farnsworth, *William C. Bullitt and the Soviet Union*, 107–9.

9. Bullitt telegram to Hull, December 24, 1933, President's Secretary's File, Russia, Box 17, Roosevelt Papers, Franklin D. Roosevelt Library (hereafter cited as P.S.F.); Bullitt to Hull, January 4, 1934, *F.R.U.S. Soviet Union*, 55–62.

10. Record of Litvinov conversation with Bullitt, December 11 and 21, record of Karakhan conversation with Bullitt, December 13, 1933, *Dokumenty vneshnei politiki, SSSR*, 16:731–32, 744–45, 758–60.

11. Troyanovsky to Stalin, February 23, 1934, ibid., 17:163–64.

12. Bullitt to Roosevelt, January 1, 1934, P.S.F., Russia, Bullitt, Roosevelt Papers; Bullitt telegram to Hull, December 24, 1933, P.S.F., Russia, Box 17, Roosevelt Papers. Bullitt later suggested to Roosevelt that Washington stay neutral in the event of a Soviet-Japanese war and trade with both sides. See Bullitt to Roosevelt, Feb. 5, 1934, in Nixon, ed., *Roosevelt*, 1:628–30.

13. Charles W. Thayer, *Diplomat*, 55. Thayer was a lively clerk and messenger in the American Embassy.

14. John Wiley to Bullitt, Aug. 16, 1934, Box 2, Wiley Papers, Franklin D. Roosevelt Library. Wiley, the counselor of the embassy, refers to Loy Henderson's assessment of Kelley. Henderson was the second secretary.

15. Litvinov to Troyanovsky, March 14, record of Litvinov conversations with Bullitt, March 18 and 21, 1934, in U.S.S.R., Soviet Ministry of Foreign Affairs, *Dokumenty vneshnei politiki, SSSR*, 17:179, 193–94. See also Bullitt telegrams to Hull, March 13, 14, and 21, 1934, *F.R.U.S. 1934*, 3:74–75, 82–83. Bullitt informed Hull that he rejected the nonaggression pact and did not relate his statements about Roosevelt's desire to keep the idea afloat. See Farnsworth, *Bullitt*, 126, for an argument that Moscow never intended to fulfill the agreement.

16. Moore memorandum, December 7, 1933, Bullitt telegram to Hull, March 2, 1934, D.S.F. 800.51 W 89 U.S.S.R.15/18, 21A; Kelley telegram to Bullitt, March 2, 1934, P.S.F., Russia, Box 17, Roosevelt Papers; Bullitt telegram to Hull, March 15, 1934, *F.R.U.S. Soviet Union*, 66–67; Litvinov to Troyanovsky, March 14, 1934, *Dokumenty vneshnei politiki, SSSR*, 17:180–81. For detailed descriptions of the negotiations, see Donald G. Bishop, *The Roosevelt-Litvinov Agreements: The American View*, 153–69; Farnsworth, *Bullitt*, 117–26.

17. Moore to Bullitt, March 19, 1934, Box 3, Robert Walton Moore Papers, Franklin D. Roosevelt Library; Hull telegram to Bullitt, March 17, Hull memorandum, March 26, 1934, *F.R.U.S. Soviet Union*, 67, 70–71; Phillips diary, April 7, 1934, Phillips Papers, Houghton Library.

18. Hull telegram to Bullitt, Bullitt telegram to Hull, April 2, 1934, *F.R.U.S. Soviet Union*, 75–77; Litvinov to Troyanovsky, April 3 and 10, record of Litvinov conversation with Bullitt, April 8, 1934, *Dokumenty vneshnei politiki, SSSR*, 17:226–27, 241–45. Although Washington had decided earlier to withhold credits, it now stressed this point to the Kremlin.

19. See Farnsworth, *Bullitt*, 127–39; Bullitt to Roosevelt, April 1, 1934, in Nixon, ed., *Roosevelt*, 2:47; Moore to Bullitt, April 10, 1934, Box 3, Robert Walton Moore Papers; Moffat diary, April 21, 1934, vol. 35, Moffat Papers.

20. Moore to Bullitt, April 24, May 8, 1934, Box 3, Moore Papers; Moore memorandum, April 30, Bullitt telegrams to Hull, May 9 and 13, Hull telegrams to Bullitt, May 11 and 15, 1934, *F.R.U.S. Soviet Union*, 86, 91–97.

21. Hull telegram to Bullitt, May 23, 1934, *F.R.U.S. Soviet Union*, 101; Moore to Bullitt, May 21 and 25, 1934, Box 3, Robert Walton Moore Papers.

22. Troyanovsky to Litvinov, April 16 and 27, Troyanovsky to Krestinsky, July 7, 1934, *Dokumenty vneshnei politiki, SSSR*, 17:261–62, 303–4, 455–57.

23. Bullitt telegrams to Hull, May 18, 21, and 23, June 14, 1934, D.S.F. 800.51 W 89 U.S.S.R./57, 60, and *F.R.U.S. Soviet Union*, 100, 106–7. The quote is from the telegram of May 21.

24. Hull telegram to Bullit, June 8, 1934, *F.R.U.S. Soviet Union*, 104; Moore to Bullitt, July 2, 9, and 23, 1934, Box 3, Robert Walton Moore Papers. The creation of a second Export-Import Bank to finance trade with all countries except Cuba and the Soviet Union stimulated some concern among firms interested in the Russian market.

25. Press conferences, May 9, August 15, 1934, in Nixon, ed., *Roosevelt*, 2:94, 177.

26. Moore to Roosevelt, August 29, Roosevelt to Moore, August 31, 1934, *F.R.U.S. Soviet Union*, 138–39.

27. Record of Litvinov conversation with Bullitt, October 10, 1934, *Dokumenty vneshnei politiki, SSSR*, 17:633–34; Nancy H. Hooker, ed., *The Moffat Papers: Selections from the Diplomatic Journals of Jay Pierrepont Moffat, 1919–1943*, 117; Phillips to Moffat, October 22, 1934, D.S.F. 500.A15A4/2600.

28. Hull telegram to Bullitt, September 15, Bullitt telegram to Hull, September 16, 1934, Kelley memorandum, January 31, 1935, *F.R.U.S. Soviet Union*, 146, 170, and D.S.F. 800.51 W 89 U.S.S.R./125; press conference, February 1, 1935, in Nixon, ed., *Roosevelt*, 2:385–86; Troyanovsky to Litvinov, January 31, 1935, *Dokumenty vneshnei politiki, SSSR*, 18:55–56.

29. For evaluations of the negotiations, see Robert P. Browder, *The Origins of Soviet-American Relations*, 182–88, who places most of the responsibility for the failure with Moscow; Farnsworth, *Bullitt*, 119–27, who criticizes Washington but suspects that Moscow never intended to make a settlement; Bishop, *Roosevelt-Litvinov Agreements*, 175–78, who also criticizes Washington; and William A. Williams, *American-Russian Relations, 1781–1947*, 240–47, who criticizes Washington's reluctance to support Moscow's foreign policies.

30. See *Washington Post*, February 2, 1935; *New York Herald Tribune*, February 4, 1935; *Courier-Journal* (Louisville), February 4, 1935; *Chicago Daily News*, February 2, 1935.

31. *Business Week*, February 16, 1935, 27–28; *Commercial and Financial Chronicle*, February 2, 1935, 685–86; *Commerce and Finance*, February 6, 1935, 119; Bertron to Howe, February 4, 1935, Official File 220 A, Russia Misc., Roosevelt Papers (hereafter cited as O.F.); *New Republic*, February 13, 1935, 1–2; *Nation*, February 13, 1935, 173; *Christian Century*, February 13, 1935, 198.

32. *Philadelphia Inquirer*, February 2, 1935; *Seattle Times*, February 8, 1935; *Boston*

Evening Transcript, February 1, 1935; *Courier-Journal* (Louisville), February 8, 1935; *Baltimore Sun*, February 2, 1935.

33. *Richmond Times-Dispatch*, February 2, 1935; *Washington Post*, February 2, 1935; *St. Louis Post-Dispatch*, February 3, 1935; *Cleveland Plain Dealer*, February 6, 1935.

34. Moore to Bullitt, April 18, June 20, 1935, Box 3, Robert Walton Moore Papers; Hornbeck memorandum, January 3, 1935, *F.R.U.S. 1935*, 3:836; Hull press release, January 31, 1935, *F.R.U.S. Soviet Union*, 173.

35. Troyanovsky to Litvinov, February 7, Litvinov to Troyanovsky, March 7, Krestinsky to Troyanovsky, March 9, 1935, *Dokumenty vneshnei politiki, SSSR*, 18:61–68, 161–69.

36. See *F.R.U.S. Soviet Union*, 192–218; *Dokumenty vneshnei politiki, SSSR*, 18:225, 269, 313–14, 381–84, 392, 404, 450–54.

37. Ralph Easley to Howard Ayres, December 16, 1933, Box 73, Easley to Edward A. Hayes, July 24, 1934, Box 74, National Civic Federation Papers, New York Public LIbrary; Moore memorandum to Hull, June 5, 1934, Box 3, Robert Walton Moore Papers; *New York Times*, November 19, 1933, July 12, 1934; *National Republic* 22, no. 8 (1935):6–7; Earl Latham, *The Communist Controversy in Washington: From the New Deal to McCarthy*, 34–38.

38. See George Wolfskill, *The Revolt of the Conservatives: A History of the American Liberty League, 1933–1940*, 22–109.

39. *New York Times*, September 1, 1934; Elizabeth Dilling, *The Red Network*. Latham discovered only a few cells of Communists and friends in the Department of Agriculture and the National Labor Relations Board (*Communist Controversy*, 72–150).

40. *Time*, April 2, 1934, 9–16; *Los Angeles Examiner*, April 12, 1934; *Saturday Evening Post*, April 7, 1934, 25; *National Republic* 21, no. 12 (1934):11; *New York Times*, April 11, 1934; *Literary Digest*, April 7, 1934, 10.

41. Moore memoranda to Hull, March 5, June 5, 1934, Box 3, Robert Walton Moore Papers; press conference, March 9, 1934, in Nixon, ed., *Roosevelt*, 2:22; Moore to Bullitt, June 26, 1934, Box 3, Robert Walton Moore Papers; Hull telegram to Bullitt, August 14, 1934, *F.R.U.S. Soviet Union*, 132–34; Wiley to Bullitt, August 28, 1934, Box 2, Wiley Papers, Franklin D. Roosevelt Library.

42. Hull telegram to Bullitt, July 3, 1935, Bullitt telegrams to Hull, October 5, 1935, July 2, 8, 9, 13, and 19, 1935, *F.R.U.S. Soviet Union*, 157, 220–24; Bullitt to Roosevelt, July 15, 1934, in Nixon, ed., *Roosevelt*, 2:556–58.

43. See Bullitt telegram to Hull, August 6, 1935, *F.R.U.S. Soviet Union*, 235–37; Kelley memorandum, August 20, 1935, MacMurray dispatch to Hull, January 10, 1936, D.S.F. 861-00 C.C.I. VII/114, 121. Minister MacMurray enclosed a 500-page memorandum prepared by the Riga legation.

44. Bullitt to Roosevelt, August 21, 1935, *F.R.U.S. Soviet Union*, 249.

45. *Denver Post*, July 30, 1935; *Detroit News*, July 26, 1935; *Des Moines Register*, July 30, 1935; *Dallas Morning News*, July 31, 1935; *Portland Oregonian*, August 2, 1935. See also *Christian Science Monitor*, July 30 and August 3, 14, and August 26, 1935, 14; *Atlanta Constitution*, August 6 and 19, 1935; *San Francisco Chronicle*, August 2 and 3, 1935; *Seattle Times*, August 1, 2, and 6, 1935; *New York Herald Tribune*, July 29, 1935; *Hartford Courant*, July 29, 1935; *Baltimore Sun*, July 27, 1935; *Washington Post*, July 27, 1935.

46. *Philadelphia Inquirer*, July 31, 1935; *Richmond Times-Dispatch*, July 31, 1935; *Portland Oregonian*, August 2, 1935; *Detroit News*, July 31, 1935.

47. Bullitt telegram to Hull, August 21, 1935, *F.R.U.S. Soviet Union*, 244–48.

48. For the rumor, see *New York Times*, August 27, 1935. Earl Browder claims that Dimitrov wanted Communist support for Roosevelt, but American Communists talked him out of it. See Earl Browder, Oral History Collection, 3:353–55, Columbia University Library.

49. See Moore to Roosevelt, August 22, 1935, O.F. 799 Bullitt, Roosevelt Papers; Hull telegram to Bullitt, August 23, Bullitt telegram to Hull, August 27, 1935, F.R.U.S. *Soviet Union*, 249–53.

50. *Atlanta Constitution*, August 27, 1935; *Philadelphia Inquirer*, August 27 and 29, 1935. See also *Los Angeles Times*, August 29, 1935; *Chicago Tribune*, August 27, 1935; *Boston Evening Transcript*, August 26 and 28, 1935; *Seattle Post-Intelligencer*, August 27 and 30, 1935; *San Francisco Chronicle*, August 27, 28, 29, 1935; *Minneapolis Tribune*, August 27, 1935.

51. *New Republic*, September 4, 86, September 11, 1935, 116–17; *Nation*, September 4, 1935, 253; *Christian Century*, September 4, 1935, 1101–2; *Common Sense 4*, no. 9 (1935):6, no. 10 (1935):5.

52. *Washington Post*, August 27 and 29, 1935; *Chicago Daily News*, August 27, 1935; *Des Moines Register*, August 27 and 29, 1935; *Baltimore Sun*, August 27 and 29, 1935. See also *Omaha Morning World-Herald*, August 27 and 31, 1935; *Hartford Courant*, August 30, 1935; *Christian Science Monitor*, August 27, 14, and August 29, 1935, 13.

53. Hull telegram to Bullitt, August 30, 1935, D.S.F. 711.61/524B; Hull statement, September 1, 1935, F.R.U.S. *Soviet Union*, 257–59.

54. *Detroit News*, September 4, 1935; *Dallas Morning News*, September 3, 1935; *Seattle Times*, September 6, 1935; *Times-Picayune* (New Orleans), September 3, 1935; *Washington Post*, September 2, 1935; *Baltimore Sun*, September 2, 1935. For a critical reaction, see *Saturday Evening Post*, Oct. 5, 1935, 22; *National Republic 23*, no. 5 (1935):10; *Los Angeles Examiner*, September 2, 1935; *Miami Herald*, September 3, 1935.

55. *New York Herald Tribune*, September 2, 1935.

56. Hull, *Memoirs*, 1:306; Bullitt telegrams to Hull, November 9, 1935, F.R.U.S. *Soviet Union*, 265, November 23, D.S.F. 711.61/577; Bishop, *Roosevelt-Litvinov Agreements*, 87–140, 211–27; Farnsworth, *Bullitt*, 153–54.

NOTES TO CHAPTER 4

1. William A. Williams, *American-Russian Relations, 1781–1947*, 231–38; Robert P. Browder, *The Origins of Soviet-American Diplomacy*, 176–213; Donald G. Bishop, *The Roosevelt-Litvinov Agreements: The American View*; Edward M. Bennett, *Recognition of Russia: An American Foreign Policy Dilemma*, 77–218; Beatrice Farnsworth, *William C. Bullitt and the Soviet Union*, 116–78; Keith D. Eagles, "Ambassador Joseph E. Davies and American-Soviet Relations, 1937–1941"; Joseph Edward O'Connor, "Laurence A. Steinhardt and American Policy toward the Soviet Union, 1939–1941"; Betty Crump Hanson, "American Diplomatic Reporting from the Soviet Union, 1934–1941." Hanson's study is the most comprehensive of these. For an earlier version of this chapter, see Thomas R. Maddux, "Watching Stalin Maneuver Between Hitler and the West: American Diplomats and Soviet Diplomacy, 1934–1939," 140–54.

2. For representative examples, see John Lewis Gaddis, *The United States and the Origins of the Cold War, 1941–1947*, 1–173; Joyce Kolko and Gabriel Kolko, *The Limits of Power: The World and United States Foreign Policy, 1945–1954*, 1–217; Thomas G. Patterson, *Soviet-American Confrontation: Postwar Reconstruction and the Origins of the Cold War* (Baltimore, 1973), 1–119; Lynn Etheridge Davis, *The Cold War Begins: Soviet-American Conflict Over Eastern Europe*. Daniel Yergin's *Shattered Peace: The Origins of the Cold War and the National Security State*, 18–41, does emphasize the "Riga Axioms," which summarized the perspective of the Russian specialists on Stalin's aims; but Yergin misses the changes in their views during the 1930s and especially the 1939–41 period.

3. See Keith D. Eagles, "Ambassador Joseph E. Davies and American-Soviet Relations, 1937–1941," *World Politics*, 220–39. Davies was a corporation lawyer for

bank and steamship companies, and his marriage in 1936 to Marjorie Post Hutton, heiress to the Post fortune, guaranteed financial security.

4. Steinhardt to John Wiley, September 21, 1939, Box 78, Steinhardt Papers, Library of Congress. Wiley was minister to the Baltic states. For Steinhardt's career, see U.S., Department of State, *Register of the State Department, 1941,* 212 (hereafter cited as *Register*); O'Connor, "Steinhardt and American Policy," 1–56.

5. Kelley memorandum to Hull, October 27, 1933, Department of State File 800.00B/227, Department of State MSS, National Archives (hereafter cited as D.S.F.); George F. Kennan, *Memoirs 1925–1950,* 61, 84; Charles E. Bohlen, *Witness to History, 1929–1969,* 39. For Kelley's and Henderson's careers, see *Register, 1941,* 152, and *Register, 1957,* 2.

6. Kennan, *Memoirs,* 24–37, 74; Bohlen, *Witness,* 3–11, 53, 57–58. Other officers who received Kelley's special training before it was curtailed by financial considerations included Edward Page, Norris B. Chipman, and Bertel T. Kuniholm. These officers were in Moscow, in the Riga legation and in Kelley's division in the thirties. Kennan was in Moscow for most of the 1934–37 period, while Bohlen returned to Washington in the spring of 1935 and did not come back until January, 1938. For the Riga experience, see Natalie Grant, "The Russian Section, A Window on the Soviet Union," 107–15.

7. See Bishop, *Roosevelt-Litvinov Agreements,* 210–32; Bullitt dispatch to Hull, April 20, 1936, D.S.F. 861.01/2120; Kennan, *Memoirs,* 69–70; Henderson to Kelley, April 30, 1937, Lane Papers, Yale University Library.

8. Bullitt dispatches to Hull, October 2, 1934, July 19, 1935, April 20, 1936, D.S.F. 861.5017–Living Conditions/769, 761.00/260, 861.01/2120. For a detailed analysis of the Moscow's embassy's views about the determinants and goals of Soviet policy, see Hanson, "American Diplomatic Reporting," 177–98.

9. Davies dispatch to Hull, June 6, 1938, in U.S., Department of State, *Foreign Relations of the United States: The Soviet Union, 1933–1939,* 557 (hereafter cited as F.R.U.S.); Faymonville G-2 report 948, September 15, 1937, in U.S., Department of Army, Military Attaché Reports, General Staff, Record Group 165, War Department Records, National Archives (hereafter cited as M.A.R.). Davies' papers must be used with caution. He frequently rewrote his letters for later publication, and sometimes the originals are missing. He also omitted parts of his letters that contained unfavorable comments about the Soviet Union in his *Mission to Moscow.* For example, in a letter to Sumner Welles, Davies removed his reference to the "menace of communism" and the "horrors of it, with attendant regimentation, its destruction of personal liberty, its denial of religious freedom." See Davies to Welles, March 26, 1938, in Davies, *Mission,* 297, and Box 7, Davies Papers, Library of Congress.

10. John Wiley dispatch to Hull, January 3, 1934. D.S.F. 861.00/11586; Bullitt dispatch to Hull, October 2, 1934, D.S.F. 861.5017–Living Conditions/769; Division of Eastern European Affairs memorandum, October 20, 1935, D.S.F. 811.00B/1608; Felix Cole memorandum to Hull, May 26, 1933, D.S.F. 811.00B/Communist International/ 135. Cole was counselor of the Riga legation from 1930 until 1936.

11. Henderson dispatches to Hull, November 16, 1936, February 18, 1938, F.R.U.S. Soviet Union, 310–11, 514–18; Bohlen, *Witness,* 39–40; Kennan memorandum, March 19, 1936, D.S.F. 761.00/269; Kennan, *Memoirs,* 70–72. For a similar assessment by another career officer, see Charles W. Thayer, *Diplomat,* 49–63. See also Kirk dispatch to Hull, November 25, Edward Page memorandum, December 21, 1938, Steinhardt dispatch to Hull, August 16, 1939, F.R.U.S. Soviet Union, 593–94n2, 779.

12. Bullitt dispatch to Hull, April 20, 1936, F.R.U.S. Soviet Union, 296; Kelley and Welles memoranda, March 10, February 7, 1934, D.S.F. 837.00/4719; R. Walton Moore to Alexander Weddell, October 4, 1935, D.S.F. 800.00B–Communist International 169. For the Chinese Communists, see Borg, *The United States and the Far Eastern Crisis of 1933–1938,* 202–33; Henderson dispatch to Hull, April 30, 1937, enclosing a Kennan memorandum, D.S.F. 761–94/965; Davies dispatch to Hull,

February 4, 1937, *F.R.U.S. 1937*, 3:22, Henderson dispatch to Hull, September 20, 1937, ibid., 538; Henderson to Kelley, April 27, 1937, D.S.F. 761.00/264.

13. Henderson dispatch and telegrams to Hull, July 31, August 4, October 17, November 19, 1936, D.S.F. 852.00/2338, 2395, 3939, *F.R.U.S. 1936*, 2:540.

14. For this interpretation of Soviet policy, see Max Beloff, *The Foreign Policy of Soviet Russia, 1929–1941*, and Adam B. Ulam, *Expansion and Coexistence: The History of Soviet Foreign Policy, 1917–1967*, 203–8 and passim. See also James E. McSherry, *Stalin, Hitler, and Europe*, 1:41–56 and passim, for a conflicting evaluation, and B. Ponomaryov et al., *History of Soviet Foreign Policy, 1917–1945*, 327–42, for an unconvincing Soviet Marxist assessment.

15. Bullitt to Moore, October 6, 1934, Box 3, Robert Walton Moore Papers, Franklin D. Roosevelt Library. See also Bullitt telegram to Hull, October 5, 1934, D.S.F. 500. A15A4/2588; Felix Cole dispatch to Hull, January 30, 1934, D.S.F. 861.00–Committee, All-Union Central Executive/45; *F.R.U.S. Soviet Union*, 53, 60–61; William E. Scott, *Alliance Against Hitler: The Origins of the Franco-Soviet Pact*, 134–36, 146–47, 199–201.

16. Hugh R. Wilson, *Diplomat Between Wars*, 254; Wilson to Hull, October 9, 1936, Corres. II, Box 39, File 93, Hull Papers, Library of Congress; Leland Harrison to Moffat, May 18, 1938, Box 28, Harrison Papers, Library of Congress. See also Cordell Hull, *Memoirs*, 1:304; Moffat diary, September 11, 1934, vol. 35, Moffat Papers, Houghton Library; Norman Davis to Hull, October 9, 1934, Corres. II, Box 37, File 79, Hull Papers; Hugh Wilson to Davis, November 21, 1934, Norman Davis Papers, Library of Congress.

17. Davis to Roosevelt, June 4, 1934, in Nixon, ed., *Franklin D. Roosevelt and Foreign Affairs, 1933–1936*, 2:137. Davis was Roosevelt's favorite delegate to European conferences. See also Wilson to Hull, September 22, 1934, Hull File, Wilson Papers, Hoover Institution; Breckinridge Long diary, March 19, 1936, Box 4, Long Papers, Library of Congress; Anthony J.D. Biddle to Roosevelt, February 24, 1936, President's Secretary's File, Norway, Box 14, Roosevelt Papers, Franklin D. Roosevelt Library (hereafter cited as P.S.F.).

18. Wiley to Kelley, April 4, 1935, Box 1, Wiley Papers, Franklin D. Roosevelt Library; Wiley to Hull, April 7, 1935, D.S.F. 862.20/837; Bohlen to William Phillips, December 2, 1935, Phillips Papers, Columbia University Library; Henderson to Hull, January 18, 1935, D.S.F. 761.00/265.

19. Bullitt dispatch to Hull, July 15, 1935, D.S.F. 761.00/260; Department of State Information Series, January 9, June 10, 1935, D.S.F. 800.00/227-228.

20. Bullitt to Roosevelt, April 8, 1935, in Nixon, ed., *Roosevelt*, 2:462–63; Wiley dispatch to Hull, November 15, 1934, D.S.F. 761.62/322. For Nazi-Soviet relations, see Gerhard L. Weinberg, *The Foreign Policy of Hitler's Germany: Diplomatic Revolution in Europe, 1933–1936*, 74–82, 180–82.

21. See Weinberg, *Foreign Policy of Hitler's Germany*, 219–23; Ulam, *Expansion and Coexistence*, 226–27. But also see, for a conflicting evaluation, McSherry, *Stalin*, 1:41–42, 56; Walter G. Krivitsky, *In Stalin's Secret Service*, 2–21. Krivitsky served as chief of Soviet military intelligence in Western Europe from 1935 until he defected to the United States.

22. Dodd to Messersmith, March 19, 1936, Box 49, Dodd Papers, Library of Congress; Messersmith to Hull, April 3, 1937, Corres. II, Box 41, File 98-A, Hull Papers; Kennan, *Memoirs*, 70–72. See also Robert Dallek, *Democrat and Diplomat: The Life of William E. Dodd*, 310.

23. Bullitt telegram to Hull, March 7, 1936, *F.R.U.S. 1936*, 1:212. See also ibid., 200–201, 233, 236; Bohlen, *Witness*, 39–40; Arnold Offner, *American Appeasement: United States Foreign Policy and Germany, 1933–1938*, 136–46.

24. Henderson to Kelley, April 27, 1937, D.S.F. 761.00/264. See also Bohlen memorandum, February 18, 1938, D.S.F. 761.00/293; Dodd telegram to Hull, June 11, 1937, D.S.F. 852.00/5836; Messersmith to Hull, April 3, 1937, Corres. II, Box 41, File

98-A, Hull Papers; Messersmith to Orsen Nielson, July 4, 1937, Box I, Messersmith Papers, University of Delaware Library; Davies to Welles, March 26, 1938, in Davies, *Mission*, 207.

25. Bullitt to Roosevelt, November 23, 1937, P.S.F., France, Bullitt Folder. For Nazi-Soviet relations, see Weinberg, *Foreign Policy of Hitler's Germany*, 311–12; McSherry, *Stalin*, 1:51–52.

26. Record of Bullitt conversation with Sir Eric Phipps, September 2, 1938, in Offner, *American Appeasement*, 251. See also Bullitt to Roosevelt, December 7 and 20, 1936, in Nixon, ed., *Roosevelt*, 3:528–30, 550–53; Bullitt to Roosevelt, December 7, 1937, May 20, 1938, P.S.F., France, Bullitt Folder; Wilson to Hull, October 9, 1936, October 11, 1938, July 12, 1939, Hull File, Wilson Papers; Hugh R. Wilson, Jr., *A Career Diplomat; The Third Chapter: Third Reich*, 35–76.

27. Davies telegram to Hull, March 26, 1938, *F.R.U.S. 1938*, 1:465; Davies to Harry Hopkins, January 18, 1939, in Davies, *Mission*, 434; Faymonville memorandum to Davies, June 6, 1938, Box 7, Davies Papers; Faymonville G-2 report 1352, October 5, 1938, M.A.R.; Messersmith to Raymond H. Geist, June 24, 1938, Box 1, Messersmith Papers.

28. Kirk telegram to Hull, August 29, 1938, *F.R.U.S. 1938*, 1:558. See also ibid., 492, 546–48, 633–34, 696–97; Kirk telegrams to Hull, August 15, September 13 and 27, 1938, D.S.F. 760F.61/569; Bohlen, *Witness*, 56–61; Kennan, *Memoirs*, 94; Moffat diary, September 23, 1938, vol. 41, Moffat Papers.

29. Kirk telegrams and dispatch to Hull, October 31, 1938, March 30, April 6, 1939, *F.R.U.S. Soviet Union*, 592, 747–50, 753. See Beloff, *Foreign Policy of Soviet Russia*, 2:120–66; Ulam, *Expansion and Coexistence*, 252–57. For an unsupported argument that Stalin never thought of aiding Czechoslovakia and encouraged a general war, see McSherry, *Stalin*, 1:68, 95, 120–21. Ponomaryov et al., *Soviet Foreign Policy*, 343–48, claim that Moscow offered military aid to Czechoslovakia on the condition that Prague request it and resist Berlin, but they present no evidence from the Soviet archives to support this argument. See also Marcia Lynn Toepfer, "The Soviet Role in the Munich Crisis: An Historiographical Debate," 341–57.

30. Bullitt telegrams to Hull, May 5 and 16, 1939, *F.R.U.S. 1939*, 1:247–51, 255. The quote is from the May 16 telegram. For the Anglo-Soviet-French negotiations, see ibid., 232–312. See also Davies memorandum to Roosevelt, April 18, 1939, Box 10, Davies Papers; Davies to Roosevelt, June 8, 1939, P.S.F., Belgium.

31. Bohlen, *Witness*, 64–65; Kirk dispatch and telegrams to Hull, March 30, April 6, May 4, 1939, *F.R.U.S. Soviet Union*, 747–50, 753, 758–59.

32. Bohlen, *Witness*, 67–77; Grummon telegrams to Hull, May 12, 22, and 24, June 2 and 22, July 1, 1939, D.S.F. 740.00/1442, 741.61/636, 662, 722, and 761.62/517, 530.

33. Bohlen, *Witness*, 77–82; Steinhardt to Welles, August 16, 1939, D.S.F. 741.61/836. See also Steinhardt dispatch to Hull, August 16, 1939, *F.R.U.S. Soviet Union*, 775–79; memoranda by Henderson, June 2, July 22, 1939, D.S.F 741.6111/57 1/2. For Nazi-Soviet relations in the summer of 1939, see Gerhard L. Weinberg, *Germany and the Soviet Union, 1939–1941*, 5–40; Philipp W. Fabry, *Der Hitler-Stalin-Pakt 1939–1941*, 9–133.

34. See Weinberg, *Germany and the Soviet Union*, 41–48. When Moscow also stated its interest in Bessarabia, Berlin denied any political interest in the Balkans. After defending the pact as a necessary move to avoid war on two fronts with Berlin and Tokyo and gain time, Ponomaryov et al. do not even mention the secret protocol on Poland (*Soviet Foreign Policy*, 359–85).

35. Bohlen, *Witness*, 82–85; Steinhardt telegram to Hull, September 1, 1939, *F.R.U.S. 1939*, 1:348; Steinhardt telegram to Bullitt, August 30, 1939, D.S.F. 761.6211/153; Henderson memorandum, September 2, 1939, D.S.F. 761.6211/194.

36. Bullitt to Alexander Kirk, September 28, 1939, Kirk File, Wilson Papers. See also

Wilson to Kirk, December 4, 1939, ibid.; Long diary, October 5, 1939, in Fred L. Israel, ed., *The War Diary of Breckinridge Long: Selections from the Years 1939–1944*, 24.

37. See Bohlen, *Witness*, 39–40, 272–73, 290–91; Kennan, *Memoirs*, 73–74, 133–34.

NOTES TO CHAPTER 5

1. For Faymonville's influence upon Davies, see Davies to Harry H. Woodring, November 3, 1937, in U.S., Department of Army, Office of the Adjutant General, File 210.681 U.S.S.R., Record Group 94, War Department Records, National Archives; Charles E. Bohlen, *Witness to History, 1929–1969*, 57. For an earlier version of this chapter, see Thomas R. Maddux, "American Diplomats and the Soviet Experiment: The View from the Moscow Embassy, 1934–1939," 468–87.

2. George F. Kennan, *Memoirs 1925–1950*, 82–83; Bohlen, *Witness*, 44–53; Henderson to Lane, March 22, 1938, Lane Papers, Yale University Library.

3. Sound treatments of Soviet industrialization include Naum Jasny, *Soviet Industrialization, 1928–1952*, 51–231; Antony C. Sutton, *Western Technology and Soviet Economic Development, 1930–1945*, 318–48; Merle Fainsod, *Smolensk Under Soviet Rule*, 238–64.

4. Bullitt dispatches to Hull, October 2, 1934, June 8, 1935, Department of State File 861.5017–Living Conditions/769, 861.00/11604, Department of State MSS, National Archives (hereafter cited as D.S.F.); Bullitt to Roosevelt, February 22, 1936, President's Secretary's File, Russia, Bullitt, Roosevelt Papers, Franklin D. Roosevelt Library; Henderson dispatches to Hull, April 20, July 30, December 2, 1936, D.S.F. 861.50/868, 871, 872.

5. Davies diary, July 28, 1937, Box 5, Davies Papers, Library of Congress. See also Davies dispatches to Hull, July 23, 1937, D.S.F. 861.61 Collective Farms/111, and 861.50/877; Joseph E. Davies, *Mission to Moscow*, 179–89; Henderson dispatches to Hull, May 13, June 2 and 18, September 2, 1937, D.S.F. 861.50/874, 877–78, and 861.60/291; Henderson to Robert Kelley, April 30, 1937, Lane Papers.

6. Davies to Sumner Welles, July 10, 1937, Davies dispatch to Hull, April 1, 1938, in Davies, *Mission*, 173, 310, and in U.S., Department of State, *Foreign Relations of the United States: The Soviet Union, 1933–1939*, 538 (hereafter cited as F.R.U.S.).

7. Henderson to Samuel Harper, February 13, 1939, Letters, 1939, Harper Papers, Institute of Current World Affairs. See also George Kennan memorandum, April 6, 1938, D.S.F. 861.60/291; Norris B. Chipman memorandum, October 27, 1938, D.S.F. 861.60/318; Alexander Kirk dispatches to Hull, January 27, May 4, April 12, 1939, D.S.F. 851.50/902, 861.5041/51, 861.50 Five-Year Plan III/4.

8. Henderson dispatch to Hull, December 9, 1935, enclosing Kennan memorandum, D.S.F. 861.504/324; Henderson dispatch to Hull, April 20, 1936, D.S.F. 861.50/868. See also Faymonville G-2 report 359, 408, October 15, November 30, 1935, in U.S., Department of Army, Military Attaché Reports, General Staff, Record Group 165, War Department Records, National Archives (hereafter cited as M.A.R.).

9. Davies to Roosevelt, March 5, 1938, Davies diary, February 12, 1937, in Davies, *Mission*, 95, 74; Davies dispatch to Hull, June 6, 1938, D.S.F. 861.00/11786.

10. Alexander Kirk dispatch to Hull, October 27, 1938, with attached Chipman and Page memoranda, D.S.F. 861.60/318; Davies dispatch to Hull, March 17, 1937, enclosing a Henderson memorandum, D.S.F. 861.01/2124; Henderson to Kelley, April 30, 1937, Lane Papers. See also Bullitt dispatches to Hull, October 2, 1934, June 22, 1935, D.S.F. 861.01/2120, 861.4055/13; Alexander Kirk dispatch to Hull, October 27, 1938, D.S.F. 861.60/318.

11. See Bullitt dispatch to Hull, April 20, 1936, D.S.F. 861.01/2120; Henderson to Kelley, April 30, 1937, Lane Papers; Davies to Steve Early, February 10, Davies to Pat Harrison, February 18, 1937, Box 3, Davies Papers. For a good discussion of the

conflicting views about Stalin's character and motivation, see Robert Conquest, *The Great Terror: Stalin's Purge of the Thirties*, 62−81.

12. Kennan, *Memoirs*, 69−70. See also George F. Kennan, *Russia and the West under Lenin and Stalin*, 248−52.

13. Henderson to Kelley, April 30, 1937, Lane Papers. See also Henderson dispatch to Hull, December 23, 1937, D.S.F. 861.00−Party, All-Union Communist/193; John Wiley dispatch to Hull, January 19, 1935, D.S.F. 861.00/11589; Leonard Schapiro, *The Communist Party of the Soviet Union*, 439−56.

14. Bullitt dispatch to Hull, April 1, 1936, D.S.F. 861.01/2119; Kennan memoranda, February 21, 1936, March 18, 1937, D.S.F. 861.00−Party, All-Union Communist/180, 186; Faymonville to Chief, Military Intelligence Division (M.I.D.), May 20, 1935, M.A.R.

15. Davies to Roy Van Bomel, January 25, 1937, Box 3, Davies Papers; Henderson dispatches to Hull, September 3 and 15, December 22, 1937, D.S.F. 861.00/11725, 861.00−Party, All-Union Communist/186, 861.00 Supreme Soviet/1; Kennan to Harper, December 23, 1937, Letters 1937, Harper Papers, University of Chicago Library; Leonard Schapiro, *The Government and Politics of the Soviet Union*, 85−101.

16. Henderson dispatch to Hull, June 18, 1936, enclosing Charles Thayer memorandum, D.S.F. 861.401/7. For Stalin's social policies, see Donald W. Treadgold, *Twentieth Century Russia*, 294−96, 341−51; Nicholas S. Timasheff, *The Great Retreat: The Growth and Decline of Communism in Russia*, 166−81, 192−225, 241−76.

17. Bullitt dispatch to Hull, June 22, 1935, D.S.F. 861.4055/13. See also Davies dispatch to Hull, March 17, 1937, D.S.F. 861.01/2124; Faymonville G-2 report 948, September 15, 1937, M.A.R.

18. Henderson dispatches to Hull, September 18 and 28, 1936, D.S.F. 861.404/403−4; Davies dispatch to Hull, March 17, 1937, enclosing Norris B. Chipman memorandum, D.S.F. 861.404/412; Davies to Eleanor Roosevelt, December 1, 1938, President's Personal File, Davies, Roosevelt Papers.

19. See Conquest, *Great Terror*, 525−35; Roy A. Medvedev, *Let History Judge: The Origins and Consequences of Stalinism*, 152−282; Alexander I. Solzhenitsyn, *The Gulag Archipelago, 1918−1956*.

20. Bohlen, *Witness*, 42−43; Bullitt dispatch to Hull, April 26, 1935, Official File, State Department, Roosevelt Papers. For the assassination, see Conquest, *Great Terror*, 43−61; Medvedev, *Let History Judge*, 152−91; and Adam Ulam, *Stalin: The Man and His Era*, 370−88.

21. Wiley telegram to Hull, December 1, Wiley dispatches to Hull, December 14, 1934, January 3, 1935, Robert Kelley memorandum, January 7, 1935, D.S.F. 861.00/11575, 11577, 11586; Henderson to Harper, December 27, 1934, Letters 1934, Harper Papers; Faymonville to Chief, M.I.D., December 7 and 31, 1934, January 3 and 31, 1935, M.A.R. Kennan became ill three days after the assassination and was sent to Vienna until November, 1935.

22. Conquest, *Great Terror*, 62−185, and Medvedev, *Let History Judge*, 152−282, thoroughly document this point. For implied agreement from the Soviet government, see Jane P. Shapiro, "Soviet Historiography and the Moscow Trials: After Thirty Years," 68−77.

23. Henderson telegrams to Hull, August 18 and 27, Henderson dispatches to Hull, September 1, December 31, 1936, D.S.F. 861.00/11629-11630, 11636, 11652.

24. Keith Eagles, "Ambassador Joseph E. Davies and American-Soviet Relations, 1937−1941," 122−30, and Richard H. Ullman, "The Davies Mission and United States−Soviet Relations, 1937−1941," 225−27, miss the ambiguity in Davies' response.

25. Davies dispatches to Hull, January 29, February 17, 1937, D.S.F. 861.00/11665, 11676; Davies to Roosevelt, February 4, 1937, Box 3, Davies Papers.

26. Davies dispatch to Hull, February 18, 1937, enclosing Kennan memorandum, February 17, 1937, D.S.F. 861.00/11675, and *F.R.U.S. Soviet Union*, 362−69; Hender-

son to Kelley, April 30, 1937, Lane Papers; Henderson to Harper, May 6, 1937, Letters 1937, Harper Papers. Unfortunately, Kennan does not discuss his views on the trial in his memoirs.

27. Davies telegram to Hull, March 13, 1938, *F.R.U.S. Soviet Union,* 532. See also Davies telegrams, D.S.F. 861.00/11755-11762; Conquest, *Great Terror,* 367–426; Stephen F. Cohen, *Bukharin and the Bolshevik Revolution: A Political Biography, 1888–1928,* 366–81.

28. Bohlen, *Witness,* 47–55. Bohlen admits that "an analytical dispatch on the trial was the only paper that I was unable to complete during my nearly forty years in the Foreign Service."

29. See Conquest, *Great Terror,* 201–35; John Erickson, *The Soviet High Command: A Military Political History, 1918–1941,* 449–73.

30. Davies to Welles, June 28, July 10, 1937, Davies, *Mission,* 160–61, 172–73; Faymonville G-2 report 776, February 24, 1937, Faymonville to Assistant Chief of Staff G-2, June 22, 1937, M.A.R.; James S. Herndon and Joseph O. Baylen, "Col. Philip R. Faymonville and the Red Army, 1934–1943," 483–505.

31. Henderson telegrams to Hull, June 8, 9, and 13, 1937, Henderson dispatches to Hull, October 2, 1937, February 18, 1938, *F.R.U.S. Soviet Union,* 378, 383–85, 591–20, and D.S.F. 861.00/11692, 11734; Kennan memorandum, January 8, 1938, D.S.F. 861.00/11747.

32. Henderson telegram to Hull, June 13, Henderson memorandum and dispatches to Hull, April 29, June 10 and 21, October 2, 1937, *F.R.U.S. Soviet Union,* 382, and D.S.F. 861.00/11702, 11708, 11713, 11734; Bohlen, *Witness,* 43–47, 50. For the general purge, see Conquest, *Great Terror,* 276–366; Medvedev, *Let History Judge,* 192–239, 258–354; Solzhenitsyn, *Gulag Archipelago.*

33. Davies dispatches to Hull, July 28, November 15, 1937, April 1, 1938, D.S.F. 861.50/877, 861.415/55, and Davies, *Mission,* 302. See also Davies to Welles, July 10, Davies to Roosevelt, February 4, 1937, in Davies, *Mission,* 172–73, and Box 3, Davies Papers.

34. Bullitt dispatch to Hull, February 21, 1936, enclosing Kennan memorandum, D.S.F. 861.00–Party, All-Union Communist/180. See also Kennan, *Memoirs,* 67–70.

35. Henderson dispatch to Hull, October 2, 1937, D.S.F. 861.00/11734.

36. See Kennan, *Memoirs,* 67, 70, and passim; Bohlen, *Witness,* 36 and passim.

NOTES TO CHAPTER 6

1. Alfred M. Bingham, "War Mongering on the Left," *Common Sense* 6, no. 6 (1937):16–18.

2. See *Christian Science Monitor,* February 2, 1934, 1, 8; *New Republic,* February 15, 1933, 8–9; William Henry Chamberlin, "Joseph Stalin and His Aides," *American Mercury* 32 (1934):315–19; William Henry Chamberlin, *Collectivism: A False Utopia* and *The Confessions of an Individualist.*

3. See Eugene Lyons, "Russia Postpones Utopia," *Reader's Digest* 28 (1936):17–19; *Moscow Carrousel; Assignment in Utopia; Stalin, Czar of All the Russia.*

4. See Demaree Bess, "Soviet Russia in 1937," address to the Chicago Council on Foreign Relations Papers, November 8, 1937, Urban Historical Collection, University of Illinois at Chicago Circle; Harold N. Denny, "My Five Years in Soviet Russia,"ibid., November 1, 1940. For Denny's articles, see *New York Times,* September 13–19, 1937.

5. See Walter Duranty, *Duranty Reports Russia, I Write As I Please,* and *The Kremlin and the People.*

6. See *Nation* (1934–36) for Fischer's frequent reports from Moscow and Louis Fischer, *Men and Politics: Europe Between the Two World Wars.*

7. Hopper to Ward [Harry?], August 25, 1938, Letters 1938, Harper Papers, Univer-

sity of Chicago Library. See also Hopper's lectures in 1937–39, Hopper Papers, Institute of Current World Affairs.

8. Harper to Donald M. Brodie, January 28, 1937, Harper Papers, Institute of Current World Affairs; Harper to Walter S. Rogers, March 2, 1937, ibid.; Harper to Loy Henderson, April or May, 1937, Paul V. Harper, ed., *The Russia I Believe In: The Memoirs of Samuel N. Harper, 1902–1941*, 247–48. Rogers was the director and Brodie the secretary of the institute.

9. Hazard memorandum, December 22, 1937, vol. 2, Hazard Papers, Institute of Current World Affairs.

10. Anna Louise Strong, *I Change Worlds: The Remaking of an American*, 300–422; Williams to Gumberg, January 21, 1938, Box 15, Gumberg Papers, State Historical Society of Wisconsin. See Sylvia R. Margulies, *The Pilgrimage to Russia: The Soviet Union and the Treatment of Foreigners, 1924–1937*, for a thorough study of Soviet policy.

11. See Margulies, *Pilgrimage to Russia*, 74–75, 217n25; Peter G. Filene, *Americans and the Soviet Experiment, 1917–1933*, 369n1; *New York Times*, July 19, 1936.

12. See *Nation*, September 17, 1938, 265–67; Rothschild report, 1935, Articles and Reports 1935, Harper Papers, University of Chicago Library.

13. *Nation*, December 19, 1934, 696, May 15, 1935, 566–568; *New Republic*, December 12, 1934, 115, December 19, 1934, 151; *Soviet Russia Today*, 2, no. 11 (1935):17; *Common Sense* 4, no. 1 (1935):5; *Christian Century*, January 2, 1935, 5.

14. *Minneapolis Tribune*, December 7, 1934; *Hartford Courant*, December 5 and 9, 1934; *Seattle Times*, December 5, 1934; *Denver Post*, December 6, 1934; *Cincinnati Enquirer*, December 11, 1934; *Richmond Times-Dispatch*, December 10, 1934; *Cleveland Plain Dealer*, December 3, 1934; *Dallas Morning News*, December 7, 1934.

15. *Common Sense* 4, no. 1 (1935):5; *New Republic*, December 19, 1934, 151; *Nation*, December 19, 1934, 696. For an analysis of the news media's comparison of Stalinism and Nazism, see Thomas R. Maddux, "Red Fascism, Brown Bolshevism: The American Image of Totalitarianism in the 1930s," 85–103.

16. *Omaha Morning World-Herald*, December 7, 1934; *Chicago Tribune*, December 8, 1934; *Philadelphia Inquirer*, December 8 and 9, 1934; *Kansas City Star*, December 7, 1934; *Baltimore Sun*, December 7, 1934; *St. Louis Post-Dispatch*, July 7, December 7, 1934; *New York Times*, January 25, 1935.

17. William Henry Chamberlin, "Russia and Germany—Parallels and Contrasts," *Atlantic Monthly* 156, no. 3 (1935):359–68. See also Chamberlin, "Behind the Events in Russia: Is a New Opposition Arising?", *New York Times*, January 6, 1935; *America*, September 14, 1935, 532; *National Republic* 23, no. 6 (1935):10–11, no. 8 (1935):10; *Catholic World* 140 (1935):514–19.

18. *Christian Century*, September 19, 1934, 1163, August 7, 1935, 1005, March 11, 1936, 388; *Nation*, June 13, 1934, 662, June 27, 1934, 128–29, September 13, 1934, 282, May 1, 1935, 494, May 29, 1935, 615, August 7, 1935, 145; *New Republic*, July 25, 1934, 277; *Common Sense* 3, no. 10 (1934), 5, and 4, no. 9 (1935):6, and 5, no. 8 (1936):4; Frank A. Warren, III, *Liberals and Communism: The "Red Decade" Revisited*, 89–126.

19. *Christian Science Monitor*, May 6, 1935, 18; *Kansas City Star*, September 20, 1934; *Des Moines Register*, September 13, 1934; *Portland Oregonian*, September 18, 1934; *Atlanta Constitution*, May 8, 1935; *Hartford Courant*, May 4 and 6, 1935; *New York Herald Tribune*, May 4, 1935.

20. *Cincinnati Enquirer*, September 19, 1934; *Philadelphia Inquirer*, September 11, 1934; *Baltimore Sun*, September 17 and 20, 1934; *St. Louis Post-Dispatch*, September 18, 1934; *Omaha Morning World-Herald*, September 17, 1934.

21. *New York Times*, May 31, September 19, 1934. See also *Christian Science Monitor*, July 9, 1934, 14, September 19, 1934, 14; *Detroit News*, September 18, 1934; *Seattle Times*, September 23, 1934, May 6, 1935.

22. *America*, October 6, 1934, 607–9, August 24, 1935, 465–67; *Commonweal*, September 28, 1934, 495–96; *National Republic* 23, no. 5 (1935):8, and 24, no. 3 (1936):11, 30.

23. *New Republic*, June 24, 1936, 192–93; *Nation*, June 17, 1936, 761–62, 772–74. See also *Soviet Russia Today* 4, no. 1 (1935):2, no. 10 (1935):7–8; *Foreign Policy Bulletin*, June 26, 1936.

24. *Chicago Tribune*, June 13, 1936; *Kansas City Star*, February 3, 1935; *St. Louis Post-Dispatch*, August 25, 1936; *Newsweek*, June 20, 1936, 22.

25. *Richmond Times-Dispatch*, November 27, 1936; *New York Herald Tribune*, November 26, 1936; *Seattle Times*, November 30, 1936; *Pittsburgh Post-Gazette*, December 3, 1936; *Boston Evening Transcript*, November 27, 1936; *Courier-Journal* (Louisville), November 28, 1936; *New York World-Telegram*, November 27, 1936.

26. *New Republic*, December 9, 1936, 160–61; *American Mercury* 42 (1937):181–84. See also *Christian Century*, June 24, 1936, 896–97, December 9, 1936, 1644, December 22, 1937, 1580; *Common Sense* 4, no. 1 (1937):5; *National Republic* 24, no. 3 (1936):11, no. 9 (1937):11, and 25, no. 5 (1937):11; *Commonweal*, September 4, 1936, 441–42.

27. *San Francisco Chronicle*, August 20, 1936; *Courier-Journal*, August 21, 1936; *American Mercury* 40 (1937):37–45. See also *America*, September 5, 1936, 507; *Saturday Evening Post*, March 6, 1937, 24; *Time*, August 31, 1936, 16–18, February 1, 1937, 18–20.

28. *Dallas Morning News*, August 21, 1936, 2. See also *New York Herald Tribune*, August 22, 1936, 10, August 26, 1936, 18; *New Republic*, August 26, 1936, 58, September 2, 1936, 89; *Common Sense* 5, no. 10 (1936):7; *Nation*, August 29, 1936, 226, October 10, 1936, 409; *Christian Century*, September 2, 1936, 1147–48, September 9, 1936, 1181; Warren, *Liberals and Communism*, 171–91.

29. *Boston Evening Transcript*, January 25, 1937; *New York Times*, January 25, 1937; *Cincinnati Enquirer*, January 27, 1937; *Omaha Morning World-Herald*, January 25, 1937.

30. *Des Moines Register*, January 29, 1937; *Cleveland Plain Dealer*, January 25, 1937; *Kansas City Star*, January 26, 1937; *Times-Picayune* (New Orleans), January 31, 1937; *New York World-Telegram*, January 16, 1937.

31. *Washington Post*, January 26, 1937; *Baltimore Sun*, January 31, 1937; *New York Times*, February 4, 1937; *Chicago Tribune*, January 26, 1937; *Atlanta Constitution*, January 31, 1937.

32. *Nation*, January 30, 1937, 114, February 6, 1937, 143–45; *New Republic*, February 3, 1937, 399–400, February 17, 1937, 33–34; *Common Sense* 4, no. 3 (1937):20; *Christian Century*, February 3, 1937, 131–32.

33. *Cincinnati Enquirer*, March 4, 1938; *Richmond Times-Dispatch*, March 1, 1938; *San Francisco Chronicle*, March 10, 1938; *Portland Oregonian*, March 17, 1938; *Kansas City Star*, March 9, 1938.

34. *Philadelphia Inquirer*, March 4, 1938; *New York Times*, March 13, 1938; *Christian Science Monitor*, March 2, March 5, 1938, 20; *Baltimore Sun*, March 1, 1938.

35. *Seattle Times*, March 11, 1938; *Los Angeles Times*, June 18, 1937; *Charlotte Observer*, August 5, 1938; *New York Times*, September 13, 1937; *Washington Post*, June 13, 1937; *Omaha Morning World-Herald*, March 7, 1938; *Philadelphia Inquirer*, June 14, 1937; *Boston Evening Transcript*, June 14, 1937; *Times-Picayune* (New Orleans), June 14, 1937.

36. *Nation*, May 22, 1937, 578; *New Republic*, June 23, 1937, 174, January 5, 1938, 240–41; *Christian Century*, June 23, 1937, 797.

37. *San Francisco Chronicle*, August 3, 1938; *New York Herald Tribune*, March 4, 1938; *Kansas City Star*, July 24, 1936, March 9, 1938; *Omaha Morning World-Herald*, January 25, June 14, 1937. See also Maddux, "Red Fascism, Brown Bolshevism," 89–94.

38. *Philadelpha Inquirer,* November 27, 1938; *Times-Picayune* (New Orleans), August 25, 1936, June 14, 1937; *Dallas Morning News,* November 27, 1936, June 13, 1937; *Charlotte Observer,* March 7, 1937.

39. *American Mercury* 42 (1937):181−86, 41 (1937):211−15. See also Chamberlin, *Collectivism;* Upton Sinclair and Eugene Lyons, *Terror in Russia? Two Views,* 16−19, 37−46; Lyons, "Dictators into Gods,"*American Mercury* 46 (1939):265−68; *Catholic World* 143 (1936):645−46, and 145 (1937):524−31; *National Republic* 25, no. 9 (1938):30, no. 10 (1938):3−4.

40. *Cleveland Plain Dealer,* June 12, 1937; *Christian Century,* April 26, 1939, 542−46; Warren, *Liberals and Communism,* 123−25, 182−84.

41. *New Republic,* March 16, 1938, 151−52; *Christian Century,* March 30, 1938, 388; *Soviet Russia Today* 6, no. 1 (1938):4, no. 4 (1938):7; *Nation,* March 3, 1938, 261.

42. *Washington Post,* July 29, 1936; *Baltimore Sun,* July 20, 23, and 28, 1936; *New York Herald Tribune,* July 22, 1936; *Courier-Journal* (Louisville), July 26 and 31, 1936; *New York World-Telegram,* July 23, 1936.

43. *Seattle Times,* July 29, 1936; *Boston Evening Transcript,* July 29, 1936; *Richmond Times-Dispatch,* July 21 and 24, 1936; *Dallas Morning News,* July 21, 1936; *America,* August 29, 1935, 491−93; *American Mercury* 40 (1937):158−66; *Commonweal,* June 5, 1936, 141−42, June 26, 1936, 237−39, August 14, 1936, 373−74; *National Republic* 24, no. 5 (1936):10.

44. *Pittsburgh Post-Gazette,* August 10, 1936; *Cleveland Plain Dealer,* August 22, 1936; *Hartford Courant,* August 5, 1936; *Philadelphia Inquirer,* August 19, 1936; *Cincinnati Enquirer,* August 20, 1936; *Christian Science Monitor,* August 19, 1936, 16, August 24, 1936, 16; *Common Sense* 5, no. 9 (1936):6−7; *Christian Century,* August 12, 1936, 1075−76, September 2, 1936, 1147, October 22, 1936, 1382−83.

45. *New York Times,* October 11, 12, and 25, 1936; *Hartford Courant,* August 5, 1936; *Cincinnati Enquirer,* August 21, 1936; *Nation,* July 25, 1936, 85−86, October 31, 1936, 508−9, February 13, 1937, 172, August 21, 1937, 186; *New Republic,* October 21, 1936, 295−96; Warren, *Liberals and Communism,* 127−42.

46. *Richmond Times-Dispatch,* August 16, 1936; *Charlotte Observer,* August 20, November 28, 1936; *Los Angeles Examiner,* August 21 and 24, 1936; *Christian Science Monitor,* August 22, 1936; *Time,* January 25, 1937, 18; *National Republic* 24, no. 1 (1936):11, 30, and 26, no. 7 (1938):11−12; *American Mercury* 41 (1937):6−18, 46 (1939):12−21; Chamberlin, *Collectivism,* 150−55.

47. *Atlanta Constitution,* November 26, 1936; *Des Moines Register,* November 27, 1936; *Courier-Journal,* November 28, 1936; *Minneapolis Tribune,* November 26, 1936; *Philadelphia Inquirer,* November 26, 1936.

48. *Time,* August 8, 1938, 14, August 15, 1938, 13; *Washington Post,* August 4, 1938; *Cincinnati Enquirer,* August 1 and 4, 1938; *New York Herald Tribune,* August 2, 1938; *Baltimore Sun,* August 6, 1938. See John Erickson, *The Soviet High Command: A Military-Political History, 1918−1941,* 494−97; James E. McSherry, *Stalin, Hitler, and Europe,* 1:17−22; Alvin D. Coox, *The Anatomy of a Small War: The Soviet-Japanese Struggle for Changkufeng/Khasan, 1938.*

49. *Courier-Journal,* August 4 and 10, 1938; *Newsweek,* August 1, 1938, 15−16, August 8, 1938, 13, August 15, 1938, 17; *Cincinnati Enquirer,* August 13, 1938; *Cleveland Plain Dealer,* August 12, 1938; *Hartford Courant,* August 12, 1938; *Philadelphia Inquirer,* August 8, 1938.

50. *Richmond Times-Dispatch,* March 15, 1938; *New York Times,* May 4, July 25, 1938.

51. *Washington Post,* September 20, 1938; *New York World-Telegram,* September 19 and 22, 1938; *Portland Oregonian,* September 26, 1938; *Cleveland Plain Dealer,* September 20 and 29, 1938; *New York Times,* September 18, 1938; *Dallas Morning News,* September 27 and 28, 1938; *Nation,* March 3, 1938, 261, July 2, 1938, 2, October 8, 1938, 340−41, October 29, 1938, 440; *Christian Century,* October 12, 1938, 1225, November 2, 1938, 1317, December 21, 1938, 1564.

52. *Portland Oregonian*, October 3, 1938; *Christian Science Monitor*, September 29, 1938; *Seattle Times*, September 30, 1938; *National Republic* 46, no. 7 (1938):11–12; *American Mercury* 46 (1939):12–21.

53. *Denver Post*, October 3 and 5, 1938; *Des Moines Register*, October 3, 1938; *Cleveland Plain Dealer*, September 30, 1938; *Cincinnati Enquirer*, September 29, 1938.

54. *Philadelphia Inquirer*, September 30, 1938.

NOTES TO CHAPTER 7

1. Bullitt dispatch to Hull, April 20, 1936, in U.S., Department of State, *Foreign Relations of the United States: The Soviet Union, 1933–1939* (hereafter cited as *F.R.U.S.*).

2. See Robert A. Divine, *The Illusion of Neutrality*, 122–28; and Richard P. Traina, *American Diplomacy and the Spanish Civil War*, 46–99, 178–239.

3. See Ernest C. Bolt, Jr., *Ballots before Bullitts: The War Referendum Approach to Peace in America, 1914–1941*, 152–85.

4. George Wolfskill, *The Revolt of the Conservatives: A History of the American Liberty League, 1933–1940*, 152; *New York Times*, July 17, August 3, 24, 1936; Elizabeth Dilling, *The Roosevelt Red Record and Its Background*, 3; David H. Bennett, *Demagogues in the Depression: American Radicals and the Union Party, 1932–1936*, 11–12, 19, 51–57, 139–44, 227–30, 238.

5. Wolfskill, *Liberty League*, 217; Hull telegram to Henderson, Henderson telegram to Hull, August 27, 1936, Department of State File 800.00B–Communist International/188B. 193, Department of State MSS, National Archives (hereafter cited as D.S.F.).

6. Roscoe Baker, *The American Legion and American Foreign Policy*, 79; George Q. Flynn, *Roosevelt and Romanism: Catholics and American Diplomacy, 1937–1945*, 137–42.

7. Walter Goodman, *The Committee: The Extraordinary Career of the House Committee on Un-American Activities*, 16–55; August Raymond Ogden, *The Dies Committee: A Study of the Special House Committee for the Investigation of Un-American Activities, 1938–1943*, 43–103; *Public Opinion Quarterly* 3, no. 6 (1939):595.

8. See Richard Polenberg, "Franklin Roosevelt and Civil Liberties: The Case of the Dies Committee," 165–79.

9. Bullitt dispatch to Hull, April 20, 1936, *F.R.U.S. Soviet Union*, 296; Henderson dispatch to Hull, November 16, 1936, D.S.F. 711.61/611; Kelley memorandum, March 5, May 26, 1936, D.S.F. 711.61/597, 861.01/2120.

10. United Fruit Company to Ivan V. Boyeff, November, 1936, Michael S. Batt to A.A. Pollan, January 27, 1937, Box 13A, Gumberg Papers, State Historical Society of Wisconsin. See also U.S., Department of Commerce, Bureau of Foreign and Domestic Commerce, Record Group 151, File 448, Russia–Trade with the U.S.; Floyd J. Fithian, "Soviet-American Relations, 1918–1933: American Business in Russia During the Period of Non-Recognition," 280–83, 344–48; Anthony C. Sutton, *Western Technology and Soviet Economic Development*, 161–63, 207–48, and passim.

11. For Stalin's naval strategy, see Robert W. Herrick, *Soviet Naval Strategy*, 28–46. For the battleship episode, see Thomas R. Maddux, "United States–Soviet Naval Relations in the 1930's: The Soviet Union's Effort to Purchase Naval Vessels," 28–37.

12. Kelley memorandum, March 24, 1937, *F.R.U.S. Soviet Union*, 465–66. See also Green memorandum, December 3, 1936, and Hull to Claude A. Swanson, secretary of the navy, March 26, 1937, ibid., 458–59, 467–69.

13. See Leahy diary, April 14, December 9, 1937, July 21, 1938, Leahy Papers, Library of Congress.

14. Ickes diary, April 3, 1937, in Harold L. Ickes, *The Secret Diary of Harold L. Ickes*, vols. 2, 3; Leahy diary, April 15, 1937, Leahy Papers.

15. See Green memorandum, April 17, 1937, *F.R.U.S. Soviet Union*, 469–70.

16. See Green memoranda, September 22, November 15, 1937, July 27, 1939, ibid., 480–82, 488–89, 893–94. See also Green to Hugh Wilson, May 5, 1938, Wilson Papers, Herbert Hoover Presidential Library.

17. Green memorandum, September 24, 1937, F.R.U.S. Soviet Union, 482–83; Leahy diary, April 14, December 9, 1939, Leahy Papers.

18. See F.R.U.S. Soviet Union, 680–81, 692; Leahy diary, April 8, 1938, Leahy Papers; Green to Wilson, May 5, 1938, Wilson Papers.

19. See F.R.U.S. Soviet Union, 689–99; Moffat diary, June 8, 1938, vol. 40, Moffat Papers, Houghton Library; Leahy diary, June 1, July 21, 1938, Leahy Papers.

20. Green memorandum, May 27, June 21, 1939, F.R.U.S. Soviet Union, 882, 884–85.

21. See Bullitt to Hull, July 19, 1937, Corres. II, Box 41, File 99-A, Hull Papers, Library of Congress; Bullitt to Moore, June 15, July 5, 1937, Box 3, Robert Walton Moore Papers, Library of Congress; and George F. Kennan, Memoirs 1925–1950, 83–84. Moore told Bullitt he would privately tell him about the "big shake-up."

22. See Vladimir Petrov, A Study in Diplomacy: The Story of Arthur Bliss Lane, 87–92. Lane also opposed a transfer of Kelley to the Moscow embassy (Lane to Moore, June 18, 1937, Lane Papers, Yale University Library). See also George Kennan to John Wiley, November 28, 1938, Box 7, Wiley Papers, Franklin D. Roosevelt Library.

23. Charles E. Bohlen, Witness to History, 39–41; Kennan, Memoirs, 84–86.

24. Troyanovsky to Litvinov, December 14, 1937, in U.S.S.R., Soviet Ministry of Foreign Affairs, Dokumenty vneshnei politiki, SSSR, 20:658.

25. Davies diary, January 2, 1937, in Joseph E. Davies, Mission to Moscow, 6; Keith D. Eagles, "Ambassador Joseph E. Davies and American-Soviet Relations, 1937–1941," 91–97; Kennan, Memoirs, 82.

26. Davies dispatches to Hull, March 26, 1937, June 6, 1938, D.S.F. 852.00/5091, 861.00/11786; Bullitt to Roosevelt, Nov. 24, 1936, in Edgar B. Nixon, ed., Franklin D. Roosevelt and Foreign Affairs, 1933–1936, 3:500; Kennan, Memoirs, 83.

27. See Traina, American Diplomacy and the Spanish Civil War, 111–17; Arnold A. Offner, American Appeasement: United States Foreign Policy and Germany, 1933–1938, 176–82, 190–94; Francis L. Loewenheim, "An Illusion That Shaped History: New Light on the History and Historiography of American Peace Efforts before Munich," 177–220.

28. See Dorothy Borg, The United States and the Far Eastern Crisis of 1933–1938, 369–98; Offner, American Appeasement, 191–92.

29. See Max Beloff, The Foreign Policy of Soviet Russia, 1929–1941, 2:179–80; Adam B. Ulam, Expansion and Coexistence: The History of Soviet Foreign Policy, 1917–1967, 248; New York Times, March 5, 1936; Henderson telegrams to Hull, January 13, 17, 1936, F.R.U.S. Soviet Union, 284–88; Bullitt telegrams to Hull, February 17, March 2, 1936, D.S.F. 711.61/594-595.

30. Davies to Roosevelt, February 17, 1937, Box 3, Davies Papers, Library of Congress; Davies dispatch to Hull, February 18, 1937, D.S.F. 800.51 W 89 U.S.S.R./ 232.

31. Troyanovsky to the Soviet Foreign Affairs Ministry, June 15, Troyanovsky to Litvinov, October 21, December 1, 1936, Dokumenty vneshnei politiki, SSSR, 19:303–5, 503–7, 623–25.

32. Troyanovsky to Litvinov, January 9, 1937, ibid., 20:19–23.

33. Soviet Foreign Affairs Ministry to Troyanovsky, June 18 and 21, Troyanovsky to Soviet Foreign Affairs Ministry, June 29, 1937, ibid., 337–38n133, 731–32; B. Ponomaryov et al., History of Soviet Foreign Policy, 1917–1945, 317–18.

34. Robert Dallek, Democrat and Diplomat: The Life of William E. Dodd, 310; Dodd diary, October 19, 1937, in William E. Dodd, Jr., and Martha Dodd, eds., Ambassador Dodd's Diary, 1933–1938, 428.

35. Messersmith to Hull, October 11, 1937, F.R.U.S. 1937, 1:140–45. See also

Robert Dallek, "Beyond Tradition: The Diplomatic Careers of William E. Dodd and George S. Messersmith, 1933–1938," 233–44.

36. Carr Diary, Aug. 19, 1937, Box 6, Carr Papers, Library of Congress.

37. Henderson to Lane, June 18, 1937, Lane Papers. See also Henderson dispatches to Hull, July 3, September 2, 1937, D.S.F. 761.94/973, 983; F.R.U.S. 1937, 3:484–85, 562–66, 922–28; Hull telegram to Davies, July 2, 1937, D.S.F. 761.9415 Amur River/7A. When Davies intervened in the Amur River clash and urged both sides to localize the conflict, Hull angrily told him to keep out of the dispute.

38. Stimson diary, March 24, 1938, vol. 37, Stimson Papers, Yale University Library. See also Moore to Lane, Feb. 23, 1937, Box 8, Robert Walton Moore Papers.

39. Hornbeck memorandum, January 3, 1935, F.R.U.S. 1935, 3:836–37.

40. Moffat diary, October 10, 1937, vol. 39, Moffat Papers; Hamilton memorandum, October 12, 1937, F.R.U.S. 1937, 3:586.

41. Welles memorandum, October 2, 28, 1937, F.R.U.S. 1937, 3:570–72, D.S.F. 852.00/6788; Moffat diary, October 28, November 4, 8, and 9, 1937, vol. 39, Moffat Papers; Davis memoranda, November 4, 5, and 8, 1937, Box 4, Norman Davis Papers, Library of Congress; Borg, Far Eastern Crisis, 399–442.

42. Litvinov to Soviet Foreign Affairs Ministry, November 5 and 6, Litvinov to Troyanovsky, November 13 and 26, 1937, Dokumenty vneshnei politiki, SSSR, 20:593–601, 605–6, 621–23.

43. Dodd to Hull, November 15, 1937, Corres. II, Box 42, File 102, Hull Papers; Hull memorandum to Roosevelt, January 24, Roosevelt memorandum to Hull, January 25, 1938, ibid.

44. See John McVickar Haight, Jr., "Franklin D. Roosevelt and a Naval Quarantine of Japan," 203–26; Offner, American Appeasement, 217–25; Loewenheim, "American Peace Efforts," 185–206; Lawrence Pratt, "The Anglo-American Naval Conversations on the Far East of January 1938," 745–63.

45. Davies dispatch to Hull, January 17, 1939, D.S.F. 800.51 W 89 U.S.S.R./247. Davies summarized the episode in this dispatch.

46. Messersmith memorandum to Hull, January 3, 1938, F.R.U.S. Soviet Union, 505. The original text (D.S.F. 711.00/814) has the underlinings. See also Kennan memorandum, November 24, 1937, D.S.F. 124.61/119; Hull memorandum, January 13, 1938, Box 61, File 250, Hull Papers.

47. Davies dispatch to Hull, January 17, 1939, D.S.F. 800.51 W 89 U.S.S.R./247; Moffat diary, March 24, 1938, vol. 39, Moffat Papers. See also Hull, Memoirs, 1:658–59; D.S.F. 124.61/122, 126, 130, 134; F.R.U.S. Soviet Union, 629–69.

48. Davies dispatch to Hull, June 9, 1938, F.R.U.S. Soviet Union, 567–82; Davies memoranda, June 9 and 10, 1938, Boxes 8 and 9, Davies Papers. Davies did not mention the military liaison in his formal report to Hull. Unfortunately Dokumenty vneshnei politiki, SSSR, vol. 21, does not contain any references to Roosevelt's proposal, Davies' meeting with Stalin, or even Troyanovsky's meeting with Hull.

49. Hull memoranda, June 7 and 18, 1938, Box 51, File 250, Hull Papers; Davies diary, June 24–28, July 4–5, 1938, in Davies, Mission, 370–75; Davies dispatch to Hull, January 17, Davies to Roosevelt, January 18, 1939, D.S.F. 800.51 W 89 U.S.S.R./257.

50. See Offner, American Appeasement, 226–69; John McVickar Haight, Jr., American Aid to France, 1938–1940, 7–99; William L. Langer and Samuel E. Gleason, The Challenge to Isolation, 1937–1940, 32–90, 122–59. See also Frederick C. Adams, "The Road to Pearl Harbor: A Reexamination of American Far Eastern Policy, July 1937–December 1938," 73–92, for a conflicting although unconvincing argument that Washington's basic stance toward Japan crystalized by the end of 1938 instead of 1940.

51. Troyanovsky to Litvinov, January 26, March 2, April 13, 1938, Dokumenty vneshnei politiki, SSSR, 21:51–54, 109–11, 190–93.

52. Morgenthau diary, June 30, 1939, vol. 199, 428–37, Morgenthau Papers,

Franklin D. Roosevelt Library. In a memorandum to Hull (April 27, 1939), Roosevelt agreed to accept Oumansky but suggested that Washington "double the guard!" (Elliott Roosevelt, ed., *F.D.R.: His Personal Letters, 1928–1945*, 880). See also Hull, *Memoirs*, 1:743.

53. See *F.R.U.S. 1938*, 3:441–48; *F.R.U.S. 1939*, 3:1–73; Grew diary, July 1939, vol. 93, Grew Papers, Houghton Library; Henderson memorandum, July 2, 1939, D.S.F. 761.99/324; Hull telegrams to Roosevelt, July 27, August 5, 1939, Official File 200-ccc, Trips of the President, Roosevelt Papers, Franklin D. Roosevelt Library.

54. Berle diary, March 16, 1939, Beatrice Bishop Berle and Travis Beal Jacobs, eds., *Navigating the Rapids, 1918–1971: From the Papers of Adolf A. Berle*, 199.

55. Davies diary, July 18, 1939, Davies, *Mission*, 450; Welles to Steinhardt, August 4, 1939, Box 27, Steinhardt Papers, Library of Congress.

56. *Nation*, April 1, 1939, 365, May 13, 1939, 548; *New Republic*, May 31, 1939, 91–93, June 24, 1939, 172; *Christian Century*, April 12, 1939, 471–72, May 17, 1939, 628; *Common Sense* 6 (1939):18; *New York Times*, April 14, May 21, 1939; *Washington Post*, April 12 and 14, 1939; *Richmond Times-Dispatch*, April 9 and 19, 1939.

57. *New York Herald Tribune*, April 2, 4, and 22, 1939; *Philadelphia Inquirer*, April 6, 1939; *Pittsburgh Post-Gazette*, May 6, 1939; *Miami Herald*, May 4, 1939; *St. Louis Post-Dispatch*, May 4, 1939; *Cleveland Plain Dealer*, May 5, 1939; *Chicago Daily News*, May 5, 1939; *Detroit News*, May 5, 1939.

58. *National Republic* 26 (1939):12; *Catholic World* 49 (1939):389; *Commonweal*, May 5, 1939, June 23, 1939, 233–35; *Christian Science Monitor*, May 4, 1939, 1; *Saturday Evening Post*, April 15, 1939, 115–22, April 22, 1939, 16–17, 71–77, April 29, 1939, 85–89. Krivitsky was a former chief of Soviet military intelligence in Western Europe. See also *Baltimore Sun*, May 9, 1939; *Courier-Journal* (Louisville), May 5, 1939; *Dallas Morning News*, May 9, 1939; *Denver Post*, May 4, 1939.

59. *Washington Post*, May 9, 1939; *St. Louis Post-Dispatch*, May 9, 1939; *Minneapolis Tribune*, May 5, 1939; *Portland Oregonian*, May 11, 1939; *Des Moines Register*, May 5, 1939; *Chicago Tribune*, May 5, 1939.

60. *America*, May 20, 1939, 133–34; *Charlotte Observer*, May 10, 1939; *New York Herald Tribune*, June 1, 1939; *Philadelphia Inquirer*, May 6, June 8, 1939; *Atlanta Constitution*, May 6, 1939; *New York World-Telegram*, June 2, 1939.

61. See *Omaha Morning World-Herald*, May 5, June 7, 1939; *Hartford Courant*, May 5, 1939; *Seattle Times*, June 6, 1939; *Chicago Tribune*, June 2, 1939.

NOTES TO CHAPTER 8

1. *Philadelphia Inquirer*, August 23, 1939; *Cincinnati Enquirer*, August 25, 1939; *Boston Evening Transcript*, August 22 and 23, 1939; *St. Louis Post-Dispatch*, August 22, 1939.

2. *Detroit News*, August 23, 1939; *Philadelphia Inquirer*, August 25, 1939; *Pittsburgh Post-Gazette*, August 23 and 25, 1939; *Chicago Daily News*, August 22, 1939; *Kansas City Star*, August 26, 1939.

3. Louis Fischer, *Stalin and Hitler*, 4–5, 38–61; Louis Fischer, *Men and Politics: Europe Between the Two World Wars*, 604; *New Republic*, August 30, 1939, 88–89, September 6, 13, 1939, 118, 150–51; *Nation*, August 26, 1939, 211–12; *Common Sense* 8, no. 10 (1939):18; *Christian Century*, August 30, 1939, 1035, September 6, 1939, 1062; Frank A. Warren, III, *Liberals and Communism: The "Red Decade" Revisited*, 197–204.

4. *American Mercury* 48 (1939):224–28; Chamberlin, *The Confessions of an Individualist*, 178–79, 265–67; *Pittsburgh Post-Gazette*, August 25, 1939; *America*, September 2, 1939, 484–85. See also *Newsweek*, September 4, 1939, 48; *Atlanta Constitution*, August 28, 1939; *Charlotte Observer*, August 23, 1939; *Times-Picayune* (New Orleans), August 23, 1939; *Denver Post*, August 23, 1939; *Dallas Morning News*, August 22, 1939; *Philadelphia Inquirer*, August 28, 1939.

5. *Omaha Morning World-Herald*, August 25, 1939; *Pittsburgh Post-Gazette*, August 23 and 25, 1939; *Portland Oregonian*, August 24, 1939; *New York Times*, August 26, September 12, 1939.

6. *Pittsburgh Post-Gazette*, August 30, 1939; *Times-Picayune* (New Orleans), August 23, 1939; *San Francisco Chronicle*, August 23, 1939; *Los Angeles Times*, September 13, 1934; *Christian Science Monitor*, August 24, 1939, 20; *Charlotte Observer*, August 23, 1939; *Chicago Daily News*, August 22, 1939.

7. *Nation*, (August 26, 1939), 212; *New Republic*, September 6, 1939; *Christian Century*, September 6, 1939, 1062.

8. *Des Moines Register*, August 23, 1939; *Seattle Times*, August 24, 1939; *Detroit News*, August 28, 1939; *Times-Picayune* (New Orleans), August 23, 1939; *Time*, August 28, 1939, 10, September 4, 1939, 17.

9. *Kansas City Star*, August 26, 1939; *St. Louis Post-Dispatch*, August 22, 1939; *San Francisco Chronicle*, August 23, 1939; *Richmond Times-Dispatch*, August 26, 1939; *Atlanta Constitution*, August 29, 1939.

10. *Omaha Morning World-Herald*, August 25, 1939; *American Mercury* 48 (1939):224–28; *Pittsburgh Post-Gazette*, August 25, 1939; *Christian Science Monitor*, September 16, 1939, 20; *Wall Street Journal*, August 23, 1939; *Boston Evening Transcript*, August 22, 1939.

11. *Des Moines Register*, October 31, 1939; *San Francisco Chronicle*, September 18, 1939; *Cleveland Plain Dealer*, September 17, 1939; *St. Louis Post-Dispatch*, September 17, 1939; *Philadelphia Inquirer*, October 1, 1939; *Dallas Morning News*, September 18, 1939; *Courier-Journal*, September 17, 1939.

12. *Cincinnati Enquirer*, September 19, 1939; *St. Louis Post-Dispatch*, September 18, 1939; *Baltimore Sun*, September 18, 1939; *Chicago Tribune*, September 18, 1939; *Pittsburgh Post-Gazette*, September 19, 1939.

13. *Nation*, September 23, 1939, 309–10, October 21, 1939, 427–28, November 1, 1939, 511–12; *Christian Century*, September 2, 1939, 1155–56, October 11, 1939, 1227, November 1, 1939, 1326–27; *New Republic*, September 27, 1939, 197–98, 200–201, October 11, 1939, 254–55, 257–58, October 18, 1939, 281, October 25, 1939, 323, November 15, 1939, 98–99, November 29, 1939, 154–55.

14. *New York Times*, September 18, 1939; *New York Herald Tribune*, September 18, 1939; *Pittsburgh Post-Gazette*, September 22, 1939; *Denver Post*, September 18 and 23, 1939; *San Francisco Chronicle*, September 18, 1939; *Seattle Post-Intelligencer*, September 20, 1939.

15. *Minneapolis Tribune*, October 11, 1939; *Christian Science Monitor*, September 18, 1939, 19; *New York Times*, September 18, 1939; *San Francisco Chronicle*, September 30, 1939; *Hartford Courant*, September 18, 1939; *Denver Post*, September 18, 1939; *Dallas Morning News*, September 18, 1939.

16. *Nation*, September 23, 1939, 309–10; *Times-Picayune* (New Orleans), September 19 and 20, 1939; *Richmond Times-Dispatch*, September 18, 1939; *Christian Century*, September 27, 1939, 1155–56; *Foreign Policy Bulletin*, September 22, 1939.

17. *Time*, September 25, 1939, 23–24; *Atlanta Constitution*, September 18, 1939; *Baltimore Sun*, September 18 and 19, 1939; *Washington Post*, September 18, 1939; Raymond Gram Swing broadcast, September 29, 1939, Box 8, Swing Papers, Library of Congress.

18. *Cincinnati Enquirer*, September 18, 19, and 29, 1939; *Cleveland Plain Dealer*, September 17, 18, 19, and 29, 1939; *Boston Evening Transcript*, September 18 and 27, 1939; *St. Louis Post-Dispatch*, Sept. 18 and 25, 1939.

19. *Hartford Courant*, September 18, 21, and 28, 1939; *Chicago Daily News*, September 19 and 22, 1939.

20. *San Francisco Chronicle*, September 19, 1939; *Philadelphia Inquirer*, September 18, October 12, 1939; *Charlotte Observer*, September 30, 1939; *Atlanta Constitution*, October 12, 1939; *Omaha Morning World-Herald*, September 14, October 9, 1939; H.V. Kaltenborn broadcast, October 31, 1939, Box 156, Kaltenborn Papers, State Historical

Society of Wisconsin; *National Republic* 27, no. 6 (1939):7–8, 30, and no. 7 (1939):11–12; *America*, October 28, 1939, 61.

21. *Nation*, November 1, 1939, 511–12; *New Republic*, October 11, 1939, 257–58; *Times-Picayune* (New Orleans), October 3, 1939; *Time*, October 9, 1939, 28–29; *Newsweek*, October 9, 1939, 18, October 16, 1939, 19–21, October 23, 1939, 19.

22. *Philadelphia Inquirer*, October 12, 1939; *Boston Evening Transcript*, September 29, October 5, 1939; *Atlanta Constitution*, October 12, 1939; *National Republic* 27, no. 7 (1939):12.

23. *Cleveland Plain Dealer*, September 29 and 30, October 9, 1939; *Pittsburgh Post-Gazette*, Oct. 12, 13, and 17, 1939; *Cincinnati Enquirer*, September 29, October 9, 1939; *Christian Science Monitor*, September 30, 1939, 20, October 16, 1939, 14; *Christian Century*, October 11, 1939, 1227, November 1, 1939, 1326–27.

24. *Washington Post*, September 30, 1939; *Baltimore Sun*, September 19, 1939; *Richmond Times-Dispatch*, September 27 and 30, 1939; *Dallas Morning News*, October 3, 1939; *Seattle Times*, October 12, 1939.

25. *National Republic* 27, no. 7 (1939):11; Ronald Earnest Magden, "Attitudes of the American Religious Press toward Soviet Russia, 1939–1941," 52–63, 78–89; *Atlanta Constitution*, October 10, 1939; *Portland Oregonian*, October 12, 1939; *Detroit News*, October 9, 1939; *Philadelphia Inquirer*, September 28, October 5, 1939.

26. *Los Angeles Times*, September 19, 1939; *Boston Evening Transcript*, September 18, October 10, 1939; *Atlanta Constitution*, September 18, 1939; *Miami Herald*, September 17 and 18, 1939; *Minneapolis Tribune*, September 19, 1939; *America*, October 21, 1939, 38–39.

27. *Cleveland Plain Dealer*, September 19 and 30, 1939; *Pittsburgh Post-Gazette*, October 13, 1939; *New York Herald Tribune*, September 18, 1939; *Washington Post*, September 18, 1939; *American Mercury* 48 (1939):226.

28. Walter Goodman, *The Committee: The Extraordinary Career of the House Committee on Un-American Activities*, 65; August Raymond Ogden, *The Dies Committee: A Study of the Special House Committee for the Investigation of Un-American Activities, 1938–1943*, 134–79; *Newsweek*, September 11, 1939, 60.

29. See Hadley Cantril, ed., *Public Opinion, 1935–1946*, 164.

30. Moffat diary, September 18, 1939, vol. 43, Moffat Papers, Houghton Library; John Wiley to Lane, October 31, 1939, Lane Papers, Yale University Library; Wiley telegram to Hull, September 29, 1939, Department of State File 7601.61/38, Department of State MSS, National Archives (hereafter cited as D.S.F.).

31. Berle diary, September 3, 1939, in William L. Langer and Samuel E. Gleason, *The Challenge to Isolation, 1937–1940*, 203. This statement is not included in Beatrice Berle and Travis Jacobs, eds., *Navigating the Rapids, 1918–1971: From the Papers of Adolf A. Berle*, 249–51.

32. Steinhardt telegrams to Hull, September 17, 22, 26, 27, 29, October 4, 1939, D.S.F. 740.0011 European War 1939/352, 496, 554, 760D.61/218, and U.S., Department of State, *Foreign Relations of the United States 1939*, 1:455–56, 482 (hereafter cited as *F.R.U.S.*); Charles E. Bohlen, *Witness to History, 1929–1969*, 82–90.

33. Cordell Hull, *The Memoirs of Cordell Hull*, 1:685; Long diary, September 2, 1939, in Fred L. Israel, ed., *The War Diary of Breckinridge Long: Selections from the Years 1939–1944*, 18.

34. Berle diary, September 22, 1939, in Berle and Jacobs, eds., *Papers*, 258.

35. Moffat diary, September 1, 1939, in Nancy H. Hooker, ed., *The Moffat Papers: Selections from the Diplomatic Journals of Jay Pierrepont Moffat, 1919–1943*, 261; Bullitt to Alexander Kirk, September 28, 1939, Wilson to Bullitt, October 16, 1939, Wilson to Kirk, Dec. 4, 1939, Wilson Papers, Hoover Institution; Long diary, October 5, 1939, in Israel, ed., *War Diary*, 24; Berle diary, September 13 and 18, 1939, in Langer and Gleason, *Challenge to Isolation*, 245, and Berle and Jacobs, eds., *Papers*, 254–56.

36. See Holger H. Herwig, "Prelude to *Weltblitzkrieg*: Germany's Naval Policy toward the United States of America, 1939-1941," 649–68.

37. Long diary, October 11, 1939, in Israel, ed., *War Diary*, 39; Wilson to Kirk, December 4, 1939, Wilson Papers; Berle diary, September 14, 1939, in Berle and Jacobs, eds., *Papers*, 255.

38. Ickes diary, Oct. 14, 1939, in Harold L. Ickes, *The Secret Diary of Harold L. Ickes*, 3:37. Hull (*Memoirs*, 1:685) and Langer and Gleason (*Challenge to Isolation*, 245) overemphasize the influence of potential Nazi-Soviet conflict on Washington's calculations in the fall of 1939.

39. Grew to Roosevelt, November 6, 1939, President's Secretary's File, Japan 1938-1940, Box 13, Roosevelt Papers, Franklin D. Roosevelt Library (hereafter cited as P.S.F.); Long diary, September 15 and 19, 1939, in Israel, ed., *War Diary*, 14–17; *F.R.U.S. 1939*, 3:62–63, 67–73, 76–78, 93–94, 261–262.

40. Welles memoranda, November 21, December 6, 1939, Langer and Gleason, *Challenge to Isolation*, 305; *F.R.U.S. 1939*, 3:96–97; Hull, *Memoirs*, 1:720-27; Hull memorandum, December 15, 1939, *F.R.U.S. 1939*, 3:98–99.

41. Biddle to Roosevelt, December 4, Roosevelt to Biddle, December 28, 1939, P.S.F., Poland, 1939, Box 17.

42. Morgenthau diary, December 19, 1939, vol. 230, 408, Morgenthau Papers, Franklin D. Roosevelt Library; John Blum, *From the Morgenthau Diaries: Years of Urgency, 1938–1941*, 123–25; record of Hull conversation with Hornbeck, December 11, 1939, Box 61, Hornbeck Papers, Hoover Institution.

43. See Gerhard L. Weinberg, *Germany and the Soviet Union, 1939–1941*, 87–88; Adam B. Ulam, *Expansion and Coexistence: The History of Soviet Foreign Policy, 1917–1967*, 289–90; James E. McSherry, *Stalin, Hitler, and Europe*, 17–38.

44. Long diary, October 11, 1939, in Israel, ed., *War Diary*, 27.

45. Moffat diary, October 25–28, 1939, vol. 43, Moffat Papers. See also John Garry Clifford, "The Odyssey of the *City of Flint*," 100–116; Hull, *Memoirs*, 1:704–5; *F.R.U.S. Soviet Union*, 984–1013. After the *City of Flint* finally left Murmansk, it put into another Norwegian port, where the officials interned the German crew and released the ship to the American crew.

46. Ickes to Raymond Robins, Oct. 17, 1939, Box 28, Robins Papers, State Historical Society of Wisconsin.

47. Hull telegram to Steinhardt, October 11, 1939, *F.R.U.S. 1939*, 1:967. See also Berle diary, October 6, November 29, 1939, in Berle and Jacobs, eds., *Papers*, 263–64, 273.

NOTES TO CHAPTER 9

1. *Philadelphia Inquirer*, December 1, 1939; *San Francisco Chronicle*, December 1, 1939; *Portland Oregonian*, December 1, 1939; *New York Herald Tribune*, December 1, 1939; *Boston Evening Transcript*, December 1, 1939; *Detroit News*, December 1, 1939.

2. *Washington Post*, December 1, 1939; *New York Times*, November 30, December 1, 1939; *Pittsburgh Post-Gazette*, December 1, 1939; *Charlotte Observer*, December 2, 1939; *Christian Science Monitor*, December 1, 1939; *Courier-Journal* (Louisville), December 1, 1939; *Dallas Morning News*, December 1, 1939; *Atlanta Constitution*, December 1, 1939; *Times-Picayune* (New Orleans), December 1, 1939; *Cleveland Plain Dealer*, December 1, 1939.

3. *New Republic*, December 13, 1939, 218–19; *Nation*, December 2, 1939, 640, December 16, 1939, 665; *Common Sense* 9, no. 1 (1940):16, 18; *Christian Century*, December 13, 1939, 1535.

4. *Christian Century*, December 13, 1939, 1534; *Los Angeles Times*, January 23, 1940; *Time*, Dec. 11, 1939, 26–27; *Common Sense* 9, no. 1 (1940):18; *New Republic*,

December 13, 1939, 218–19; *Denver Post,* December 3, 1939; *Omaha Morning World-Herald,* December 12, 1939.

5. *Courier-Journal* (Louisville), December 1, 1939; *Pittsburgh Post-Gazette,* December 6, 1939; *Portland Oregonian,* Dec. 17, 1939; *St. Louis Post-Dispatch,* December 14, 1939; *Hartford Courant,* December 1 and 7, 1939; *Des Moines Register,* December 1, 1939; *Washington Post,* December 1, 1939.

6. *Cincinnati Enquirer,* December 2 and 16, 1939; *Cleveland Plain Dealer,* December 23, 1939; *Philadelphia Inquirer,* December 1 and 2, 1939; *Baltimore Sun,* December 3 and 4, 1939; *Boston Evening Transcript,* December 1 and 4, 1939.

7. *San Francisco Chronicle,* December 2, 1939, 12; *Pittsburgh Post-Gazette,* December 6, 1939; *Atlanta Constitution,* December 1 and 6, 1939; *Dallas Morning News,* December 2, 1939; *America,* March 23, 1940, 646.

8. *New York Herald Tribune,* December 1, 1939; *Charlotte Observer,* January 17, 1940; *Chicago Daily News,* December 1, 1939; *Omaha Morning World-Herald,* December 1, 1939; Dorothy Thompson in *Pittsburgh Post-Gazette,* December 5, 1939; *Boston Evening Transcript,* December 4, 1939.

9. *St. Louis Post-Dispatch,* December 15, 1939; *Pittsburgh Post-Gazette,* December 15, 1939; *Washington Post,* December 10 and 14, 1939; *Cleveland Plain Dealer,* December 15, 1939; *Baltimore Sun,* December 15, 1939; *San Francisco Chronicle,* December 15, 1939.

10. *Pittsburgh Post-Gazette,* December 2, 4, and 6, 1939; *National Republic* 27, no. 10 (1940):12; *America,* December 9, 1939, 326, December 16, 1939, 254, 266–67; *Los Angeles Examiner,* December 2, 1939; *Denver Post,* December 1, 1939; *Detroit News,* December 6, 1939; *Seattle Times,* December 5, 1939; *New York World-Telegram,* December 4, 1939.

11. *San Francisco Chronicle,* December 4, 1939; *Newsweek,* December 18, 1939, 15–16; *Dallas Morning News,* December 7, 1939; *St. Louis Post-Dispatch,* December 4, 1939; *Atlanta Constitution,* December 20, 1939; *Baltimore Sun,* December 5, 1939; *Cincinnati Enquirer,* December 7, 1939; *Hartford Courant,* December 4, 1939; *New York Herald Tribune,* December 3, 1939; *Philadelphia Inquirer,* December 3, 1939.

12. *Congressional Record,* 76th Cong., 3rd sess., January 11, 1940, 290–91, February 7, 1940, 1175–92; McCormack to Hull, December 3, 1939, Department of State File 711.61/688, Department of State MSS, National Archives (hereafter cited as D.S.F.); Vandenberg to Hull, Dec. 7, 1939, D.S.F. 711.61/691.

13. Roosevelt to Grew, November 30, Roosevelt to William A. White, December 14, 1939, in Elliott Roosevelt, ed., *F.D.R.: His Personal Letters, 1927–1945,* 2:961, 967–68; Roosevelt to Lincoln MacVeagh, December 1, 1939, President's Personal File 1192, Roosevelt Papers, Franklin D. Roosevelt Library. MacVeagh was minister to Greece.

14. George H. Gallup, *The Gallup Poll: Public Opinion, 1935–1973,* 1:197, 207; *Public Opinion Quarterly* 4, no. 2 (1940):358–59; Hadley Cantril, ed., *Public Opinion, 1935–1946,* 970; Peggy M. Mulvihill, "The United States and the Russo-Finnish War," 71–93.

15. Moffat diary, Nov. 30, 1939, vol. 43, Moffat Papers, Houghton Library; Henderson to Samuel Harper, December 9, 1939, Letters 1939, Harper Papers, University of Chicago Library; Henderson to Wiley, December 19, 1939, Box 7, Wiley Papers, Franklin D. Roosevelt Library; Steinhardt to Henderson, December 13, 1939, Box 78, Steinhardt Papers, Library of Congress; Moore to Bullitt, December 27, 1939, Box 3, Robert Walton Moore Papers, Franklin D. Roosevelt Library; Berle diary, December 4–5, 1939, Beatrice Berle and Travis Jacobs, *Navigating the Rapids, 1918–1971: From the Papers of Adolf A. Berle,* 274–75.

16. Roosevelt memorandum to Hull and Welles, December 22, 1939, D.S.F.

124.61/144½; Key Pittman to Hull, January 19, Hull to Pittman, January 30, 1940, D.S.F. 711.61/704; Arthur Vandenberg diary, December 5 and 8, 1939, vol. 12, Vandenberg Papers, William L. Clements Library; Henderson memorandum to Hull, December 11, 1939, D.S.F. 711.61/691.

17. John Blum, *From the Morgenthau Diaries: Years of Urgency, 1938−1941,* 126−30; Steve Early memorandum to Hull, December 14, Hull to Early, December 15, 1939, Official File 249-Official, Roosevelt Papers (hereafter cited as O.F.); presidential press conference, December 1, 1939.

18. Moffat diary, December 28, 1939, vol. 43, Moffat Papers; Berle diary, December 15, 18, and 27, 1939, in Berle and Jacobs, eds., *Papers,* 277−78, 280.

19. *Boston Evening Transcript,* December 6 and 22, 1939; *Philadelphia Inquirer,* December 20 and 22, 1939; *Richmond Times-Dispatch,* December 14 and 15, 1939; *Pittsburgh Post-Gazette,* December 4, 1939; *Times-Picayune* (New Orleans), December 4, 1939.

20. *New York Herald Tribune,* December 8, 1939; *Washington Post,* December 3, 1939; *Baltimore Sun,* December 12, 1939; *Charlotte Observer,* December 14, 1939; *St. Louis Post-Dispatch,* December 3, 1939.

21. *Detroit News,* December 26, 1939; *Richmond Times-Dispatch,* December 22, 1939; *Hartford Courant,* December 8 and 16, 1939; *Seattle Post-Intelligencer,* December 20, 1939; *San Francisco Chronicle,* February 14, 1940; *Chicago Tribune,* December 20, 1939; *Philadelphia Inquirer,* February 15, 1940; *Los Angeles Examiner,* February 13, 1940.

22. Steinhardt telegrams to Hull, December 1, 6, and 18, 1939, in U.S., Department of State, *Foreign Relations of the United States: The Soviet Union, 1933−1939,* 1:1015, 1032−33 (hereafter cited as F.R.U.S.), and D.S.F. 761.61/161. The quote is from the December 18 telegram.

23. Steinhardt to Henderson, January 6, 29, 1940, Steinhardt to H.F. Arthur Schoenfeld, December 2 and 9, 1939, Steinhardt to Mrs. Ina M. Hofman, February 1, 1940, Box 78, Steinhardt Papers. Schoenfeld was minister to Finland.

24. Bullitt to Roosevelt, December 19, 1939, President's Secretary's File, France, Bullitt, Roosevelt Papers (hereafter cited as P.S.F.); Beatrice Farnsworth, *William C. Bullitt and the Soviet Union,* 167−68; Welles telegram to John J. Muccio, December 5, 1939, Laurence Duggan memorandum, December 17, 1939, F.R.U.S. 1939, 5:129, 136. Muccio was the chargé in Panama. Duggan was chief of the Division of American Republics.

25. Cordell Hull, *The Memoirs of Cordell Hull,* 1:709−10; William L. Langer and Samuel E. Gleason, *The Challenge to Isolation, 1937−1940,* 333−40, 401; Berle memorandum to Roosevelt, February 1, 1940, O.F. 220 Russia, Roosevelt Papers; Roosevelt memorandum, January 10, 1940, P.S.F., Russia, Box 18, Roosevelt Papers.

26. Hull, *Memoirs,* 1:707−10.

27. Moffat diary, January 5, 15, 16, 30, 1940, vol. 43, Moffat Papers; Long diary, January 15, 1940, in Fred L. Israel, ed., *The War Diary of Breckenridge Long: Selections from the Years 1939−1944,* 52−53; Ickes diary, December 24, 1939, Harold L. Ickes, *The Secret Diary of Harold L. Ickes,* 3:97.

28. Presidential press conference, February 9, 1940; *Congressional Record,* 76th Cong., 3rd sess., Feb. 9−13, 1940, 1271−1300, 1376−1405, February 27−28, 1940, 2034−2116; Robert Sobel, *The Origins of Interventionism: The United States and the Russo-Finnish War,* 123−45.

29. *New York Herald Tribune,* January 18, 1940; *Washington Post,* January 17, 1940; *New York Times,* January 17, 1940; *Chicago Daily News,* January 16 and 19, 1940; *Christian Science Monitor,* January 19, 1940; Walter Lippman and Dorothy Thompson, *Pittsburgh Post-Gazette,* January 17, 19, and 20, 1940.

30. *Richmond Times-Dispatch*, January 18, 1940; *Los Angeles Examiner*, January 20, 1940; *Seattle Post-Intelligencer*, January 19, 1940; *Omaha Morning World-Herald*, January 18, 1940; *Hartford Courant*, January 17 and 19, 1940.

31. *Courier-Journal* (Louisville), February 17, 1940; *Washington Post*, February 15 and 29, 1940; *Cleveland Plain Dealer*, February 15, 1940.

32. Hull telegrams to Steinhardt, January 27, March 7–8, Steinhardt telegrams to Hull, February 2, March 8, 1940, *F.R.U.S. 1940*, 1:281–86, 300–302; Henderson memorandum, March 2, 1940, D.S.F. 760D.61/1184; Steinhardt to Henderson, March 2, 1940, Box 79, Steinhardt Papers; Berle diary, January 26, March 7, 1940, in Berle and Jacobs, eds., *Papers*, 287, 293–94.

33. *San Francisco Chronicle*, March 14, 1940; *New York Times*, March 13 and 14, 1940; *Charlotte Observer*, March 15, 1940; *Times-Picayune* (New Orleans), March 14, 1940; *Newsweek*, March 25, 1940, 25; *Time*, March 25, 1940, 25; *Cincinnati Enquirer*, March 14, 1940; *St. Louis Post-Dispatch*, March 13, 1940; *Christian Science Monitor*, March 15, 1940, 22.

34. *Charlotte Observer*, December 28, 1939; *Baltimore Sun*, December 28, 1939; *St. Louis Post-Dispatch*, December 23, 1939; *Cleveland Plain Dealer*, December 22, 1939; *Dallas Morning News*, December 15, 1939.

35. Walter Lippman, *Los Angeles Times*, March 7, 1940; *Baltimore Sun*, March 13, 1940; *Charlotte Observer*, March 14, 1940; *Des Moines Register*, December 25, 1939; *Chicago Daily News*, December 7, 1939; *Kansas City Star*, December 20, 1939; *Courier-Journal* (Louisville), March 15, 1939; *Washington Post*, March 15, 1940; Kirke I. Simpson, *Cincinnati Enquirer*, March 14, 1940; *Christian Science Monitor*, March 13, 1940, 22; *Dallas Morning News*, March 18, 1940; *San Francisco Chronicle*, March 15, 1940.

36. *New York Herald Tribune*, March 13, 1940; *Chicago Tribune*, March 18, 1940; *Richmond Times-Dispatch*, March 14, 1940; *Omaha Morning World-Herald*, March 14, 1940; *Times-Picayune* (New Orleans), March 14, 1940; *Philadelphia Inquirer*, March 14, 1940; *Detroit News*, March 14, 1940.

37. Hull memorandum, April 2, 1940, *F.R.U.S. 1940*, 3:267; Pittman to Hull, March 16, Hull to Pittman, March 25, 1940, D.S.F. 711.61/718.

38. See *F.R.U.S. 1940*, 1:545–47, 3:197, 245–58, 263, 267–87, 291, 295, 370–71; Gerhard L. Weinberg, *Germany and the Soviet Union, 1939–1941*, 66–75.

39. See Richard J. Whalen, *The Founding Father: The Story of Joseph P. Kennedy*, 310–20; Long diary, June 8, 21, and 24, 1940, in Israel, ed., *War Diary*, 103, 111, 113–15.

40. See August R. Ogden, *The Dies Committee: A Study of the Special House Committee for the Investigation of Un-American Activities, 1938–1943*, 42, 207–10; Richard Polenberg, "Franklin Roosevelt and Civil Liberties: The Case of the Dies Committee," 172–73, 176–77; Long diary, May 8 and 17, June 4 and 5, 1940, in Israel, ed., *War Diary*, 88, 95, 100–101. In 1938 Roosevelt had approved a law requiring the registration of foreign agents, and in 1939 he had instructed the Justice Department to increase its surveillance of suspected agents.

41. Harold Moseley memorandum, June 6, Hull telegram to Thurston, May 27, Henderson memorandum, May 23, 1940, *F.R.U.S. 1940*, 3:303–4, 311.

42. Henderson memorandum, July 26, 1940, ibid., 326.

43. Henderson memoranda, June 1, 6, 7, and 10, August 1, 1940, ibid., 305–15, 340–48. Amtorg sued over the *Wildwood* but lost the case when the U.S. Supreme Court denied a review on June 14, 1943.

44. Steinhardt dispatch to Hull, April 15, 1940, D.S.F. 761.62/661.

45. Berle memorandum to Hull, May 29, 1940, in Langer and Gleason, *Challenge to Isolation*, 643; Hull memorandum, June 12, Henderson memorandum, June 7, 1940, *F.R.U.S. 1940*, 3:314, 317–18.

NOTES TO CHAPTER 10

1. Sumner Welles, *The Time for Decision,* 169; Henderson to Steinhardt, December 13, 1940, Box 29, Steinhardt Papers, Library of Congress; Hornbeck to Welles, June 1, 12, and 21, 1940, Boxes 61 and 161, Hornbeck Papers, Hoover Institution.
2. Ickes diary, June 5, 1940, in Harold L. Ickes, *The Secret Diary of Harold L. Ickes,* 3:200–201.
3. Walter Thurston telegrams to Hull, June 17 and 20, August 27, 1940, Department of State File 740.0011 European War 1939/4031, 4112, 741.61/898, Department of State MSS, National Archives (hereafter cited as D.S.F.). The quote is from the last telegram. Washington had received an earlier report from the London embassy. See also Hull telegram to Bullitt, May 21, Welles memorandum, June 18, 1940, in U.S., Department of State, *Foreign Relations of the United States 1940,* 3:322, 600–601 (hereafter cited as *F.R.U.S.*).
4. Morgenthau diary, June 20, 1941, vol. 274, 262–63, Morgenthau Papers, Franklin D. Roosevelt Library.
5. Walter Johnson, *The Battle Against Isolation,* 62–68; Mark Lincoln Chadwin, *The Hawks of World War II,* 44–73.
6. *New York Herald Tribune,* June 23, 1940; *Washington Post,* June 28, 1940; *Courier-Journal* (Louisville), June 17, July 25, 1940; *Time,* July 15, 1940, 23; *Chicago Daily News,* June 20, 1940; *Kansas City Star,* June 18, 1940; *Portland Oregonian,* June 30, July 2, 1940.
7. Raymond Gram Swing broadcasts, June 17, 27, and 29, 1940, Box 20, Swing Papers, Library of Congress; *Times-Picayune* (New Orleans), June 29, 1940; *Cleveland Plain Dealer,* June 17 and 28, July 22, 1940; *Charlotte Observer,* July 26, 1940; *Philadelphia Inquirer,* July 22, 1940; *Richmond Times-Dispatch,* July 16, 1940; *Boston Evening Transcript,* June 18, 1940; *New York Times,* June 17, 1940.
8. Henderson memorandum, July 15, 1940, *F.R.U.S. 1940,* 1:390.
9. William L. Langer and Samuel E. Gleason, *The Challenge to Isolation, 1937–1940,* 646; *F.R.U.S. 1940,* 1:401–2; Welles telegram to Thurston, August 9, 1940, ibid., 416.
10. Welles memorandum, July 27, 1940, *F.R.U.S. 1940,* 3:327–30. I have reversed the order of phrases in the second quotation.
11. Henderson memorandum, August 7, 1940, ibid., 360–61.
12. Henderson memoranda, August 12 and 15, 1940, ibid., 362–69, 372–79; Roosevelt memorandum to Welles, August 15, Welles to Roosevelt, August 19, 1940, Official File 220 Russia, Roosevelt Papers, Franklin D. Roosevelt Library (hereafter cited as O.F.).
13. See Gerhard L. Weinberg, *Germany and the Soviet Union, 1939–1941,* 107–32; James E. McSherry, *Stalin, Hitler, and Europe,* 2:90–158; Philipp Fabry, *Der Hitler-Stalin-Pakt 1939–1941,* 307–64.
14. Thurston dispatch to Hull, August 22, 1940, *F.R.U.S. 1940,* 3:216; Steinhardt telegram to Hull, Oct. 2, 1940, ibid., 1:615–17. See also ibid., 1:503, 507, 562–64, 610–13, 653–55.
15. Henderson to Samuel Harper, September 19, 1940, Letters 1940, Harper Papers, University of Chicago Library; Long diary, October 8, 1940, Fred L. Israel, ed., *The War Diary of Breckinridge Long: Selections from the Years 1939–1944,* 137–38. See also Berle memorandum, October 9, 1940, *F.R.U.S. 1940,* 3:959.
16. Cordell Hull, *The Memoirs of Cordell Hull,* 2:967–68.
17. John M. Blum, *From the Morgenthau Diaries: Years of Urgency, 1938–1941,* 347.
18. Stimson diary, September 27, 1940, vol. 30, Stimson Papers, Yale University Library. For Roosevelt's remark, see Blum, *Years of Urgency,* 362. See also Morgenthau

diary, September 19, 20, and 25, 1940, vols. 307:65, 71, 141, 148, 308:156–57, Morgenthau Papers; Ickes diary, September 28, 1940, in Ickes, *Secret Diary*, 3:340.

19. Blum, *Years of Urgency*, 358–59; Long diary, September 25, 1940, in Israel, ed., *War Diary*, 132.

20. Stimson diary, October 23, 1940, vol. 31, Stimson Papers; Hull memorandum, October 14, Hull telegrams to Steinhardt, October 9 and 26, 1940, *F.R.U.S. 1940*, 1:439–40, 3:392–93, 399–400; William L. Langer and Samuel E. Gleason, *The Undeclared War, 1940–1941*, 126.

21. *National Republic* 28, no. 9 (1941):11; Eugene Lyons, "Must Russia Fight Hitler?", *American Mercury* 52 (1941):24–32; *United States News*, November 1, 1940, 28.

22. *Seattle Post-Intelligencer*, November 14, 1940; *Richmond Times-Dispatch*, November 12, 1940; *Portland Oregonian*, November 16, 1940; *Des Moines Register*, November 25, 1940.

23. *Cincinnati Enquirer*, November 24, 1940; *Baltimore Sun*, November 24, 1940; *Hartford Courant*, November 15 and 28, 1940; *Cleveland Plain Dealer*, November 13, 1940; *Times-Picayune* (New Orleans), November 25, 1940.

24. Henderson to Harper, July 20, 1940, Letters 1940, Harper Papers; Henderson to Steinhardt, December 13, 1940, Box 29, Steinhardt Papers. The second quote is from the letter to Steinhardt. See also Edward Page memorandum, October 3, Page memorandum to Welles, October 17, 1940, *F.R.U.S. 1940*, 3:224–30, 396–97.

25. Steinhardt telegrams to Hull, November 10, 14, and 19, 1940, *F.R.U.S. 1940*, 1:574, 580–81, 584–86; Charles E. Bohlen, *Witness to History, 1929–1969*, 104. Molotov hoped to obtain an annexation of Finland and Southern Bukovina from Rumania. Instead, Hitler replied with vague statements about a Soviet sphere in the Persian Gulf area, since he wanted only to smooth over differences as a cover for his military preparations. After the Berlin conference, Molotov offered to join the Tripartite Pact in exchange for bases in Bulgaria and the withdrawal of German troops from Finland. Hitler never bothered to make a formal reply. See Weinberg, *Germany and the Soviet Union*, 137–45; Adam B. Ulam, *Expansion and Coexistence: The History of Soviet Foreign Policy, 1917–1967*, 304–5.

26. Steinhardt telegrams to Hull, October 30, November 1, 20, and 28, December 27, 1940, *F.R.U.S. 1940*, 3:400–403, 1:670–71, 674, 676–77, 688.

27. Steinhardt to Henderson, n.d., Ray Atherton memorandum, November 26, 1940, ibid., 3:406–8; Steinhardt telegrams to Hull, December 26, 1940, January 6, 1941, ibid., 438–40, and *F.R.U.S. 1941*, 1:117–18. See also Division of European Affairs memorandum, November 26, 1940, *F.R.U.S. 1940*, 3:413–14; Henderson memorandum to Welles, November 27, 1940, D.S.F. 711.61/800; Long diary, December 29, 1940, in Israel, ed., *War Diary*, 166.

28. Henderson memorandum, December 13, 1940, *F.R.U.S. 1940*, 3:420–33, Hull telegrams to Steinhardt, December 3 and 13, 1940, ibid., 416–17.

29. Henderson memorandum, January 8, 1941, *F.R.U.S. 1941*, 1:667–81; Welles to Roosevelt, January 9, 1941, O.F., 200 Russia, Roosevelt Papers. See also Welles' comment to Oumansky about their common interest in the status quo in the Pacific (Welles memorandum, January 15, 1941, *F.R.U.S. 1941*, 4:3–4).

30. Hull telegram to Steinhardt, January 24, 1941, ibid., 1:696–97; Hull, *Memoirs*, 2:969.

31. *Congressional Record*, 77th Cong., 1st sess., February 3, 1941, 466, February 7, 1941, 762; August Raymond Ogden, *The Dies Committee: A Study of the Special House Committee for the Investigation of Un-American Activities, 1938–1943*, 227–31; *Cincinnati Enquirer*, January 23, 1941; *Portland Oregonian*, January 23, 1941; *Hartford Courant*, January 23, 1941; *Omaha Morning World-Herald*, January 23, 1941.

32. *Courier-Journal* (Louisville), January 23, 1941; *Washington Post*, January 24, 1941; *Pittsburgh Post-Gazette*, January 24, 1941; *Philadelphia Inquirer*, January 25, 1941; *Seattle Times*, January 25, 1941; *New Republic*, February 10, 1941, 165.

33. See Langer and Gleason, *Undeclared War*, 213–57; Raymond H. Dawson, *The Decision to Aid Russia, 1941: Foreign Policy and Domestic Politics*, 21–26.

34. *Congressional Record*, 77th Cong., 1st sess., February 7, 1941, 761–64, March 3, 1941, 1645–48, March 7, 1941, 1984; Dawson, *Decision to Aid Russia*, 26–41; Warren F. Kimball, *The Most Unsordid Act: Lend-Lease, 1939–1941*, 166–216.

35. See *F.R.U.S. 1941*, 1:125–26, 690–94, 700–711, 715.

36. Hull memorandum, February 5, 1941, ibid., 157–59; Hull memorandum to Morgenthau, February 14, 1941, in Blum, *Years of Urgency*, 334–35.

37. Clapper report, March 5, 1941, Personal File–Diaries, 1941, Clapper Papers, Library of Congress; Langer and Gleason, *Undeclared War*, 336–37; Long diary, February 21, March 24, 1941, in Israel, ed., *War Diary*, 182–84, 188–89; Welles, *Time for Decision*, 170–71; Hull telegrams to Steinhardt, March 1 and 4, Steinhardt telegram to Hull, March 3, Welles memorandum, March 20, 1941, *F.R.U.S. 1941*, 1:712–14, 727.

38. Steinhardt telegrams to Hull, March 9, April 6 and 12, 1941, *F.R.U.S. 1941*, 1:297, 136–37, 301–2. See Weinberg, *Germany and the Soviet Union*, 148–58; Ulam, *Expansion and Coexistence*, 305–8.

39. Henderson to Steinhardt, March 31, 1941, Box 33, Steinhardt Papers; Welles memorandum, March 22, Henderson memorandum, March 27, 1941, *F.R.U.S. 1941*, 1:725–29. Moscow had outstanding orders of $53 million with 60 percent under export control and other restrictions and bottlenecks.

40. Welles memorandum, March 20, Hull telegram to Grew, March 1, 1941, *F.R.U.S. 1941*, 4:920, 55–56. Hull also warned Japan against an agreement.

41. Hull telegram to Steinhardt, April 15, 1941, D.S.F. 761.9411; *New York Times*, April 14 and 15, 1941; Hornbeck to Welles, April 29, 1941, Box 61, Hornbeck Papers; McSherry, *Stalin*, 2:215–19. The most direct evidence of Hitler's plans in April came from Richard Sorge's espionage activity in Tokyo and German air photo reconnaissance; one German plane, while taking pictures, had to make an emergency landing inside the Soviet Union.

42. *Cleveland Plain Dealer*, April 14, 1941; *Philadelphia Inquirer*, April 15, 1941; Joseph Alsop and Robert Kinter in *San Francisco Chronicle*, April 17, 1941; *Charlotte Observer*, April 21, 1941; *National Republic* 29, no. 1 (1941):12; *Baltimore Sun*, April 15, 1941.

43. *Washington Post*, April 14, 1941; Kaltenborn broadcast, April 13, 1941, Box 156, Kaltenborn Papers, State Historical Society of Wisconsin; Swing broadcast, April 14, 1941, Box 14, Swing Papers; *New York Herald Tribune*, April 14, 1941; Walter Lippmann in *Cincinnati Enquirer*, April 15, 1941; *Courier-Journal* (Louisville), April 14, 1941; *New York Times*, April 14, 15, and 21, 1941.

44. *Cincinnati Enquirer*, April 15, 1941; *Times-Picayune* (New Orleans), April 15, 1941; *Los Angeles Times*, April 15, 1941; *San Francisco Chronicle*, April 15, 1941; *Chicago Daily News*, April 15, 1941; *St. Louis Post-Dispatch*, April 14, 1941; *Hartford Courant*, April 14, 1941; *Omaha Morning World-Herald*, April 15, 1941; *Seattle Post-Intelligencer*, April 15, 1941.

45. *Washington Post*, May 11, 1941; *Baltimore Sun*, April 10, 1941; *St. Louis Post-Dispatch*, March 1, May 2, 1941; Walter Lippman in *Pittsburgh Post-Gazette*, March 7, 1941; *Richmond Times-Dispatch*, March 4, 1941; *Dallas Morning News*, April 19, May 1 and May 8, June 19, 1941; *Chicago Daily News*, April 10, 1941.

46. See Weinberg, *Germany and the Soviet Union*, 160–63; McSherry, *Stalin*, 2:220–37; John Erickson, *The Soviet High Command: A Military-Political History, 1918–1941*, 559–93.

47. Paul Mallon in *Seattle Post-Intelligencer*, May 2, 1941; *Newsweek*, June 9, 1941, 23; Joseph Alsop and Robert Kinter in *Seattle Times*, March 5, 1941.

48. *Hartford Courant*, June 20, 1941; *Cincinnati Enquirer*, June 20, 1941; *Cleveland Plain Dealer*, June 20, 1941; *New Republic*, May 26, 1941, 715–16.

49. *Philadelphia Inquirer*, May 10, 1941; *Hartford Courant*, April 12, 8, May 8, 1941;

Seattle Times, March 5, 1941; *Catholic World* 153 (1941):132; *Courier-Journal* (Louisville), May 7, 1941; *Pittsburgh Post-Gazette*, May 9, 1941.

50. Steinhardt dispatch to Hull, June 4, Steinhardt telegrams to Hull, June 7 and 12, 1941, D.S.F. 861.00/11891, *F.R.U.S. 1941*, 620–21, 754–57.

51. Dawson, *Decision to Aid Russia*, 56. See also Stimson to Roosevelt, June 23, 1941, President's Personal File 20, Roosevelt Papers; Knox to Roosevelt, June 23, 1941, President's Secretary's File, Frank Knox, Roosevelt Papers.

52. Hull memorandum, May 14, 1941, *F.R.U.S. 1941*, 1:745–47.

53. Hull telegram to Steinhardt, June 14, 1941, ibid., 757–58.

54. Welles memorandum, June 15, 1941, ibid., 759–61.

55. Steinhardt telegram to Hull, June 17, 1941, ibid., 764–66.

56. Atherton and Henderson memorandum, June 17, 1941, ibid., 764–66.

57. Churchill to Roosevelt, June 14, 1941, Corres. II, Box 49, File 145, Hull Papers, Library of Congress; Hull, *Memoirs*, 2:967; Langer and Gleason, *Undeclared War*, 531–32.

NOTES TO CHAPTER 11

1. Hull telegram to Steinhardt, June 23, 1941, in U.S., Department of State, *Foreign Relations of the United States*, 1:767–68 (hereafter cited as *F.R.U.S.*); Raymond H. Dawson, *The Decision to Aid Russia, 1941: Foreign Policy and Domestic Politics*, 117–21. In discussing the Lend-Lease decision, I have relied heavily on Dawson's thorough analysis, except in reporting the editorial opinions in American newspapers.

2. Fish broadcast, June 30, 1941, America First bulletin, June 23, 1941, Hoover address, June 29, 1941, Boxes 9 and 31, America First Papers, Hoover Institution. See also Wayne S. Cole, *Charles A. Lindbergh and the Battle Against American Intervention in World War II*, 97–98; *Catholic World* 153 (1941):516–19; *America*, July 5, 1941, 338.

3. *Cleveland Plain Dealer*, June 22, 23, 24, 26, and 27, 1941. See also *Los Angeles Examiner*, June 27 and 30, 1941; *Wall Street Journal*, June 24, 25, and 28, 1941; *United States News*, July 4, 1941, 26–27.

4. Walter Johnson, *The Battle Against Isolation*, 313; Mark L. Chadwin, *The Hawks of World War II*, 235–47; Raymond Gram Swing broadcast, June 23, 1941, Box 14, Swing Papers, Library of Congress; round-table conference, June 22, 1941, Box 156, Kaltenborn Papers, State Historical Society of Wisconsin; *National Republic* 29, no. 4 (1941):3–4; Eugene Lyons, "The End of Joseph Stalin," *American Mercury* 53 (1941):135–43, Lyons' editorial, ibid., 583–89; William Henry Chamberlin, "The Struggle for Continents," *Atlantic Monthly* 168, no. 2 (1941):274–80.

5. *Chicago Daily News*, June 27 and 30, 1941; *Dallas Morning News*, June 25, 1941; *Charlotte Observer*, June 24, 1941; *Portland Oregonian*, June 24, 1941; Dorothy Thompson in *Pittsburgh Post-Gazette*, July 3, 1941; *Christian Century*, July 2, 1941, 855–56; *Commonweal*, July 4, 1941, 243–44

6. *Washington Post*, June 29, 1941; *St. Louis Post-Dispatch*, June 23, 24, and 25, 1941; *Christian Science Monitor*, June 24, 25, and 28, 1941; *Kansas City Star*, June 26, 1941; *Pittsburgh Post-Gazette*, June 24, 1941; *Philadelphia Inquirer*, June 23 and 24, 1941; *New York Herald Tribune*, June 23, 24, and 25, 1941; *Courier-Journal* (Louisville), June 23 and 28, 1941.

7. *Hartford Courant*, July 6, 1941; *Times-Picayune* (New Orleans), June 24, 1941; *San Francisco Chronicle*, June 24 and 25, July 2, 1941; *Richmond Times-Dispatch*, June 23 and 25, July 1, 1941; *Cincinnati Enquirer*, June 24 and 25, 1941; *Seattle Times*, June 23, 1941.

8. Welles memorandum, June 22, 1941, *F.R.U.S. 1941*, 4:275. See also Kennan to Henderson, June 24, 1941, in George F. Kennan, *Memoirs, 1925–1950*, 133–34.

9. Steinhardt telegrams to Hull, June 26 and 28, 1941, *F.R.U.S. 1941*, 1:886, 177, Stimson to Roosevelt, June 23, 1941, President's Personal File 20, Roosevelt Papers,

Franklin D. Roosevelt Library (hereafter cited as P.P.F.); Knox to Roosevelt, June 23, 1941, President's Secretary's File, Frank Knox, ibid.; Yeaton reports to Chief, Military Intelligence Division, 1941, in U.S., Department of Army, Military Attaché Reports, General Staff, Record Group 165, War Department Records, National Archives; Henderson to Harper, June 27, 1941, Data–Post Conf., Harper Papers, University of Chicago.

10. Davies journal, June 23, Davies memorandum to Hopkins, July 18, 1941, Joseph E. Davies, *Mission to Moscow,* 475, 493–97; Robert E. Sherwood, *Roosevelt and Hopkins: An Intimate History,* 321–22. In July, Davies served as an unofficial lobbyist for the Soviet embassy.

11. Henderson memorandum, July 2, 1941, *F.R.U.S. 1941,* 1:781–86.

12. Berle to Hoover, July 10, Berle memorandum, July 30, 1941, ibid., 789–90, 798–99. See also Berle diary, July 11 and 31, Berle memorandum to Harry Hopkins, July 30, 1941, in Beatrice Berle and Travis Jacobs, eds., *Navigating the Rapids, 1918–1971: From the Papers of Adolf A. Berle,* 373–75.

13. See Holger H. Herwig, "Prelude to *Weltblitzkrieg:* Germany's Naval Policy toward the United States of America, 1939–1941," 662–63.

14. Steinhardt telegrams to Hull, August 5, 17, and 23, 1941, *F.R.U.S. 1941,* 1:635, 641, 644; Dawson, *Decision to Aid Russia,* 128–31, 146–47.

15. See Dawson, *Decision to Aid Russia,* 136, 292–94; George C. Herring, *Aid to Russia, 1941–1946: Strategy, Diplomacy, the Origins of the Cold War,* 26–30, 48.

16. Kennan, *Memoirs,* 133–34.

17. Welles memorandum, June 22, 1941, *F.R.U.S. 1941,* 4:275; Division of Far Eastern Affairs memoranda, June 23 and 25, 1941, ibid., 276–80; Hornbeck memoranda, June 24, July 3, 16, 23, 1941, Boxes 39, 20, 161, Hornbeck Papers, Hoover Institute.

18. Division of Far Eastern Affairs memoranda, June 23 and 25, 1941, *F.R.U.S. 1941,* 4:276, 279.

19. Welles telegram to Grew, July 4, 1941, ibid., 994. Foreign Minister Matsuoka denied the rumors and, in reply, asked if the United States intended to intervene in Europe. Washington also tried to immobilize Japan by stopping Tokyo's purchase of oil after Japan accelerated its advance into Indochina on July 24.

20. Hornbeck memorandum, September 5, 1941, ibid., 426–28. This question arose in August when Prince Konoye asked for a conference with Roosevelt. See Robert J.C. Butow, "Backdoor Diplomacy in the Pacific: The Proposal for a Konoye-Roosevelt Meeting, 1941," 48–72.

21. Hadley Cantril, ed., *Public Opinion, 1935–1946,* 1187; American Institute of Public Opinion poll, July 12, 1941, *Public Opinion Quarterly* 5, no. 4 (1941):675.

22. Dawson, *Decision to Aid Russia,* 149, 180, 218–32; *America,* July 12, 1941, 373–74; *Commonweal,* July 4, 1941, 243–44; *Catholic World* 153 (1941):517–19, 154 (1941):136; *National Republic* 29, no. 6 (1941):3, 12, 32.

23. *San Francisco Chronicle,* September 25, 1941; *New York Herald Tribune,* July 10, 1941; *Hartford Courant,* September 30, 1941. For continuing opposition, see *Chicago Tribune,* July 1, 1941.

24. *Cleveland Plain Dealer,* September 23, 1941; *Christian Science Monitor,* September 23, 1941; *Dallas Morning News,* September 29, 1941; *Des Moines Register,* September 26, 1941; *Portland Oregonian,* September 29, 1941.

25. See Dawson, *Decision to Aid Russia,* 152–71, 198–212; Sherwood, *Roosevelt and Hopkins,* 321–48; *F.R.U.S. 1941,* 1:837–51.

26. Dawson, *Decision to Aid Russia,* 269–82.

27. *Charlotte Observer,* November 8, 1941, 12; *Chicago Daily News,* November 8, 1941; *Times-Picayune* (New Orleans), November 12, 1941; *Pittsburgh Post-Gazette,* November 10, 1941; *Richmond Times-Dispatch,* November 8, 1941; *Chicago Tribune,* November 8, 1941; *Los Angeles Examiner,* November 10, 1941.

28. See Hull telegram to Steinhardt, October 2, Hull memorandum, September 11, Steinhardt telegrams to Hull, October 4 and 6, 1941, *F.R.U.S. 1941*, 1:832, 1002–1003; Dawson, *Decision to Aid Russia,* 258–65.

29. *Omaha Morning World-Herald,* November 9, 1941; *Dallas Morning News,* November 8, 1941; *Des Moines Register,* September 26, 1941; *Portland Oregonian,* September 29, 1941; *Pittsburgh Post-Gazette,* November 10, 1941.

30. Edward Page memorandum, October 3, 1940, *F.R.U.S. 1940,* 3:229.

31. Roosevelt address to American Youth Congress, February 10, 1940, Speech File 1272, Roosevelt Papers.

32. Roosevelt to Admiral William D. Leahy, June 26, 1941, in Elliott Roosevelt, ed., *F.D.R.: His Personal Letters, 1928–1945,* 2:1177. See also Roosevelt to Fulton Oursler, June 25, 1941, P.P.F. 212. Oursler, a personal friend of Roosevelt and the editor of *Liberty* magazine, was also a strong critic of Moscow.

Bibliographical Essay

Official records and personal papers of the participants in Soviet-American relations provide the most significant sources for this study. The records of the Department of State, deposited in the National Archives, are of course indispensable. Purport books, which contain short descriptions of each document as well as cross references, not only ease progress through the files bearing directly upon Soviet-American relations but also reveal material pertinent to the Kremlin's relations with other countries and foreign Communist movements. The Department of State's *Foreign Relations of the United States*—including several volumes covering each year, and a special volume, *The Soviet Union, 1933–1939*—provide excellent documentation, but they are necessarily selective and in no way eliminate the necessity for research in the original records.

The Franklin D. Roosevelt Papers, at the Franklin D. Roosevelt Library in Hyde Park, New York, are an important collection divided into three central files—the Official File, President's Personal File, and President's Secretary's File. Roosevelt's correspondence with his ambassadors and the letters, memoranda, and notes exchanged with the State Department furnish information about his involvement in recognition, the issues of propaganda and debts, and formal relations after 1935. Edgar B. Nixon's *Franklin D. Roosevelt and Foreign Affairs* adequately covers the

207

1933–36 period, but further research in the Roosevelt collection is still required.

The Roosevelt Library also has the papers of Henry Morgenthau, Jr., Robert Walton Moore, and John Cooper Wiley. Secretary Morgenthau's diary has material about recognition and about his attempts to further cooperation with the Soviet Union in the Far East after 1937. Moore's correspondence with Roosevelt and Ambassadors Bullitt and Dodd adds data about the president and Bullitt. Wiley's correspondence with Russian specialists is helpful.

The records of the Department of the Army, the Department of Commerce, and Congress are of less importance. Army records are not as well indexed as the Department of State files, and many of the records for the 1930s are restricted. However, the reports of Philip R. Faymonville, military attaché at Moscow, contain interesting information. The Department of Commerce records, also in the National Archives, supply much data about American interest in the Russian market. The published surveys of the Department of Commerce also present interesting evaluations of Soviet industrialization. There are very infrequent discussions about Soviet-American relations in the *Congressional Record* and the unpublished files of the House Committee on Foreign Affairs and the Senate Committee on Foreign Affairs and the Senate Committee on Foreign Relations, deposited in the National Archives.

The Manuscript Division of the Library of Congress has several valuable collections, notably the papers of Raymond Clapper, Joseph E. Davies, William E. Dodd, Cordell Hull, Nelson T. Johnson, Laurence A. Steinhardt, and Raymond Gram Swing. Clapper's diary is helpful on the subject of recognition. The papers of Davies and Steinhardt yield significant insights into their attitudes toward the Soviet Union, while those of Dodd and Johnson contain evaluations of Soviet foreign policy in Europe and Asia. The Hull Papers contain many letters from American diplomats; Hull's perfunctory replies, however, contribute very little. The collection of Swing's radio broadcasts is complete and valuable.

There are several important collections in New York City, although the Oral History Collection at Columbia University Library is disappointing. The Institute of Current World Affairs, a private educational organization, granted permission for research in the correspondence and files of Samuel Harper, John Hazard, and Bruce Hopper, three academic specialists on the Soviet Union. The papers of the National Civic Federation, located in the Manuscript Division of the New York Public Library, contain material about anti-Communism in the thirties.

The Houghton Library in Cambridge, Massachusetts, has three important collections. Ambassador Joseph Grew's diary documents his hostile attitude toward the Soviet Union. Jay Pierrepont Moffat, who was head of the European desk in the State Department from 1933 to 1935 and from 1937 to 1940, kept a voluminous diary that provides background information about the formulation of policy toward the Soviet Union, particularly in 1939–40. William Phillips' diary has some material on recognition, although Phillips probably revised his original entries considerably.

The Arthur Bliss Lane and Henry L. Stimson papers at the Yale University Library in New Haven, Connecticut, are useful. Stimson's diary while secretary of war in 1940–41 yields information about Washington's policies toward Moscow. Lane's collection has copies of valuable letters from Loy W. Henderson to Robert Kelley, both Russian specialists.

Three other diplomatic collections of some importance are the George S. Messersmith Papers at the University of Delaware Library, the Hugh R. Wilson Papers at the Herbert Hoover Presidential Library in West Branch, Iowa, and the Stanley K. Hornbeck collection at the Hoover Institution on War, Revolution and Peace in Stanford, California. Messersmith's memoranda from his tenures as minister to Austria and assistant secretary of state demonstrate his excellent grasp of European developments. Wilson's letters document his opposition to cooperation with the Soviet Union, expressed from his positions in Geneva and Washington. Hornbeck's voluminous collection of correspondence and memoranda added some new material on the Far Eastern dimension of Washington's relations with the Soviet Union. George Kennan's correspondence and diaries at Princeton are still closed.

The University of Chicago Library has the Samuel Harper Papers, a rewarding collection of Harper's letters, correspondence with Loy Henderson and other Russian specialists, and information about various pro-Soviet organizations. The papers of Alexander Gumberg and Raymond Robins at the Wisconsin Historical Society are also valuable. Gumberg's files contain not only his letters but also material about the American-Russian Chamber of Commerce. Robins is irresistible although somewhat unbalanced. His flamboyant letters are worth reading, although he was not very active after recognition because of illness.

Newspapers and periodicals are also significant sources of opinion about the Soviet Union and Roosevelt's Soviet policy. The major liberal journals and a few conservative publications (including *American Mercury* and *National Republic*) provided the most useful assessments.

Interlibrary loan and the Center for Research Libraries in Chicago provided access to thirty-six newspapers. From the newspapers that were available, a systematic selection was made, based upon geographical location, political outlook, and circulation figures. After determining what events attracted commentary, the editorials and columnists were covered for selected periods during the years 1933–41.

The standard accounts of American relations with the Soviet Union are Robert P. Browder's concise *The Origins of Soviet-American Diplomacy* and William A. Williams' *American-Russian Relations, 1781–1947*. Browder's study of the pressures for and against recognition from 1917 to 1933 as well as formal relations until 1936 is still valuable, although he did not consult the unpublished records of the State Department. Williams' study is very suggestive, though thin for the years after 1935 because the official records for those years were closed when he wrote. Williams correctly redirects attention to economic considerations in Washington's policies, although this influence is easily exaggerated. Like too many revisionists, Williams does not apply the same critical standards to Moscow's policies that he applies to Washington's.

More recent studies include Edward M. Bennett's *Recognition of Russia: An American Foreign Policy Dilemma* and Joan Hoff Wilson's *Ideology and Economics: U.S. Relations with the Soviet Union, 1918–1933*. Bennett's study, which uses official and several private manuscript collections, effectively criticizes Roosevelt's tactics on recognition. Focusing on the issue of economic influences upon the policy of nonrecognition and Roosevelt's reversal in 1933, Wilson vigorously challenges Williams' interpretation. Nevertheless, she too thoroughly dismisses Roosevelt's interest in the Soviet market and the trial-balloon aspect of the President's economic maneuvers in 1933.

The most important source on the Soviet Union's policies toward the United States is the documentary publication by the Soviet Ministry of Foreign Affairs, *Dokumenty vneshnei politiki SSSR*, with one volume on each year since 1917 and the most recent volume on 1938. This collection is necessarily very selective but still contains telegrams and letters exchanged between Moscow and the Soviet embassy in Washington as well as records of conversations between Soviet and American officials in Moscow.

Although no thorough analysis of the 1933–41 period has been written, some accounts cover aspects of Soviet-American relations. Donald G. Bishop's *The Roosevelt-Litvinov Agreements: The American View* is a comprehensive study of the problems and resolutions involved in the agreements. Raymond H. Dawson's *The Decision to Aid Russia, 1941: Foreign Policy and Domestic Politics* is an excellent analysis of the strategic and domestic pressures upon Washington's policy in 1941. There are two useful studies of American opinion about the Soviet Union. Peter G. Filene's *Americans and Soviet Experiment, 1917–1933* effectively analyzes attitudes prior to recognition, and Frank A. Warren's *Liberals and Communism: The "Red Decade" Revisited* adequately covers liberal spokesmen through 1939.

The most detailed and reliable account of Soviet foreign policy for the 1933–41 period is still Max Beloff's two-volume *The Foreign Policy of Soviet Russia, 1929–1941*. Adam B. Ulam's *Expansion and Coexistence: The History of Soviet Foreign Policy, 1917–1967* is more suggestive than Beloff's work though not as reliable for the 1939–41 period as Gerhard L. Weinberg's *Germany and the Soviet Union, 1939–1941*. James E. McSherry's *Stalin, Hitler, and Europe* is thoroughly researched, but the first volume lacks adequate organization and a sustained, documented argument. The most recent Soviet assessment, B. Ponomaryov's *History of Soviet Foreign Policy, 1917–1945*, which is based in part on Soviet archives, is neither revealing nor persuasive. Of special general value is Gerhard Weinberg's *The Foreign Policy of Hitler's Germany: Diplomatic Revolution in Europe, 1933–1936*, which has surpassed earlier assessments because of its exhaustive research and cogent interpretations.

A few important American officials have published memoirs or have received biographies containing important material on Washington's relations with Moscow. Secretary of State Cordell Hull's two-volume *The Memoirs of Cordell Hull* occasionally refers to Soviet-American relations but is riddled with hindsight. George F. Kennan and Charles E. Bohlen, who initiated their specialization in Soviet-American relations during the thirties, have written the most valuable memoirs. Kennan's *Memoirs 1924–1950* and Bohlen's *Witness to History, 1929–1969* contain not only interesting evaluations of Soviet policies but also perceptive assessments of other American officials. Beatrice Farnsworth's *William C. Bullitt and the Soviet Union* is a balanced analysis of Bullitt's three years as ambassador in Moscow, though his private papers for this period are unavailable. Joseph E. Davies' *Mission to Moscow* is useful but not always reliable, and Richard H. Ullman's article "The Davies Mission and United States–Soviet Relations, 1937–1941" should be consulted. The Moscow embassy's reports, especially those on Soviet diplomacy and the purge, receive thorough treatment in Betty Crump Hanson's dissertation,

"American Diplomatic Reporting from the Soviet Union, 1934–1941."
My analysis in this volume, which covers more aspects of Soviet policies,
differs most significantly from Hanson's over the embassy's preoccupation with Soviet ideological expansion in the thirties.

A number of recent analyses of Washington's general policies provide
insights on Soviet-American relations. The best study of the politics of
isolationism is Robert A. Divine's *The Illusion of Neutrality*. Lloyd C.
Gardner's *Economic Aspects of New Deal Diplomacy* covers a neglected
area of Washington's policies, though Gardner sometimes fails to evaluate economic concerns in a larger political context, especially after 1936.
John P. Diggins' *Mussolini and Fascism: The View from America* makes
suggestive comparisons between American opinion on Mussolini and on
Stalin. Dorothy Borg's *The United States and the Far Eastern Crisis of
1933–1938* is a superb account of Washington's cautious response to
Japan. The same insight with respect to Roosevelt's European policies is
found in Arnold Offner's *American Appeasement: United States Foreign
Policy and Germany, 1933–1938* and in Richard P. Traina's *American
Diplomacy and the Spanish Civil War*. The best accounts of America's
initial response to World War II are still William L. Langer and Samuel E.
Gleason's *The Challenge to Isolation, 1937–1940* and *The Undeclared
War, 1940–1941*.

Selected Bibliography

PRIMARY SOURCES

Government Records (Manuscripts)

National Archives, Washington, D.C.
  U.S., Congress, Historical Division
    House Committee on Foreign Affairs
    Senate Committee on Foreign Relations
  U.S., Department of the Army, Historical Division
    Office of the Adjutant General, Central Files, Record Group 94, War Department
      Records
    Military Attaché Reports, Record Group 165, War Department Records
  U.S., Department of Commerce, Historical Division
    Bureau of Foreign and Domestic Commerce, Record Group 151
    Office of the Secretary, General Correspondence, Record Group 40
  U.S., Department of State, Historical Division
    General Files, 1933–1941, Record Group 59
Franklin D. Roosevelt Library, Hyde Park, New York

Published Documents

France
  Commission Publication des Documents Relatifs aux Origines de la Guerre
  1932–1945. *Documents Diplomatiques Français 1932–1939.* 1st series
  (1932–35), 5 vols. in progress. 2nd series (1936–39), 3 vols. in progress. Paris:
  Imprimerie Nationale, 1963.

U.S., Congress
  Congressional Record. 72nd–77th Congress. Vols. 77–87, 1933–41. Washington, 1933–41.
U.S., Department of Commerce
  Annual Report of the Secretary of Commerce, 1933–41. Washington, 1934–42.
  Economic Review of Foreign Countries, 1937–41. Washington, 1938–42.
  Foreign Trade of the United States, 1933–41. Washington, 1934–41.
  World Economic Review, 1933–36. Washington, 1934–37.
U.S., Department of State
  Foreign Relations of the United States 1933. 5 vols. Washington, 1949–52.
  —— *1934.* 5 vols. Washington, 1950–52.
  —— *1935.* 4 vols. Washington, 1952–53.
  —— *1936.* 5 vols. Washington, 1953–54.
  —— *1937.* 5 vols. Washington, 1954.
  —— *1938.* 5 vols. Washington, 1954–56.
  —— *1939.* 5 vols. Washington, 1955–57.
  —— *1940.* 5 vols. Washington, 1955–61.
  —— *1941.* 7 vols. Washington, 1956–63.
  —— *Japan: 1931–1941.* 2 vols. Washington, 1943.
  —— *The Soviet Union, 1933–1939.* Washington, 1952.
  Nazi-Soviet Relations, 1939–1941; Documents from Archives of the German Foreign Office. Edited by Raymond James Sontag and James Stuart Beddie. Washington, 1948.
  Peace and War: United States Foreign Policy, 1931–1941. Washington, 1943.
  Register of the State Department, 1933–1941. Washington, 1934–42.
U.S.S.R.
  Soviet Ministry of Foreign Affairs. *Dokumenty vneshnei politiki, SSSR.* 21 vols. in progress. Moscow: Political Literary Publishing House, 1957–.

Personal Records (Manuscripts)

University of Chicago Library
  Samuel Harper
  Robert M. Hutchins
  Salmon O. Levinson
  Robert Morse Lovett
William L. Clements Library, Ann Arbor, Michigan
  Arthur H. Vandenberg
Library of Congress (Manuscript Division), Washington, D.C.
  Frederick Lewis Allen   Leland Harrison   Eric Sevareid
  Joseph Alsop   Cordell Hull   Laurence A. Steinhardt
  William E. Borah   Nelson T. Johnson   Raymond Gram Swing
  Wilbur J. Carr   Jesse H. Jones   William Boyce Thompson
  Raymond Clapper   William D. Leahy   Henry A. Wallace
  Bainbridge Colby   Breckinridge Long   William A. White
  Thomas Connally   William G. McAdoo
  Josephus Daniels   Charles C. McNary
  Joseph E. Davies   George Fort Milton
  Elmer Davis   John Bassett Moore
  James J. Davis   Reinhold Niebuhr
  Norman H. Davis   George W. Norris
  William E. Dodd   Key Pittman
  Henry P. Fletcher   Donald Richberg
  Theodore F. Green   Francis Bowe Sayre

Columbia University Library, New York City
    Lincoln Steffens
    Oral History Collection
        Boris Bakmeteff   Nelson T. Johnson
        Claude G. Bowers   Arthur Krock
        Earl Browder   Corliss Lamont
        Cass Canfield   Herbert C. Pell
        Malcolm W. Davis   William Phillips
        Samuel Dickstein   De Witt Clinton Poole
        Eddie Dowling   Upton Sinclair
        Florence J. Harriman   Norman Thomas
        Quincy Howe   Rexford G. Tugwell
University of Delaware Library, Wilmington
    George S. Messersmith
Firestone Memorial Library, Princeton University
    Bernard Baruch
    John Foster Dulles
    James Forrestal
    George Frost Kennan
    Ivy Lee
    John Van Antwerp MacMurray
    Harry Dexter White
Hoover Institution on War, Revolution and Peace, Stanford, California
    America First
    Stanley K. Hornbeck
Herbert Hoover Presidential Library, West Branch, Iowa
    Hugh R. Wilson
Houghton Library, Harvard University, Cambridge
    Joseph Clark Grew
    Jay Pierrepont Moffat
    William Phillips
    Oswald Garrison Villard
University of Illinois at Chicago Circle Library (Urban Historical Collection)
    Chicago Council on Foreign Relations
Institute of Current World Affairs, New York City
    Samuel Harper
    John Hazard
    Bruce Hopper
Newberry Library, Chicago
    Sherwood Anderson
    Malcolm Cowley
    Graham Taylor
New York Public Library (Manuscript Division)
    Victor F. Calverton
    Emma Goldman
    National Civic Federation
    Norman Thomas
Franklin D. Roosevelt Library, Hyde Park, New York
    John Carmody   Franklin D. Roosevelt
    Leon Henderson   Samuel I. Rosenman
    Harry L. Hopkins   Charles W. Taussig
    Robert Walton Moore   Elbert Thomas
    Henry Morgenthau, Jr. John Cooper Wiley
    Herbert C. Pell

Russian Library of the New York University Libraries
  American Council on Soviet Relations
  American-Russian Chamber of Commerce
  American-Russian Institute for Cultural Relations with the Soviet Union
State Historical Society of Wisconsin, Madison
  American Federation of Labor
  Cecil Brown
  Alexander Gumberg
  John Gunther
  H. V. Kaltenborn
  De Witt Clinton Poole
  Raymond Robins
Swarthmore College Library (Swarthmore Peace Collection), Swarthmore,
  Pennsylvania
    America First
    American Peace Mobilization
    League Against War and Fascism
    League for Peace and Democracy
Tamiment Library, New York City
  General Files
  League for Industrial Democracy
  Algernon Lee
  Rand School
Yale University Library, New Haven, Connecticut
  Arthur Bliss Lane
  Henry L. Stimson
  Dorothy Thompson

Memoirs, Autobiographies, Published Diaries and Papers

Anderson, Sherwood. *Sherwood Anderson's Memoirs.* New York: Harcourt, Brace and
  Co., 1942.
Berle, Beatrice Bishop, and Travis Beal Jacobs, eds. *Navigating the Rapids, 1918–1971:
  From the Papers of Adolf A. Berle.* New York: Harcourt Brace Jovanovch, Inc., 1973.
Bliss, Edward, Jr., ed. *In Search of Light: The Broadcasts of Edward R. Murrow,
  1938–1961.* New York: Alfred A. Knopf, 1967.
Bohlen, Charles E. *Witness to History, 1929–1969.* New York: W. W. Norton, 1973.
Bowers, Claude. *My Life: The Memoirs of Claude Bowers.* New York: Simon and
  Schuster, 1962.
——. *My Mission to Spain: Watching the Rehearsal for World War II.* New York: Simon
  and Schuster, 1954.
Briggs, Ellis O. *Farewell to Foggy Bottom: The Recollections of a Career Diplomat.* New
  York: David McKay Co., 1964.
Bullitt, Orville H., ed. *For the President; Personal and Secret: Correspondence Between
  Franklin D. Roosevelt and William C. Bullitt.* Boston: Houghton Mifflin Co., 1972.
Bullitt, William C. *The Great Globe Itself: A Preface to World Affairs.* New York: Charles
  Scribner's Sons, 1946.
Cantril, Hadley, ed. *Public Opinion, 1935–1946.* Princeton: Princeton University Press,
  1951.
Chamberlin, William Henry. *Collectivism: A False Utopia.* New York: Macmillan Co.,
  1937.
——. *The Confessions of an Individualist.* New York: Macmillan Co., 1940.
Cudahy, John. *The Armies March: A Personal Report.* New York: Charles Scribner's
  Sons, 1941.

Daniels, Josephus. *Shirt-Sleeve Diplomat.* Chapel Hill: University of North Carolina Press, 1947.

Davies, Joseph E. *Mission to Moscow.* New York: Simon and Schuster, 1941.

Degras, Jane, ed. *Soviet Documents on Foreign Policy.* 3 vols. London: Oxford University Press, 1951–53.

Dilling, Elizabeth. *The Red Network.* Kenilworth, Ill.: Elizabeth Dilling, 1934.

———. *The Roosevelt Red Record and Its Background.* Kenilworth, Ill., 1936.

Dodd, Martha. *Through Embassy Eyes.* New York: Harcourt, Brace and Co., 1939.

Dodd, William E., Jr., and Martha Dodd, eds. *Ambassador Dodd's Diary, 1933–1938.* New York: Harcourt, Brace and Co., 1941.

Duggan, Stephen. *A Professor At Large.* New York: Macmillan Co., 1943.

Duranty, Walter. *Duranty Reports Russia.* New York: Viking Press, 1934.

———. *I Write As I Please.* New York: Simon and Schuster, 1935.

———. *The Kremlin and the People.* New York: Reynal and Hitchcock, 1941.

Farley, James A. *Jim Farley's Story: The Roosevelt Years.* New York: McGraw-Hill Co., 1948.

Fischer, Louis. *Men and Politics: Europe Between the Two World Wars.* New York: Harper and Row, 1941.

Freedman, Max, annotator. *Roosevelt and Frankfurter: Their Correspondence, 1928–1945.* Boston: Little, Brown and Co., 1967.

Gallup, George H. *The Gallup Poll: Public Opinion, 1935–1973.* 3 vols. New York: Random House, 1972.

Grew, Joseph C. *Ten Years in Japan.* New York: Simon and Schuster, 1944.

———. *Turbulent Era: A Diplomatic Record of Forty Years, 1904–1945.* 2 vols. Boston: Houghton Mifflin Co., 1952.

Harper, Paul V., ed. *The Russia I Believe In: The Memoirs of Samuel N. Harper, 1902–1941.* Chicago: University of Chicago Press, 1945.

Hilger, Gustav, and Alfred G. Meyer. *The Incompatible Allies: A Memoir-History of German-Soviet Relations, 1918–1941.* New York: Macmillan Co., 1953.

Hooker, Nancy Harvison, ed. *The Moffat Papers: Selections from the Diplomatic Journals of Jay Pierrepont Moffat, 1919–1943.* Cambridge, Mass.: Harvard University Press, 1956.

Hoover, Calvin. *Memoirs of Capitalism, Communism and Nazism.* Durham, N.C.: Duke University Press, 1965.

Hull, Cordell. *The Memoirs of Cordell Hull.* 2 vols. New York: Macmillan Co., 1948.

Ickes, Harold L. *The Secret Diary of Harold L. Ickes.* 3 vols. New York: Simon and Schuster, 1953–55.

Israel, Fred L., ed. *The War Diary of Breckinridge Long: Selections from the Years 1939–1944.* Lincoln: University of Nebraska Press, 1966.

Johnson, Walter, ed. *Selected Letters of William Allen White.* New York: Henry Holt and Co., 1947.

Jones, Howard Mumford, ed. *Letters of Sherwood Anderson.* Boston: Little, Brown and Co., 1953.

Jones, Jesse H., and Edward Angly. *Fifty Billion Dollars: My Thirteen Years with R.F.C.* New York: Macmillan Co., 1951.

Josephson, Matthew. *Infidel in the Temple: A Memoir of the Nineteen-Thirties.* New York: Alfred A. Knopf, 1967.

Kennan, George F. *From Prague After Munich: Diplomatic Papers 1938–1940.* Princeton, N.J.: Princeton University Press, 1968.

———. *Memoirs 1925–1950.* Boston: Little, Brown and Co., 1967.

Krivitsky, Walter G. *In Stalin's Secret Service.* New York: Harper & Brothers, 1939.

Lamont, Corliss. *Soviet Civilization.* New York: Philosophical Library, 1952.

Lamont, Corliss, and Margaret Lamont. *Russia Day By Day: A Travel Diary.* New York: Covici and Friede, 1933.

Lamont, Corliss, ed. *The Trial of Elizabeth Gurley Flynn by the American Civil Liberties Union.* New York: Horizon Press, 1968.

Lamont, Thomas W. *Across World Frontiers.* New York: Harcourt, Brace and Co., 1951.

Lyons, Eugene. *Assignment in Utopia.* New York: Harcourt, Brace and Co., 1937.

———. *Moscow Carrousel.* New York: Alfred A. Knopf, 1935.

———. *Stalin, Czar of All the Russia.* Philadelphia: J. B. Lippincott, 1940.

Maisky, Ivan. *Memoirs of a Soviet Ambassador: The War 1939–1943.* London: Hutchinson & Co., 1967.

Moley, Raymond. *After Seven Years.* New York: Harper & Brothers, 1938.

Murphy, Robert. *Diplomat Among Warriors.* Garden City, N.Y.: Doubleday, 1964.

Nixon, Edgar B., ed. *Franklin D. Roosevelt and Foreign Affairs, 1933–1936.* 3 vols. Cambridge, Mass.: Harvard University Press, 1971.

Norris, George W. *Fighting Liberal: The Autobiography of George W. Norris.* New York: Macmillan Co., 1945.

Patterson, Jefferson. *Diplomatic Duty and Diversion.* Cambridge, Mass.: Riverside Press, 1956.

Perkins, Francis. *The Roosevelt I Knew.* New York: Viking Press, 1946.

Phillips, William. *Ventures in Diplomacy.* Boston: Beacon Press, 1952.

Roosevelt, Elliott, ed. *F.D.R.: His Personal Letters, 1928–1945.* 2 vols. New York: Duell, Sloan and Pearce, 1947–50.

Rosenman, Samuel, ed. *The Public Papers and Addresses of Franklin D. Roosevelt.* 13 vols. New York, 1938–50.

Sinclair, Upton, and Eugene Lyons. *Terror in Russia? Two Views.* New York: Richard R. Smith, 1938.

Stimson, Henry L., and McGeorge Bundy. *On Active Service in Peace and War.* New York: Harper & Brothers, 1947.

Strong, Anna Louise. *I Change Worlds: The Remaking of an American.* New York: Henry Holt, 1935.

Taracouzio, T. A. *War and Peace in Soviet Diplomacy.* New York: Macmillan Co., 1940.

Thayer, Charles W. *Diplomat.* New York: Harper & Brothers, 1959.

———. *Hands Across the Caviar.* New York: J. P. Lippincott Co., 1952.

Thomas, Lowell. *History As You Heard It.* Garden City, N.Y.: Doubleday, 1957.

Toledano, Ralph de. *Lament for a Generation.* New York: Farrar, Straus and Cudahy, 1960.

Vandenberg, Arthur H., Jr., ed. *The Private Papers of Senator Vandenberg.* Cambridge, Mass.: Houghton Mifflin Co., 1952.

Welles, Sumner. *Seven Decisions That Shaped History.* New York: Harper & Brothers, 1950.

———. *The Time for Decision.* New York: Harper & Brothers, 1944.

Wilson, Hugh R. *Diplomat Between Wars.* New York: Longmans, Green and Co., 1941.

Wilson, Hugh R., Jr. *A Career Diplomat; The Third Chapter: The Third Reich.* New York: Vantage Press, 1960.

———. *For Want of a Nail: The Failure of the League of Nations in Ethiopia.* New York: Vantage Press, 1959.

Winant, John Gilbert. *Letter from Grosvenor Square: An Account of a Stewardship.* Boston: Houghton Mifflin Co., 1947.

Winter, Ella, and Granville Hicks, eds. *The Letters of Lincoln Steffens.* 2 vols. New York: Harcourt, Brace and Co., 1938.

Wolfe, Henry C., *The Imperial Soviets.* New York: Doubleday, Doran and Co., 1940.

Interviews and Letters

Interview with Louis Fischer, November 8, 1967.

Interviews with Loy W. Henderson, June 29, November 17, 1967.

Loy W. Henderson to author, January 19, 1968.
Robert F. Kelley to author, Feburary 14, 1968.
Interview with Corliss Lamont, November 10, 1967.

Periodicals

America
American Federationist
American Mercury
American Quarterly on the Soviet Union, 1938–41
American Review
Atlantic Monthly
Barron's
Bulletin on the Soviet Union, 1936–41
Business Week
The Catholic World
Christian Century
The Commercial and Financial Chronicle
Common Sense
The Commonweal
Economic Review of the Soviet Union, 1933–35
Foreign Affairs
Foreign Policy Association Bulletin
Fortune
Harper's Magazine
Literary Digest, 1933–36
Nation
National Republic
Nation's Business
New Republic
Newsweek
Public Opinion Quarterly, 1938–41
Reader's Digest
The Saturday Evening Post
Soviet Russia Today
Time
U.S. News

Newspapers

Atlanta Constitution
Baltimore Sun
Boston Evening Transcript
Charlotte Observer
Chicago Daily News
Chicago Tribune
Christian Science Monitor
Cincinnati Enquirer
Cleveland Plain Dealer
Courier-Journal (Louisville)
The Daily Worker
Dallas Morning News
Denver Post
Des Moines Register
Detroit News
Hartford Courant
Kansas City Star
Los Angeles Examiner
Los Angeles Times
Miami Herald
Minneapolis Tribune
Moscow News
New York Herald Tribune
New York Times
New York World-Telegram
Omaha Morning World-Herald
Philadelphia Inquirer
Pittsburgh Post-Gazette

Portland Oregonian
Richmond Times-Dispatch
St. Louis Post-Dispatch
San Francisco Chronicle
Seattle Post-Intelligencer
Seattle Times
The Times-Picayune (New Orleans)
Wall Street Journal
Washington Post

SECONDARY SOURCES

Books

Aaron, Daniel. *Writers on the Left*. New York: Harcourt, Brace and World, 1961.

Adams, Frederick C. *Economic Diplomacy: The Export-Import Bank and American Foreign Policy, 1934–1939*. Columbia: University of Missouri Press, 1976.

Adler, Selig. *The Isolationist Impulse: Its Twentieth Century Reaction*. New York: Abelard-Schuman, 1957.

Aguilar, Luis. *Cuba 1933: Prologue to Revolution*. Ithaca, N.Y.: Cornell University Press, 1972.

Alexander, Robert J. *Communism in Latin America*. New Brunswick, N.J.: Rutgers University Press, 1957.

Armstrong, John A. *The Politics of Totalitarianism: The Communist Party of the Soviet Union from 1934 to the Present*. New York: Random House, 1961.

Baker, Roscoe. *The American Legion and American Foreign Policy*. New York: Bookman Associates, 1954.

Barron, Gloria. *Leadership in Crisis: FDR and the Path to Intervention*. Port Washington, N.Y.: Kennikat Press, 1973.

Beloff, Max. *The Foreign Policy of Soviet Russia, 1929–1941*. 2 vols. London: Oxford University Press, 1947–49.

Bendiner, Robert. *The Riddle of the State Department*. New York: Farrar and Rhinehart, 1942.

Bennett, David H. *Demagogues in the Depression: American Radicals and the Union Party, 1932–1936*. New Brunswick, N.J.: Rutgers University Press, 1969.

Bennett, Edward M. *Recognition of Russia: An American Foreign Policy Dilemma*. Waltham, Mass.: Ginn and Co., 1970.

Bialer, Seweryn, ed. *Stalin and His Generals: Soviet Military Memoirs of World War II*. New York: Pegasus, 1969.

Bishop, Donald G. *The Roosevelt-Litvinov Agreements: The American View*. Syracuse, N.Y.: Syracuse University Press, 1965.

Blackstock, Paul E. *The Secret Road to World War Two: Soviet Versus Western Intelligence, 1921–1939*. Chicago: Quadrangle, 1969.

Blum, John Morton. *From the Morgenthau Diaries: Years of Crisis, 1928–1938*. Boston: Houghton Mifflin Co., 1959.

———. *From the Morgenthau Diaries: Years of Urgency, 1938–1941*. Boston: Houghton Mifflin Co., 1965.

Bolt, Ernest C., Jr. *Ballots before Bullitts: The War Referendum Approach to Peace in America, 1914–1941*. Charlottesville: University Press of Virginia, 1977.

Borg, Dorothy. *The United States and the Far Eastern Crisis of 1933–1938: From the*

Manchurian Incident Through the Initial Stage of the Undeclared Sino-Japanese War.
Cambridge, Mass.: Harvard University Press, 1964.

Borkenau, Franz. *European Communism.* New York: Harper & Brothers, 1953.

Browder, Robert P. *The Origins of Soviet-American Diplomacy.* Princeton, N.J.:
Princeton University Press, 1953.

Budurowycz, Bohdan B. *Polish-Soviet Relations, 1932–1939.* New York: Columbia
University Press, 1963.

Burns, James MacGregor. *Roosevelt: The Lion and the Fox.* New York: Harcourt, Brace
and World, 1956.

———. *Roosevelt: The Soldier of Freedom.* New York: Harcourt Brace Jovanovich,
1970.

Cattell, David T. *Communism and the Spanish Civil War.* Berkeley: University of California Press, 1957.

———. *Soviet Diplomacy and the Spanish Civil War.* Berkeley: University of California
Press, 1957.

Chadwin, Mark Lincoln. *The Hawks of World War II.* Chapel Hill: University of North
Carolina Press, 1968.

Clissold, Stephen, ed. *Soviet Relations with Latin America, 1918–1968: A Documentary
Survey.* London: Oxford University Press, 1970.

Cohen, Stephen F. *Bukharin and the Bolshevik Revolution: A Political Biography,
1888–1938.* New York: Alfred A. Knopf, 1973.

Cohen, Warren I. *The American Interventionists: The Lessons of Intervention in World
War II.* Chicago: University of Chicago Press, 1967.

Cole, Wayne S. *America First: The Battle Against Intervention, 1940–1941.* Madison:
University of Wisconsin Press, 1953.

———. *Charles A. Lindbergh and the Battle Against American Intervention in World War
II.* New York: Harcourt Brace Jovanovich, 1974.

Conquest, Robert. *The Great Terror: Stalin's Purge of the Thirties.* New York: Macmillan
Co., 1968.

Coox, Alvin D. *The Anatomy of a Small War: The Soviet-Japanese Struggle for
Changkufeng/Khasan, 1938.* Westport, Conn.: Greenwood Press, 1977.

Craig, Gordon, and Felix Gilbert, eds. *The Diplomats, 1919–1939.* Princeton, N.J.:
Princeton University Press, 1953.

Culbert, David Holbrook. *News for Everyman: Radio and Foreign Affairs in Thirties
America.* Westport, Conn.: Greenwood Press, 1976.

Dallek, Robert. *Democrat and Diplomat: The Life of William E. Dodd.* New York: Oxford
University Press, 1968.

Davis, Lynn Etheridge. *The Cold War Begins: Soviet-American Conflict Over Eastern
Europe.* Princeton, N.J.: Princeton University Press, 1974.

Dawson, Raymond H. *The Decision to Aid Russia, 1941: Foreign Policy and Domestic
Politics.* Chapel Hill: University of North Carolina Press, 1959.

Deakin, F. W., and G. R. Storry. *The Case of Richard Sorge.* New York: Harper and Row,
1966.

Diggins, John P. *Mussolini and Fascism: The View from America.* Princeton, N.J.:
Princeton University Press, 1972.

———. *Up from Communism: Conservative Odysseys in American Intellectual History.*
New York: Harper & Row, 1975.

Divine, Robert A. *The Illusion of Neutrality.* Chicago: University of Chicago Press, 1962.

———. *The Reluctant Belligerent: American Entry into World War II.* New York: John
Wiley & Sons, 1965.

———. *Roosevelt and World War II.* Baltimore: Johns Hopkins Press, 1969.

Drummond, Donald F. *The Passing of American Neutrality, 1937–1941.* Ann Arbor:
University of Michigan Press, 1955.

Duroselle, Jean-Baptiste, ed. *Les relations germanosovietiques de 1933 à 1939.* Paris: Armand Colin, 1954.

Erickson, John. *The Soviet High Command: A Military-Political History, 1918–1941.* New York: St. Martin's Press, 1962.

Fabry, Philipp W. *Der Hitler-Stalin-Pakt 1939–1941.* Darmstadt, Germany: Fundus Verlag, 1962.

Fainsod, Merle. *Smolensk Under Soviet Rule.* Cambridge, Mass., 1958.

Farnsworth, Beatrice. *William C. Bullitt and the Soviet Union.* Bloomington: Indiana University Press, 1967.

Feis, Herbert. *Churchill-Roosevelt-Stalin: The War They Waged and the Peace They Sought.* Princeton, N.J.: Princeton University Press, 1957.

——. *The Road to Pearl Harbor: The Coming of the War Between the United States and Japan.* Princeton, N.J.: Princeton University Press, 1950.

Filene, Peter G. *Americans and the Soviet Experiment, 1917–1933: American Attitudes Toward Russia from the February Revolution until Diplomatic Recognition.* Cambridge, Mass.: Harvard University Press, 1967.

Fischer, Louis. *Russia's Road from Peace to War: Soviet Foreign Relations, 1917–1941.* New York: Harper & Row, 1969.

——. *Stalin and Hitler.* New York, 1940.

Flynn, George Q. *American Catholics and the Roosevelt Presidency, 1932–1936.* Lexington: University of Kentucky Press, 1968.

——. *Roosevelt and Romanism: Catholics and American Diplomacy, 1937–1945.* Westport, Conn.: Greenwood Press, 1976.

Freidel, Frank. *Franklin D. Roosevelt: Launching the New Deal.* Boston: Little, Brown and Co., 1973.

Gaddis, John Lewis. *Russia, The Soviet Union, and the United States: An Interpretive History.* New York: John Wiley & Sons, 1978.

——. *The United States and the Origins of the Cold War, 1941–1947.* New York: Columbia University Press, 1972.

Gallagher, Louis J., S.J. *Edmund A. Walsh, S.J.: A Biography.* New York: Benziger Brothers, 1962.

Gardner, Lloyd C. *Economic Aspects of New Deal Diplomacy.* Madison: University of Wisconsin Press, 1964.

Goodman, Walter. *The Committee: The Extraordinary Career of the House Committee on Un-American Activities.* New York: Farrar, Straus and Giroux, 1968.

Green, David. *The Containment of Latin America: A History of the Myths and Realities of the Good Neighbor Policy.* Chicago: Quadrangle Books, 1971.

Guttmann, Allen. *The Wound in the Heart: America and the Spanish Civil War.* Chicago: The Free Press of Glencoe, 1962.

Haight, John McVickar, Jr. *American Aid to France, 1938–1940.* New York: Atheneum, 1970.

Harris, Brice, Jr. *The United States and the Italo-Ethiopian Crisis.* Stanford, Calif.: Stanford University Press, 1964.

Herrick, Robert Waring. *Soviet Naval Strategy: Fifty Years of Theory and Practice.* Annapolis, Md.: United States Naval Institute, 1968.

Herring, George C., Jr. *Aid to Russia, 1941–1946: Strategy, Diplomacy, the Origins of the Cold War.* New York: Columbia University Press, 1973.

Howe, Irving, and Lewis Coser. *The American Communist Party: A Critical History, 1919–1957.* Boston: Beacon Press, 1957.

Ilchman, Warren F. *Professional Diplomacy in the United States, 1779–1939: A Study in Administrative History.* Chicago: University of Chicago Press, 1961.

Jasny, Naum. *Soviet Industrialization, 1928–1952.* Chicago: University of Chicago Press, 1961.

Johnson, Chalmers. *An Instance of Treason: Ozaki Hotsumi and the Sorge Spy Ring.* Stanford, Calif.: Stanford University Press, 1964.

Johnson, Walter. *The Battle Against Isolation.* Chicago: University of Chicago Press, 1944.

Jonas, Manfred. *Isolationism in America, 1935–1941.* Ithaca, N.Y.: Cornell University Press, 1966.

Kennan, George F. *Russia and the West under Lenin and Stalin.* Boston: Little, Brown and Co., 1960.

———. *Soviet-American Relations.* 2 vols. Princeton, N.J.: Princeton University Press, 1956–58.

Kimball, Warren F. *The Most Unsordid Act: Lend-Lease, 1939–1941.* Baltimore: Johns Hopkins Press, 1969.

Knipping, Franz. *Die Amerikanische Russlandpolitik in Der Zeit Des Hitler-Stalin-Pakts.* Tübingen, Germany: J.C.B. Mohr, 1974.

Kolko, Gabriel. *The Limits of Power: The World and United States Foreign Policy, 1945–1954.* New York, 1972.

Kottman, Richard N. *Reciprocity and the North Atlantic Triangle, 1932–1938.* Ithaca, N.Y.: Cornell University Press, 1968.

Krosby, Peter H. *Finland, Germany, and the Soviet Union, 1940–1941: The Petsamo Dispute.* Madison: University of Wisconsin Press, 1968.

Lafore, Laurence. *The End of Glory: An Interpretation of the Origins of World War II.* Philadelphia: J. B. Lippincott Co., 1970.

Langer, William L., and Samuel E. Gleason. *The Challenge to Isolation, 1937–1940.* New York: Harper & Brothers, 1952.

———. *The Undeclared War, 1940–1941.* New York: Harper & Brothers, 1953.

Lash, Joseph P. *Eleanor and Franklin.* New York: W. W. Norton, 1971.

Latham, Earl. *The Communist Controversy in Washington: From the New Deal to McCarthy.* Cambridge, Mass.: Harvard University Press, 1966.

Lawson, R. Alan. *The Failure of Independent Liberalism, 1930–1941.* New York: G. P. Putnam's Sons, 1971.

Leigh, Michael. *Mobilizing Consent: Public Opinion and American Foreign Policy, 1937–1947.* Westport, Conn.: Greenwood Press, 1976.

Leuchtenburg, William E. *Franklin D. Roosevelt and the New Deal, 1932–1940.* New York: Harper & Row, 1963.

Levering, Ralph B. *American Opinion and the Russian Alliance, 1939–1945.* Chapel Hill: University of North Carolina Press, 1976.

Levin, N. Gordon. *Woodrow Wilson and World Politics: America's Response to War and Revolution.* New York, 1968.

Lovenstein, Meno. *American Opinion of Soviet Russia.* Washington: American Council on Public Affairs, 1941.

Lyons, Eugene. *The Red Decade: The Stalinist Penetration of America.* New York: Bobbs-Merrill Co., 1941.

Maddox, Robert James. *William E. Borah and American Foreign Policy.* Baton Rouge: Louisiana State University Press, 1969.

Margulies, Sylvia R. *The Pilgrimage to Russia: The Soviet Union and the Treatment of Foreigners, 1924–1937.* Madison: University of Wisconsin Press, 1968.

McKenna, Marian C. *Borah.* Ann Arbor: University of Michigan Press, 1961.

McLane, Charles B. *Soviet Policy and the Chinese Communists, 1931–1946.* New York: Columbia University Press, 1958.

———. *Soviet Strategies in Southeast Asia: An Exploration of Eastern Policy Under Lenin and Stalin.* Princeton, N.J.: Princeton University Press, 1966.

McSherry, James E. *Stalin, Hitler, and Europe.* 2 vols. Cleveland: World Publishing Co., 1968–70.

Medvedev, Roy A. *Let History Judge: The Origins and Consequences of Stalinism.* Translated by Colleen Taylor and edited by David Joravsky and George Haupt. New York: Alfred A. Knopf, 1971.

Nekrich, Aleksandr M. *June 22, 1941: Soviet Historians and the German Invasion.* Translated by Vladimir Petrov. Columbia: University of South Carolina Press, 1968.

O'Brien, David J. *American Catholics and Social Reform: The New Deal Years.* New York: Oxford University Press, 1968.

Offner, Arnold A. *American Appeasement: United States Foreign Policy and Germany, 1933–1938.* Cambridge, Mass.: Harvard University Press, 1969.

———. *The Origins of the Second World War: American Foreign Policy and World Politics, 1917–1941.* New York: Praeger Publishers, 1975.

Ogden, August Raymond. *The Dies Committee: A Study of the Special House Committee for the Investigation of Un-American Activities, 1938–1943.* Washington: Catholic University of America Press, 1943.

Osgood, Robert Endicott. *Ideals and Self-Interest in America's Foreign Relations: The Great Transformation of the Twentieth Century.* Chicago: University of Chicago Press, 1953.

Pells, Richard H. *Radical Visions and American Dreams: Culture and Social Thought in the Depression Years.* New York: Harper & Row, 1973.

Petrov, Vladimir. *A Study in Diplomacy: The Story of Arthur Bliss Lane.* Chicago: Henry Regnery Co., 1971.

Ponomaryov, B., et al. *History of Soviet Foreign Policy, 1917–1945.* Translated by David Skvirsky. Moscow: Progress Publishers, 1969.

Poppino, Rollie E. *International Communism in Latin America.* Chicago: The Free Press of Glencoe, 1964.

Pratt, Julius W. *Cordell Hull, 1933–1944.* 2 vols. New York: Cooper Square Publishers, 1964.

Purcell, Edward A., Jr. *The Crisis of Democratic Theory: Scientific Naturalism and the Problem of Value.* Lexington: University of Kentucky Press, 1973.

Range, Willard. *Franklin D. Roosevelt's World Order.* Athens: University of Georgia Press, 1959.

Rich, Norman. *Hitler's War Aims: Ideology, the Nazi State, and the Course of Expansion.* New York: W. W. Norton, 1973.

Robinson, Richard A. H. *The Origins of Franco's Spain: The Right, the Republic and Revolution, 1931–1936.* London: David and Charles, 1970.

Roy, Ralph Lord. *Communism and the Churches.* New York: Harcourt, Brace and World, 1960.

Schapiro, Leonard. *The Communist Party of the Soviet Union.* New York: Random House, 1960. Rev. ed. 1971.

———. *The Government and Politics of the Soviet Union.* New York, 1965.

Schlesinger, Arthur M., Jr. *The Age of Roosevelt.* 3 vols. Boston: Houghton Mifflin Co., 1957–60.

Schwartz, Andrew J. *America and the Russo-Finnish War.* Washington: Public Affairs Press, 1960.

Scott, William E. *Alliance Against Hitler: The Origins of the Franco-Soviet Pact.* Durham, N.C.: Duke University Press, 1962.

Sherwood, Robert E. *Roosevelt and Hopkins: An Intimate History.* New York: Harper & Brothers, 1948.

Shewmaker, Kenneth E. *Americans and Chinese Communists, 1927–1945.* Ithaca, N.Y.: Cornell University Press, 1971.

Small, Melvin, ed. *Public Opinion and Historians: Interdisciplinary Perspectives.* Detroit: Wayne State University Press, 1970.

Smith, Geoffrey S. *To Save A Nation: American Countersubversives, the New Deal, and the Coming of World War II.* New York: Basic Books, 1970.

Sobel, Robert. *The Origins of Interventionism: The United States and the Russo-Finnish War*. New York: Bookman Associates, 1960.

Solzhenitsyn, Alexander I. *The Gulag Archipelago, 1918–1956: An Experiment in Literary Investigation*. Translated by Thomas P. Whitney. 3 vols. New York: Harper & Row, 1973–78.

Spaulding, Ernest Wilder. *Ambassadors Ordinary and Extraordinary*. Washington: Public Affairs Press, 1961.

Steward, Dick. *Trade and Hemisphere: The Good Neighbor Policy and Reciprocal Trade*. Columbia: University of Missouri Press, 1975.

Stuart, Graham H. *The Departure of State: A History of Its Organization, Procedure, and Personnel*. New York: Macmillan Co., 1949.

Sutton, Anthony C. *Western Technology and Soviet Economic Development, 1930–1945*. Stanford, Calif.: Hoover Institution Press, 1971.

Taylor, A. J. P. *The Origins of the Second World War*. New York: Atheneum, 1962.

Taylor, Foster Jay. *The United States and the Spanish Civil War*. Bloomington: Indiana University Press, 1956.

Thorne, Christopher. *The Approach of War, 1938–1939*. London: St. Martin's Press, 1967.

Timasheff, Nicholas S. *The Great Retreat: The Growth and Decline of Communism in Russia*. New York, 1946.

Tompkins, C. David. *Senator Arthur H. Vandenberg: The Evolution of a Modern Republican, 1884–1945*. East Lansing: Michigan State University Press, 1970.

Tompkins, Pauline. *American-Russian Relations in the Far East*. New York: Macmillan Co., 1949.

Traina, Richard P. *American Diplomacy and the Spanish Civil War*. Bloomington: Indiana University Press, 1968.

Treadgold, Donald W. *Twentieth Century Russia*. 3rd rev. ed. Chicago: Rand McNally and Co., 1972.

Triska, Jan F., and David Finley. *Soviet Foreign Policy*. New York: Macmillan Co., 1968.

Tucker, Robert C. *Stalin as Revolutionary, 1879–1929: A Study in History and Personality*. New York: W. W. Norton, 1972.

Tull, Charles J. *Father Coughlin and the New Deal*. Syracuse, N.Y.: Syracuse University Press, 1965.

Ulam, Adam B. *Expansion and Coexistence: The History of Soviet Foreign Policy, 1917–1967*. New York: Frederick A. Praeger, 1968.

———. *Stalin: The Man and His Era*. New York: Viking Press, 1973.

Van Slyke, Lyman P. *Enemies and Friends: The United Front in Chinese Communist History*. Stanford, Calif.: Stanford University Press, 1967.

Walker, J. Samuel. *Henry A. Wallace and American Foreign Policy*. Westport, Conn.: Greenwood Press, 1976.

Warren, Frank A., III. *Liberals and Communism: The "Red Decade" Revisited*. Bloomington: Indiana University Press, 1966.

Warth, Robert D. *Soviet Russia in World Politics*. New York: Twayne Publishers, 1963.

Weinberg, Gerhard L. *The Foreign Policy of Hitler's Germany: Diplomatic Revolution in Europe, 1933–1936*. Chicago: University of Chicago Press, 1970.

———. *Germany and the Soviet Union, 1939–1941*. Leiden, Netherlands: E. J. Brill, 1954.

Welsh, William. *American Images of Soviet Foreign Policy: An Inquiry into Recent Appraisals from the Academic Community*. New Haven, Conn.: Yale University Press, 1970.

Whalen, Richard J. *The Founding Father: The Story of Joseph P. Kennedy*. New York: New American Library, 1964.

Williams, William Appleman. *American-Russian Relations, 1781–1947*. New York: Rinehart and Co., 1952.

Wilson, Joan Hoff. *Ideology and Economics: U.S. Relations with the Soviet Union, 1918–1933.* Columbia: University of Missouri Press, 1974.

Wilson, Theodore A. *The First Summit: Roosevelt and Churchill at Placentia Bay 1941.* Boston: Houghton Mifflin, 1969.

Wiltz, John E. *In Search of Peace: The Senate Munitions Inquiry, 1934–1936.* Baton Rouge: Louisiana State University Press, 1963.

Wolfskill, George. *The Revolt of the Conservatives: A History of the American Liberty League, 1933–1940.* Boston: Houghton Mifflin Co., 1962.

Wolfskill, George, and John A. Hudson. *All But the People: Franklin D. Roosevelt and His Critics, 1933–1939.* New York: Macmillan Co., 1969.

Wood, Bryce. *The Making of the Good Neighbor Policy.* New York: Columbia University Press, 1961.

Yergin, Daniel. *Shattered Peace: The Origins of the Cold War and the National Security State.* Boston: Houghton Mifflin Co., 1977.

Articles

Adams, Frederick C. "The Road to Pearl Harbor: A Reexamination of American Far Eastern Policy, July 1937–December 1938." *Journal of American History* 58, no. 1 (1971):73–92.

Adler, Les K., and Thomas G. Paterson. "Red Fascism: The Merger of Nazi Germany and Soviet Russia in the American Image of Totalitarianism, 1930's–1950's." *American Historical Review* 75, no. 4 (1970):1046–64.

Andreyeva, M., and L. Vidyasova. "The Struggle of the U.S.S.R. for Collective Security in Europe during 1933–1935." *International Affairs* 9 (1963), no. 6:107–16, no. 7:116–23, no. 8:132–39, no. 10:112–20.

Bowers, Robert E. "American Diplomacy, the 1933 Wheat Conference, and Recognition of the Soviet Union," *Agricultural History* 40, no. 1 (1966):39–53.

———. "Hull, Russian Subversion in Cuba, and Recognition of the U.S.S.R." *Journal of American History,* 53, no. 3 (1966):542–55.

Bullitt, William C. "How We Won the War and Lost the Peace." *Life,* August 30, 1948, 83–97, September 6, 1948, 86–100.

Butow, Robert J. C. "Backdoor Diplomacy in the Pacific: The Proposal for a Konoye-Roosevelt Meeting, 1941." *Journal of American History* 61, no. 1 (1971):48–72.

Clifford, John Garry. "The Odyssey of the *City of Flint.*" *American Neptune* 32, no. 2 (1972):100–116.

Dallek, Robert. "Beyond Tradition: The Diplomatic Careers of William E. Dodd and George S. Messersmith, 1933–1938." *South Atlantic Quarterly* 66, no. 2 (1967):233–44.

Davies, R. W., and S. G. Wheatcroft. "Further Thoughts on the First Soviet Five-Year Plan." *Slavic Review* 34 (1975):790–802.

Dewey, Donald O. "America and Russia, 1939–1941: The Views of the *New York Times.*" *Journalism Quarterly* 44 (1967): 62–70.

Dreifort, John E. "The French Popular Front and the Franco-Soviet Pact, 1936–1937." *Journal of Contemporary History* 11 (1976):217–36.

Drummond, Donald F. "Cordell Hull." In *An Uncertain Tradition: American Secretaries of State in the Twentieth Century,* edited by Norman Graebner. New York: McGraw-Hill Co., 1961.

Eagles, Keith D. "Ambassador Joseph E. Davies and American-Soviet Relations, 1937–1941." *World Politics* 9 (1956–57):220–39.

Feuer, Lewis S. "Travelers to the Soviet Union, 1917–1932: The Formation of a Component of New Deal Ideology." *American Quarterly* 14, no. 2, part 1 (1962):119–50.

Grant, Natalie. "The Russian Section, A Window on the Soviet Union." *Diplomatic History* 2, no. 1 (1978):107–15.

Haight, John McVickar, Jr. "Franklin D. Roosevelt and a Naval Quarantine of Japan." *Pacific Historical Review* 40, no. 2 (1971):203–26.

Herndon, James S., and Joseph O. Baylen. "Col. Philip R. Faymonville and the Red Army, 1934–1943." *Slavic Review* 34 (1975):483–505.

Herwig, Holger H. "Prelude to *Weltblitzkrieg*: Germany's Naval Policy toward the United States of America, 1939–1941." *Journal of Modern History* 43, no. 4 (1971):649–68.

Hunter, Holland, et al. "The Overambitious First Soviet Five Year Plan." *Slavic Review* 32, no. 2 (1973):237–91.

Itakovlev, N. N. "F. Roosevelt—Proponent of Collaboration with the Soviet Union." *Soviet Studies in History* 12 (1974):3–29.

Libbey, James K. "Liberal Journals and the Moscow Trials of 1936–1938." *Journalism Quarterly* 52, no. 1 (1975):85–92.

Loewenheim, Francis L. "An Illusion That Shaped History: New Light on the History and Historiography of American Peace Efforts before Munich." In *Some Pathways in Twentieth-Century History*, edited by Daniel R. Beaver. Detroit: Wayne State University Press, 1969.

Maddux, Thomas R. "American Diplomats and the Soviet Experiment: The View from the Moscow Embassy, 1934–1939." *South Atlantic Quarterly* 74, no. 4 (1975): 468–87.

———. "Red Fascism, Brown Bolshevism: The American Image of Totalitarianism in the 1930s." *Historian* 40, no. 1 (1977):85–103.

———. "United States–Soviet Naval Relations in the 1930's: The Soviet Union's Efforts to Purchase Naval Vessels," *Naval War College Review* 29, no. 2 (1976):28–37.

——— "Watching Stalin Maneuver Between Hitler and the West: American Diplomats and Soviet Diplomacy, 1934–1939." *Diplomatic History* 1, no. 2 (1977):140–54.

Offner, Arnold A. "Appeasement Revisited: The United States, Great Britain, and Germany, 1933–1940." *Journal of American History* 64, no. 2 (1977):373–93.

Petrov, Vladimir. "A Missing Page in Soviet Historiography: The Nazi-Soviet Partnership." *Orbis* 11, no. 4 (1968):1113–36.

Polenberg, Richard. "Franklin Roosevelt and Civil Liberties: The Case of the Dies Committee." *Historian* 30, no. 2 (1968):165–79.

Pratt, Lawrence. "The Anglo-American Naval Conversations on the Far East of January 1938." *International Affairs* 47 (1976):745–63.

Ropes, E. C. "American-Soviet Trade Relations." *Russian Review* 3, no. 1 (1943):89–95.

———. "Russian-American Cultural Relations." *Russian Review* 6, no. 6 (1947):3–9.

Shapiro, Jane P. "Soviet Historiography and the Moscow Trials: After Thirty Years." *Russian Review* 27, no. 1 (1968):68–77.

Small, Melvin. "Buffoons and Brave Hearts: Hollywood Portrays the Russians, 1939–1944." *California Historical Quarterly* 52 (1973):326–37.

——— "How We Learned to Love the Russians: American Media and the Soviet Union During World War II." *Historian* 36, no. 3 (1974):455–78.

Toepfer, Marcia Lynn. "The Soviet Role in the Munich Crisis: An Historiographical Debate." *Diplomatic History* 1, no. 4 (1977):341–57.

Ullman, Richard H. "The Davies Mission and United States–Soviet Relations, 1937–1941." *World Politics* 9 (1957):220–39.

Vinson, J. Chal. "War Debts and Peace Legislation: The Johnson Act of 1934." *Mid-America* 50, no. 3 (1968):206–22.

Walker, Samuel. "Communists and Isolationism: The American Peace Mobilization, 1940–1941." *Maryland Historian* 4 (1973):1–12.

Wilson, Joan H. "American Business and the Recognition of the Soviet Union." *Social Science Quarterly* 52, no. 2 (1971):349–68.

Dissertations

Bennett, Edward Moore. "Franklin D. Roosevelt and Russian-American Relations, 1933–1939." Ph.D. dissertation, University of Illinois, 1961.

Eagles, Keith David. "Ambassador Joseph E. Davies and American-Soviet Relations, 1937–1941." Ph.D. dissertation, University of Washington, 1966.

Fithian, Floyd James. "Soviet-American Economic Relations, 1918–1933: American Business in Russia During the Period of Non-Recognition." Ph.D. dissertation, University of Nebraska, 1964.

Hanson, Betty Crump. "American Diplomatic Reporting from the Soviet Union, 1934–1941." Ph.D. dissertation, Columbia University, 1966.

Lowenfish, Lee Elihu. "American Radicals and Soviet Russia, 1917–1940." Ph.D. dissertation, University of Wisconsin, 1968.

Magden, Ronald Earnest. "Attitudes of the American Religious Press Toward Soviet Russia, 1939–1941." Ph.D. dissertation, University of Washington, 1964.

Mulvihill, Peggy M. "The United States and the Russo-Finnish War." Ph.D. dissertation, University of Chicago, 1964.

O'Connor, Joseph Edward. "Laurence A. Steinhardt and American Policy Toward the Soviet Union, 1939–1941." Ph.D. dissertation, University of Virginia, 1968.

Papachristous, Judith R. "American-Soviet Relations and United States Policy in the Pacific, 1933–1941." Ph.D. dissertation, University of Colorado, 1968.

Thornton, Sandra Winterberger. "The Soviet Union and Japan, 1939–1941." Ph.D. dissertation, Georgetown University, 1964.

Williams, William Appleman. "Raymond Robins and Russian-American Relations, 1917–1938." Ph.D. dissertation, University of Wisconsin, 1950.

Index